The Q&A Guide to Photo Techniques

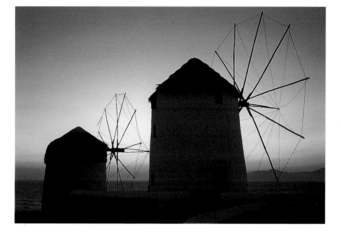

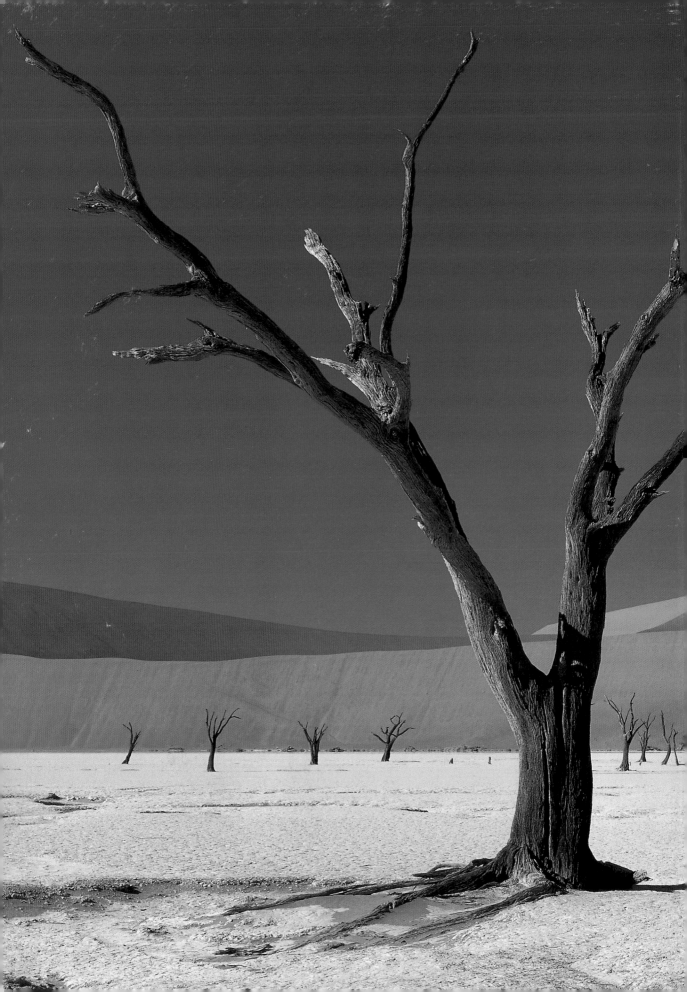

The Q&A Guide to Photo Techniques

LEE FROST

David & Charles

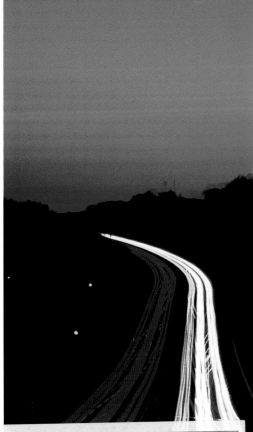

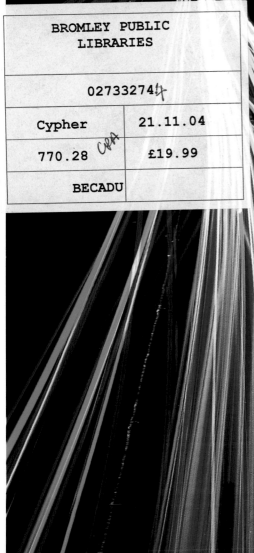

For my children, Noah and Kitty

A DAVID & CHARLES BOOK

David & Charles is a subsidiary of F+W (UK) Ltd.,
an F+W Publications Inc. company

First published 1995
First paperback edition 1997
New revised, expanded and updated edition, 2004

Distributed in North America
by F+W Publications, Inc.
4700 East Galbraith Road
Cincinnati, OH 45236
1-800-289-0963

A catalogue record for this book is available from the British Library.

ISBN 0 7153 1813 6 hardback
ISBN 0 7153 1814 4 paperback (USA only)

Illustrations by Steven Handley and Ethan Danielson
Line drawings by Greg Volichenko

Printed in China by SNP Leefung
for David & Charles
Brunel House   Newton Abbot   Devon

Commissioning editor Neil Baber
Desk editor Ame Verso
Executive art editor Ali Myer
Book designer Sarah Underhill
Production controller Kelly Smith

Visit our website at www.davidandcharles.co.uk

David & Charles books are available from all good bookshops;
alternatively you can contact our Orderline on (0)1626 334555
or write to us at FREEPOST EX2110, David & Charles Direct,
Newton Abbot, TQ12 4ZZ (no stamp required UK mainland).

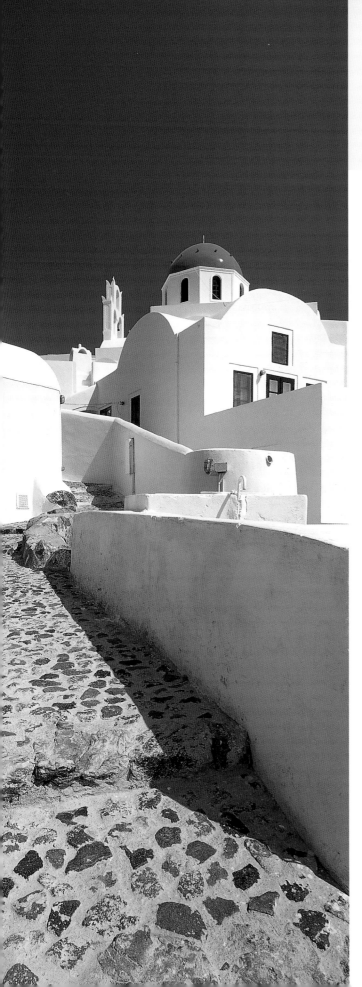

Contents

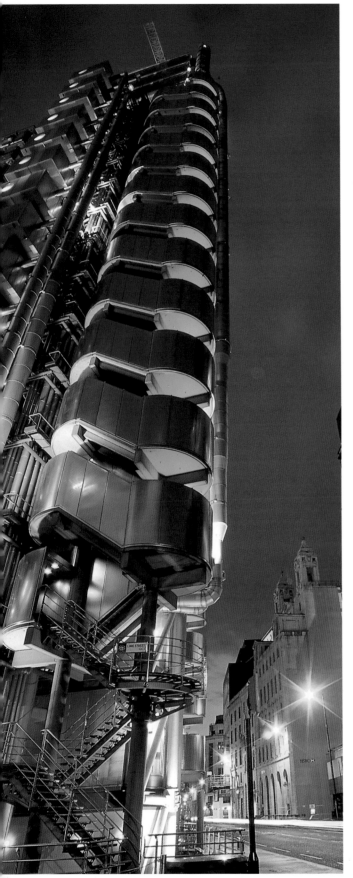

Introduction

In recent years photography has become more accessible, more affordable, and easier than ever before. Equipment manufacturers have gone to incredible lengths to develop cameras that make the whole picture-taking process as simple as possible, and with digital cameras now available that offer superb quality at affordable prices, we have a viable alternative to film for the first time ever.

When I first became interested in photography 20 years ago, the idea of a camera that didn't need film was the stuff of science fiction, but it's here – and it's here to stay. At the same time, film is far from dead, and despite the advances made in digital technology, and its growing popularity, manufacturers are still investing and developing traditional equipment and materials, and silver-based photography has a long life ahead of it – so don't worry if you've yet to jump on the digital bandwagon.

The most important thing to remember is that whether you shoot digitally or use film, photography is still a creative process that depends more upon the skill and judgment of you, the photographer, than on which camera you own, or how many lenses you have. You can own the most expensive, up-to-date equipment available, but without knowledge, guidance and inspiration, your efforts will more than likely be in vain.

Which is where this book comes in. Using a handy question-and-answer format, this fact-packed guide has been carefully compiled to provide all the information you're likely to require as your interest in photography develops, from being a complete beginner to an advanced enthusiast. No need to spend hours reading through huge chapters to find those small golden nuggets of information you seek. Just locate the relevant section, and you will find the solutions to your problems clearly explained.

Part 1 discusses equipment and looks at everything from choosing and using cameras and lenses, to making the most of filters and film, mastering the intricacies of electronic flash and deciding which accessories you need to complete your system.

Part 2 then takes a look at the techniques that are essential to successful picture-taking. Depth of field, exposure, composition, understanding colour and mastering light are explored in detail to give you a thorough grounding in the fundamentals of photography, along with how to process and print your first pictures.

Finally, Part 3 takes all this information and applies it to a wide range of the subjects you're most likely to photograph: portraits, kids, travel, candids, landscapes, sport and action, night and low-light shots, nature, close-ups, buildings, still lifes and special effects.

I hope you enjoy reading it, and in doing so gain as much enjoyment as I have from the fascinating art of photography.

Lee Frost

part one
equipment

Cameras

With such a vast range of models available, choosing a camera can be difficult. Fortunately, camera design and technology have reached such heights of sophistication that any model can produce high-quality results. All cameras are designed to perform the same task – they're just a lightproof box containing a shutter that allows a controlled amount of light to fall on a piece of film or digital chip placed behind it. Don't be misled into thinking that the latest feature-packed models will automatically turn you into a master photographer. All they do is free you from some of the decisions that have to be made so you can dedicate more thought to the creative aspects of photography. But ultimately, any camera is only as good as the person using it.

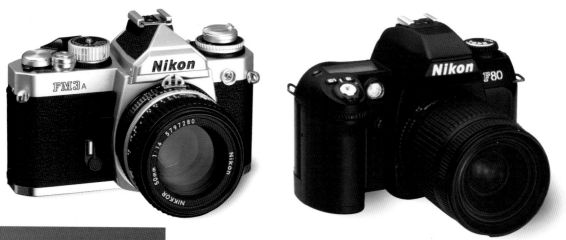

Q Which type of camera would you recommend for an aspiring amateur photographer?

The vast majority of 35mm SLRs in use today are modern autofocus models like the Nikon F80 above – they boast a vast array of features and functions and harness the latest microchip technology to make picture-taking as easy as possible. Some manufacturers continue to produce more traditional models, however, and these are favoured by photographers who like to keep things simple. The Nikon FM3A (above left) is the latest incarnation of a classic SLR.

The answer is quite simple – a 35mm single lens reflex (SLR) camera. This is by far the most widely used type of camera, for several key reasons.

First, it offers a good compromise between ease of use, control and image quality. If you're new to photography, you can rely on the camera to produce successful results, but as your experience grows it allows you to take more control.

Second, 35mm SLRs can be fitted with a vast range of lenses, flashguns, close-up equipment and filters that allow you to photograph every subject imaginable.

Third, when you peer through the viewfinder of an SLR you see almost exactly what's going to appear on the final picture, as shown on the right, because the viewing system allows you to see directly through the lens. This is especially useful when using filters such as polarizers and graduates that require careful alignment (see Filters, page 22).

THE SLR VIEWING SYSTEM

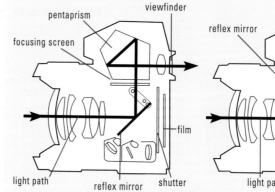

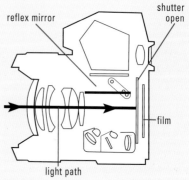

The heart of the SLR lies in the viewing system, which uses a reflex mirror to reflect the image passing through the lens up to the viewfinder pentaprism. When you trip the camera's shutter, the mirror flips up so light entering the lens can reach the film. When the exposure ends, the mirror drops back to its original position.

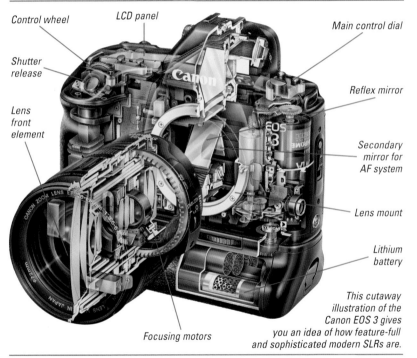

The features that you should look for really depend on how much you can afford to spend and what kind of camera you're looking for. Most of the SLRs being made today are autofocus (AF) models that use the latest in microchip technology and are packed with a myriad of electronic features, some of which you may never come to use. But it's still possible to buy traditional manual cameras that contain just the very basic features if you like to keep things simple. To give you an idea of the features you should expect to find, let's take a journey around a typical AF SLR.

Liquid crystal display (LCD) Used instead of or in conjunction with conventional dials, this allows you to access the camera's many electronic functions via input dials or mode buttons. Information such as frame number, aperture and shutter speed, exposure mode, exposure compensation, metering pattern, flash mode and battery condition are displayed on the screen.

Metering The metering system is the most important part of an SLR, because it determines how much control you have over the exposure set. The simplest traditional models use fully manual metering and rely on you to set the aperture and shutter speed required, but the majority of SLRs use a whole host of automatic exposure

Shutter speed range Most pictures are taken using shutter speeds from 1 to 1/1000sec, but a typical range on a modern SLR is 30 to 1/4000sec. Some models offer faster speeds, but longer shutter speeds are actually more useful because they allow you to take pictures at night with your camera set to an automatic exposure mode such as aperture priority AE. Make sure the shutter also has a 'Bulb' (B) setting, so you can hold the shutter open indefinitely (see Night and low light, page 118).

Depth of field preview This feature stops the lens iris down to the aperture (f/number) it is set to. By doing so you can assess depth of field – what will be in and out of sharp focus in the final picture. Although by no means essential, it will prove very useful and is well worth having (see Depth of field, page 44).

Film speed range Modern SLRs set the film speed automatically using a system known as DX-coding, usually in an ISO range of 6 to 6400. Ideally you also need to be able to set film speed manually, as some specialist films such as infrared are not DX-coded, and there may be times when you want to change the recommended ISO of a film (see Film, page 30).

Integral flash Many SLRs have a small flash unit built into the pentaprism. It's handy for taking snapshots, or for fill-in flash outdoors, but the power output is quite low so the working range is limited.

Built-in motor winder Not essential, but useful as it ensures the film is always wound on to the next frame and ready for use so you never miss a shot. An advance rate of two frames per second is the average speed, though professional SLRs can operate at up to ten frames per second.

Lens mount Each brand of camera, with a few exceptions, has its own unique bayonet mount to accept interchangeable lenses. This means that if you buy a Canon SLR, for example, only Canon lenses or independent lenses with the Canon mount can be fitted.

Other features You might also want to consider a cable release socket in the shutter release button or camera body, a flash sync socket so you can use off-camera or studio flash, a self-timer, and a multiple-exposure facility.

Control wheel

LCD panel

Main control dial

Shutter release

Reflex mirror

Lens front element

Secondary mirror for AF system

Lens mount

Lithium battery

Focusing motors

This cutaway illustration of the Canon EOS 3 gives you an idea of how feature-full and sophisticated modern SLRs are.

The viewfinder As well as allowing you to see exactly what's going to appear in your final pictures, the viewfinder on many models provides important information such as the aperture and shutter speed set, under- or overexposure warnings, a 'flash ready' lamp, if any exposure compensation has been applied and so on. The viewfinder on manual-focus SLRs also incorporates a handy focusing screen to aid accurate focusing, while AF SLRs use one or more focusing sensors.

Bright, crisp viewfinders are a joy to work with because they aid accurate focusing and composition – AF SLRs are better in this respect than manual-focus models.

modes and metering patterns. A typical 35mm AF SLR these days will offer manual, aperture priority AE, shutter priority AE and program exposure modes plus multi-pattern and spot or partial metering patterns (see Exposure, page 49).

Exposure compensation Camera meters don't always give accurate results – something you will learn more about later on – so some kind of facility that allows you to override the exposure set and avoid error is essential. Most SLRs allow you to increase or reduce the exposure by up to three stops, in third-, half- or full-stop increments (see Exposure, page 46).

Which type of camera would you recommend for a beginner?

If your main interest is taking snapshots at parties, get-togethers and holidays, a 35mm compact camera will almost certainly suit you perfectly.

The main advantage of compact cameras is that they're so easy to use. Everything is there in one neat package, so all you have to do is switch on, point, and shoot. Being small and light they can also be carried in a pocket, so you never miss a chance to grab a great picture.

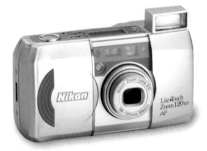

The Nikon Lite Touch Zoom 120 is typical of today's zoom compacts, featuring a powerful 38–120mm macro zoom but still being relatively small so it can be carried anywhere.

Why are some SLRs tagged 'professional' models?

Certain SLRs, such as the Nikon F5 and Canon EOS 1v, earn this distinction because they're built to endure rigorous daily use by professional photographers, who tend to treat their equipment more like tools of the trade than expensive jewellery.

Pro-spec SLRs are built from tougher materials so they can withstand regular knocks and, heaven forbid, drops. Their bodies also tend to be better sealed, so they'll continue to function in wet weather; there's usually some provision for manual operation should the batteries fail; and they boast a wider range of features than 'amateur' SLRs – such as a faster motor drive and wider shutter speed range.

You have to pay more for this, but for professionals it's money well spent because their reputation and livelihood are dependent on their ability to come up with the goods. One downside of 'Pro' SLRs is that they're bigger and heavier.

The simplest models have a fixed lens – usually a slightly wide 35mm – fixed focusing, automatic exposure and a simple integral flashgun that fires automatically in low light. They're very handy for general snapshots, but image quality isn't that high, and they don't offer any creative control.

If you like the idea of a truly compact compact, but want a camera that has more features, then you could go for a more expensive fixed-lens model. All the major camera manufacturers produce pocketable compacts that incorporate a more advanced design to give perfectly exposed results in all lighting conditions, a better flash, and improved image quality.

Moving up the size and price scale we arrive at dual-lens, or twin-lens, compacts. These cameras, as their names suggest, offer the choice of two focal lengths – usually 35mm and 50mm – so your options

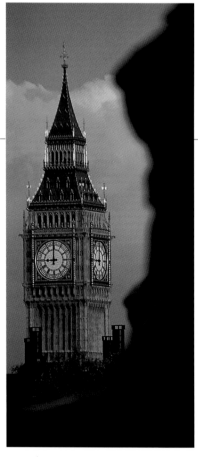

Big Ben, London, England Aperture priority is the most practical exposure mode for general use as it allows you to control depth of field.
Camera Nikon F90x Lens 80–200mm zoom Film Fujichrome Velvia 50

are increased. Again, the amount you pay will determine the model's sophistication, so it's worth inspecting a variety before making a decision.

Finally, if you want optimum versatility and don't mind paying a bit more for it, nothing beats the optical freedom offered by a zoom compact. A continuous zoom lens means you can photograph a much broader range of subjects, and compose your pictures with far greater precision. The focal length varies from model to model, with the smallest covering a range from 35 to 60mm or 35 to 70mm and the largest covering 38 to 115mm or more. As this range increases, so does the size of the camera and the price.

Zoom compacts also tend to be packed with other features, such as a sophisticated flash offering fill-in, slow sync and night modes, a wider shutter speed range, exposure compensation, and sometimes even a multiple exposure mode, so you can produce top-quality results with ease.

The drawback with all compact cameras is that you are limited to the lens the camera comes with, and even the best models offer little control over exposure, so once your interest in photography develops you are likely to find that they are somewhat restricting.

My camera has so many functions I never know which to use. What do you suggest?

This can be a problem for many novice photographers. Modern SLRs are packed with so many different functions that you're spoilt for choice, and until you know what each one is capable of, deciding which to use when can cause a great deal of confusion. That said, just because a camera has lots of features, you don't have to use them, and you'll find that once you have become accustomed to your own camera you will probably use only a fraction of the features offered.

In the beginning, you'll find working in program or fully auto mode the easiest option. The camera will set the exposure for you, if there's an integral flash it will cut in automatically, and all you have to do is look for interesting subjects, compose your pictures and press the shutter release.

As your experience grows, you can move away from program mode and make use of

TYPES OF SHUTTER

There are two very different types of shutter used in cameras today. The most popular is the focal plane shutter, which you'll find in all SLRs and some medium-format models, while compacts, most medium-format and all large-format cameras use a leaf shutter. Both types use the same system of shutter speeds, but they work in totally different ways.

Focal plane shutters (below) are fitted inside the camera body and comprise two blades that move in front of the film to allow light to reach it.

When you trip the camera's shutter release, the first blade moves across the shutter gate so light can pass through, then soon after the second blade follows to close it. At slow shutter speeds these two actions are distinct, but at fast shutter speeds, both blades move almost instantaneously to create a narrow slit passing very quickly in front of the film.

The advantage of the focal plane shutter is it makes faster shutter speeds possible – the fastest currently available is 1/12,000sec on the Minolta Dynax 9. The disadvantage is that electronic flash has to be used at a slow shutter speed for synchronization to occur.

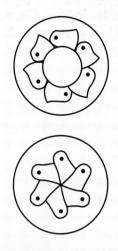

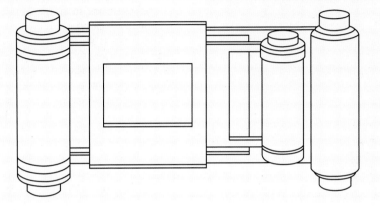

Leaf shutters (above) are found in the lens rather than the body of the camera, and close down centrally, like the blades in the lens's aperture.

This design prevents such fast shutter speeds being used – the highest is usually 1/500sec. However, electronic flash can be synchronized at any shutter speed, so it's ideal for fill-in flash in bright sunlight, for example, or high-speed flash photography when shooting action.

features that give you more control. You'll begin to experiment with the other exposure modes – aperture priority AE is the best one for general use – and try alternative metering patterns such as spot metering, make use of the exposure compensation facility and depth-of-field preview, exploit the full range of shutter speeds, and so on.

 What are the pros and cons of autofocusing, and how do different AF modes operate?

The first SLR to appear using a successful autofocus system was the Minolta 7000 in 1985. Since then, manufacturers have invested millions refining the methods used to produce a system that's fast, accurate, and as foolproof as possible, and the latest AF SLRs from manufacturers such as Canon, Nikon, Pentax and Minolta are as good as they're ever likely to be.

The main advantage of autofocusing is that it gives you one less factor to think about, so you can respond to fleeting photo opportunities far more quickly. This isn't as important for static subjects such as

landscapes and architecture, but for sport, action and candid photography, where pictures are often spoiled by inaccurate focusing, it can be a real boon. Autofocusing can also be invaluable for portraiture, reportage and wildlife photography.

Autofocusing works using sensors in the camera body that detect subject contrast (see page 12). Motors in the body or lens then adjust the focusing distance accordingly. To achieve sharp focus, the focusing sensor in your camera's viewfinder must be centred on your main subject.

Most AF SLRs use two different focusing modes. For general use with static subjects there's 'one-shot' AF, where you focus the lens by partially depressing the shutter release, and once focus locks on, you can hold it there by keeping your finger on the shutter release.

For moving subjects, 'servo' AF is used. This works by continually adjusting the focus so that your subject remains sharp as it moves closer to, or further away from the camera, so you can track a moving subject and time your picture carefully.

A variation of this found in some SLRs is 'predictive' AF, which estimates where the subject will be at the exact moment of

exposure, and adjusts the focus as you trip the shutter to ensure a sharp result.

Autofocusing isn't totally foolproof, of course. If something crosses your path the lens is likely to hunt around. Some systems also have difficulty focusing on areas of low contrast or continuous tone, such as blue sky, green grass and snow. But if this proves to be the case, you can always switch back to manual focusing to prevent problems – most AF lenses have a manual focusing ring of some description. This is also advised for static subjects such as buildings and landscapes where you need to control exactly where the lens is focused to ensure you achieve optimum depth of field (see page 45).

Camera manufacturers invest more money in developing their AF SLRs these days, so if you want to benefit from all the latest features such as sophisticated metering, a good choice of exposure modes and so on, you will have no choice but to buy an AF SLR. If you don't need autofocusing, just make sure that the model you choose can be fitted with lenses that have substantial manual focus rings so you get the best of both worlds – some brands of SLR are better in this respect than others.

Q Is there a correct way to hold a camera so that it is stable?

The way you hold your camera is very important, because it can make all the difference between pin-sharp results and pictures ruined by camera shake.

If you can achieve a firm, stable stance you will be able to use relatively slow shutter speeds and still produce perfect results each time.

Here are a few suggestions that will help ensure your pictures are always pin-sharp.

Grip the camera body with your right hand, letting your index finger rest over the shutter release, cup the lens in your left hand, and

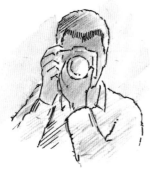

tuck your elbows into your sides. Your legs should also be slightly apart and your back as straight as possible.

When using long lenses, you will usually find the most stable position is to kneel on one knee and use your left leg to support your left arm (holding the lens).

Alternatively, sit on the ground cross-legged and rest your elbows on your legs, so that both camera and lens are well supported.

If you're forced to handhold the camera in low light when shutter speeds are low, either lean against a wall or post to increase stability, or rest the camera on a solid surface such as a wall.

Q What are the advantages of using a medium- or large-format camera?

The main reason for using medium- or large-format cameras instead of 35mm cameras is that they give far superior image quality due to the larger film size.

A medium-format camera such as the Pentax 67 or Mamiya RZ67, for example, produces negatives or transparencies that measure 6x7cm – that's almost five times the size of a 35mm original. As a result, the images can be enlarged to much bigger sizes before sharpness becomes unacceptable, and when they are reproduced in books, magazines, on calendars and posters, they look superb.

There are other reasons too. Most medium- and large-format cameras use leaf shutters in the lens, rather than a focal plane shutter like a 35mm SLR, so electronic flash can be synchronized at any shutter speed (see panel on page 35). The majority of medium-format cameras also have interchangeable backs, so you can switch to different film types and formats – including Polaroid instant film for test

HOW AUTOFOCUSING WORKS

Modern AF SLRs use a system known as 'phase detection' to ensure accurate focusing. Here's how it works:

Twin separator lenses inside the camera body project dual images of the scene you're photographing on to two rows of Charge-Coupled Devices (CCDs), which emit an electrical signal based on the amount of light hitting them. A microprocessor in the camera then compares these signals to a reference signal built into its memory, and when the signals match, sharp focus has been achieved.

If the lens has focused in front of your subject, the signals emitted by the CCD are closer together than the reference signal, while if the lens focuses behind your subject the signals are further apart. In either case the space between the signals is analyzed, and focusing motors in the lens adjust the focusing accordingly until those signals are 'in phase'. Clever stuff!

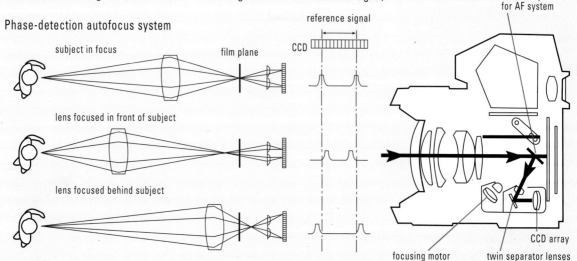

Phase-detection autofocus system

subject in focus · film plane

lens focused in front of subject

lens focused behind subject

reference signal · CCD

secondary mirror for AF system · CCD array · focusing motor · twin separator lenses

OTHER TYPES OF CAMERA

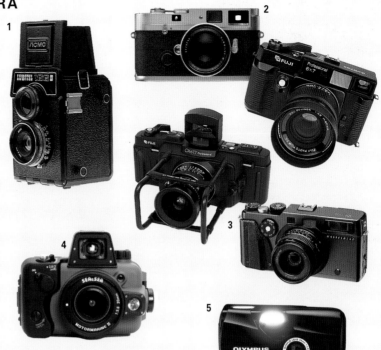

1 Rangefinder

Rangefinder, or non-reflex, cameras use separate viewing and taking systems like compacts. This can lead to parallax error caused by the taking lens not seeing exactly the same thing as the viewfinder, but most models are corrected for parallax.

Rangefinder cameras are smaller and lighter than SLRs. With no reflex mirror to flip up when you trip the shutter they're also much quieter, and the viewfinder doesn't black out during the exposure. These factors make them a favourite among photojournalists who often favour the Leica M-series of rangefinder cameras, and more recently the Hasselblad Xpan 35mm panoramic camera.

2 Twin lens reflex (TLR)

The TLR is an old-fashioned type of medium-format camera that uses two lenses – one for viewing the subject and the other for taking the picture. Most models are fitted with a fixed 80mm standard lens and produce 6x6cm images on rollfilm.

Parallax error can again be a problem at close focusing distances, and using graduated or polarizing filters is tricky because you can't see the effect obtained. Despite this, some fashion and portrait photographers still use them. One benefit is that the viewfinder doesn't black out as a picture is being taken because there's no mirror inside the camera to flip up. Secondhand models can be picked up cheaply, so they offer a budget introduction to medium-format photography.

3 Panoramic

Many 35mm compacts, all APS cameras and a few SLRs offer the option to take panoramic pictures, though they do this by masking the picture area so image quality isn't great if you want to make big enlargements.

To shoot true panoramics you need a purpose-made panoramic camera. The

Hasselblad Xpan is one of the best-selling models today as it accepts 35mm film, has a small range of interchangeable lenses, is compact and well-built and can also be set to full-frame 35mm format. Alternatives in 35mm format include models from Widelux, Horizon and Noblex that all feature a fixed rotating lens.

Rollfilm panoramic cameras are also available from Fuji, Linhof and Tomiyama (Art) in 6x17cm format (giving four shots on a 120 roll of film) and 6x12cm from Linhof, while Noblex produces a similar rollfilm model with a rotating lens.

For more specialist applications there are 360-degree panoramic cameras such as the Seitz Roundshot and Globuscope in both 35mm and rollfilm formats.

4 Underwater

The best-known underwater camera is the Nikonos, but Sea & Sea and other

manufacturers also produce cameras that can be taken underwater and several of the main camera marques also manufacture at least one underwater compact camera, like the Canon Sureshot A1. An alternative to buying an underwater camera is to purchase a waterproof housing for conventional 35mm SLR and compact.

5 Weatherproof

If you don't require full waterproofing, but would like to take your camera on the ski slopes, on the beach, or out in foul weather, there are many weatherproof compacts to choose from. Essentially they're just like normal 35mm compacts, with a sealed body to give protection against the elements.

shots, as well as black and white or colour, or fast and slow film – mid-roll.

Large-format cameras offer better image quality but they are mainly used because they allow you to adjust the position of the lens in relation to the film plane in order to control perspective and depth of field and prevent converging verticals when photographing buildings (see Architecture, page 129). This ability is known as 'camera movements'.

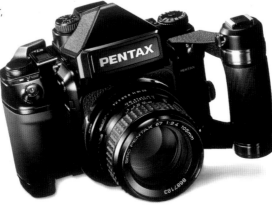

The Pentax 67II is a popular medium-format camera among both professionals and serious enthusiasts, especially for landscape and travel photography – I have used this camera for more than a decade.

Q I'm thinking about buying a digital camera. What features should I look out for?

First, you need to decide between a digital SLR or a digital compact. The former are generally more expensive, but if you buy a model from the same manufacturer as your film SLR, you can use the same lenses on both bodies. Digital compacts, on the other hand, have a fixed zoom lens. Let's assume you decide on a digital compact – here are the main features you need:

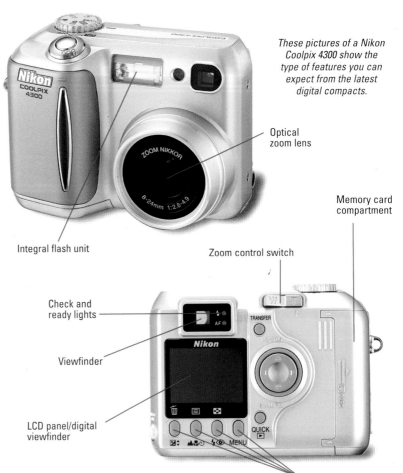

These pictures of a Nikon Coolpix 4300 show the type of features you can expect from the latest digital compacts.

Optical zoom lens

Memory card compartment

Integral flash unit

Zoom control switch

Check and ready lights

Viewfinder

LCD panel/digital viewfinder

TRANSFER

QUICK

Mode and function buttons

Resolution – the image quality a digital camera is capable of is governed mainly by how many pixels are offered – these days this number is always stated as megapixels (millions of pixels). Make sure that the camera has no less than three megapixels if you want to be able to make decent-sized prints (see below for a more detailed explanation of pixels).

Lens – the focal length of lenses for digital cameras is much smaller than for film cameras because the CCD isn't as large as a frame of 35mm film. For example, if a digital compact has a zoom range of 8–24mm, this is the same as 35–115mm on a 35mm film compact.

Optical or digital zoom – don't confuse the two. If a camera has an optical zoom, the focal length is adjusted to make the subject bigger in the frame. A digital zoom merely enlarges a central portion of the frame so image quality drops. Optical zooms are therefore preferable.

Sound and video – many digital compacts allow you to record video clips as well as still images; some record sound as well. The duration of the video is governed by the size of memory card in use.

LCD display – as well as showing the various menus and functions offered, the LCD on a digital compact can also be used as a real-time viewfinder in which you can frame your pictures, and to review pictures taken. This is useful for checking to see if a shot has turned out okay.

Chip speed – just as you can load films of different speeds (ISOs) into a film camera, so you can vary the sensitivity of the chip or CCD in a digital camera. For the

best results, this speed should be kept at ISO100, but in low light you can usually increase it as high as ISO800 or more. The higher you go, the poorer image quality becomes, and in the same way that grain becomes coarser with faster film, the digital equivalent is called 'noise' and appears on an image as random red or green pixels.

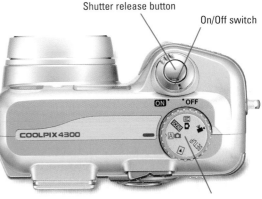

Shutter release button

On/Off switch

Mode dial

Exposure modes – most digital compacts have a range of modes from fully automatic to manual, as well as a series of subject-based auto modes. The flash status can also be varied – on, off, auto, red-eye reduction, slow sync and so on.

White balance – one of the problems with colour film is that it's designed to record light of a specific colour temperature, which is why your pictures

come out green if taken in fluorescent light or orange under tungsten. Digital cameras can correct these casts so your pictures look normal in any type of lighting.

Sockets – expect to find various sockets on a digital compact that allow you to connect the camera to a computer to download images, to a TV so you can display pictures, and so on.

Q Can you explain how digital cameras work?

Instead of using film to record an image, digital cameras use what's known as a Charge-Coupled Device (CCD). This is a chip composed of microscopic light-sensitive cells. Lightmeters have these too, but in a digital camera there can be millions.

When you trip the camera's shutter to take a photograph, light passes through the lens to the CCD and each cell (or 'pixel') generates an electronic signal based on the amount of light it receives. An image is then created from this grid of pixels.

The more cells a digital camera has in its CCD the better, because it means finer detail can be resolved – image quality is quantified by the camera's resolution, and this is stated as the number of million pixels the CCD has.

In order to produce high-quality prints up to 10x8in you really need a camera offering at least 3.5 megapixels (3.5 million pixels): digital compact cameras tend to offer this level of resolution at affordable prices. Digital SLRs have higher resolution – usually around six megapixels – though the latest professional digital SLRs, costing four times that of leading film SLRs, boast resolution of more than 11 million pixels and are said to offer quality that's superior to 35mm film.

Of course, digital technology is improving and progressing at an incredible rate, so by the time you read this, 20 or even 50 megapixel cameras may already have become available.

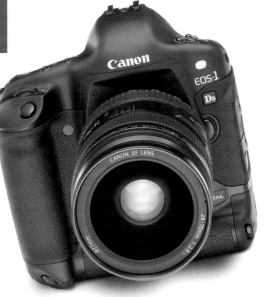

The latest breed of professional digital SLRs, led by the Canon EOS1 DS, offer resolution of over 11 million pixels and are said to be capable of achieving image quality equal, if not better, to that of rollfilm.

Q I'm still not convinced that I should buy a digital camera. What are the pros and cons?

Well, starting off on a positive note, digital cameras are extremely convenient – you can view a picture instantly and decide if it's worth keeping or not, or if it can be improved in any way, then take it again. In important situations this can be a huge benefit – which is why a lot of wedding photographers now shoot digitally. Digital cameras are also lots of fun – you can let the whole family use one, and kids are fascinated by the fact that they can take a picture then view it immediately – as well as plugging the camera into a TV or computer and viewing the pictures just seconds after they have been taken.

The initial outlay can be quite high because as well as the camera and memory cards, ideally you will also need a computer and printer – though it is possible now to buy small printers that you plug the camera directly into, so no computer is required. However, you now get a lot of technology for your money so there's never been a better time to go digital. Also, if you add up how much money you spend on film and processing each year you will see that your initial investment will soon pay for itself, especially if you take a lot of pictures.

The only downside is that to achieve image quality from a digital camera that's equivalent to film, you need to spend a lot of money on the latest pro-spec digital SLRs, and they cost four times as much as the most expensive film SLR.

Q When I take a digital picture, what happens to it?

The image is first stored in the camera's internal memory, then recorded onto a removable memory card.

In the same way that film comes in different exposures – usually 12, 24 or 36 – digital memory cards have different memory capacities – usually 16 Megabytes (MB), 32MB, 64MB, 128MB, 256MB, 512MB and 1 Gigabyte (1GB = 1,024MB).

The bigger the capacity of the memory card, the more images you can store before that card has to be removed and replaced by an empty one. The main difference between film and digital memory cards is that you can only use a roll of film once, whereas with a digital memory card you can download the images to a computer or other storage device, wipe the card clean and use it again and again.

Digital memory cards and storage media are discussed more on page 32.

Memory cards come in various sizes from 16MB to 1GB, though today's digital cameras offer such high resolution that anything smaller than 256MB isn't really worth bothering with.

Lenses

Lenses hold the key to a whole world of photographic creativity. Your camera may be capable of amazing things, but it's the lenses you fit to it that determine, more than anything, what appears on the final picture. You can use wide-angle lenses to capture sweeping views, and telephotos to isolate eye-catching details or fill the frame with distant subjects. Zooms give you the option to capture near and far subjects at the flick of your wrist, while macro lenses allow you to create stunning close-up images. Whatever your needs, you can guarantee there's a lens of some description that will satisfy them. The characteristics of different lens types can also be put to good use, helping you turn an ordinary picture into a true work of art.

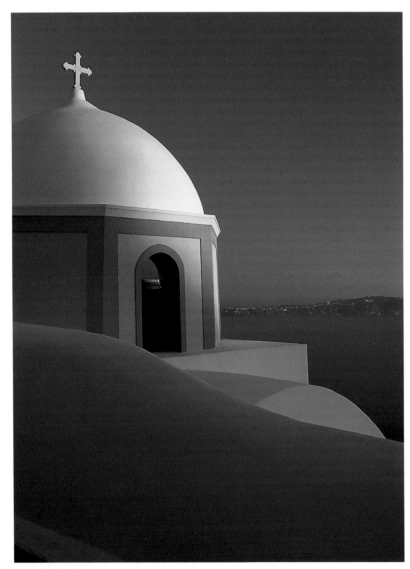

Church at Firostephani, Santorini, Greece
Lenses are the most powerful tool in your photographic armoury, making it possible to photograph any subject imaginable. I favour wide-angle lenses over telephotos as I prefer their characteristics – in this case I used a moderate wide-angle lens to create a simple, atmospheric image in the dying light of the day.
Camera Nikon F90x Lens 28mm Filter Polarizer Film Fujichrome Velvia 50

Q Could you explain how lenses are made and how they work?

Lens technology has come a long way in recent years, and modern optics are now painstakingly designed by computers to give optimum quality for minimum cost. If you take a slice through a typical lens you'll see that it comprises a series of glass elements arranged in groups of two or more. This optical configuration varies from lens to lens, but its basic purpose is to correct the optical aberrations that are caused when light rays are passed from one lens to the next, so sharp pictures with accurate colours and acceptable contrast are produced. It also determines the focal length of the lens.

Lens quality still varies considerably, but even the most inexpensive lenses are capable of producing excellent results due to improvements in design and higher standards of materials.

Internal lens elements

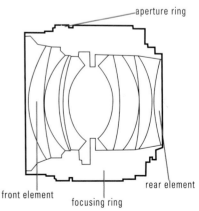

This cross-section shows the main components found in a typical lens.

APERTURES

As we'll discuss in more detail in Exposure (page 46), all lenses have a variable aperture so you can control the amount of light reaching the film to ensure the correct exposure.

The aperture scale is represented by a series of f/numbers, as shown below. The largest aperture is f/1, and as you move up the scale each subsequent f/number is half the size of the previous one and admits exactly half as much light.

If you look at the f/number scale on your lenses you'll see that the range offered varies. Most standard 50mm lenses have a maximum aperture of f/1.4 or f/2 and go down to f/16, for example, whereas on a 70–210mm telezoom the maximum aperture may be f/5.6 and the minimum aperture f/22.

The maximum aperture is particularly important because it determines the lens 'speed'. Lenses with a wide maximum aperture such as f/2.8 or wider are said to be 'fast' because they allow faster shutter speeds to be used.

Finally, all f/numbers are identical from lens to lens. An aperture of f/8 on a 28mm lens is exactly the same as f/8 on 50mm lens, 600mm lens or 80–200mm zoom, for example, and therefore allows the same amount of light to the film.

Most lenses give the sharpest results when set to an aperture of f/8 or f/11 – this is known as the 'optimum' aperture.

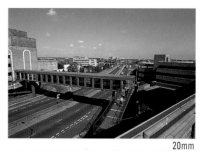

20mm

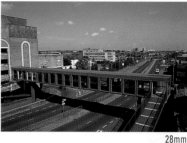

28mm

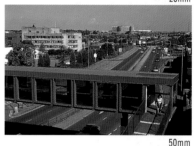

50mm

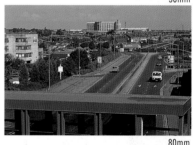

80mm

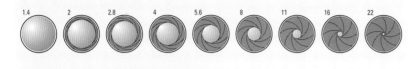

| 1.4 | 2 | 2.8 | 4 | 5.6 | 8 | 11 | 16 | 22 |

Q I'm a little confused about the terms 'focal length' and 'angle of view'. What do they mean?

Both terms are commonly used when discussing lenses, so it's important that you understand them.

Technically, focal length is the distance between the centre of the lens and the point at which the light rays passing through it focus, but it's mainly used to express the magnification of a lens.

There are basically three focal length groups: standard, wide-angle, and telephoto. The standard focal length for any given film format is equal to the diagonal measurement across one frame of that film: 50mm for 35mm film, 80mm for 6x6cm, 150mm for 5x4in and so on.

Any lens with a focal length smaller than the standard is known as wide-angle, and any lens with a focal length bigger than the standard is known as telephoto.

Angle of view is a measurement of how much a lens 'sees', and can be directly related to focal length. A wide-angle lens has a greater angle of view than a standard lens, while a telephoto lens has a smaller angle of view than a standard lens. The illustration and photographs right show the angle of view of a variety of focal lengths.

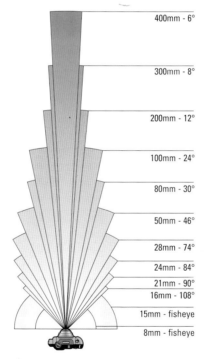

400mm - 6°
300mm - 8°
200mm - 12°
100mm - 24°
80mm - 30°
50mm - 46°
28mm - 74°
24mm - 84°
21mm - 90°
16mm - 108°
15mm - fisheye
8mm - fisheye

This illustration shows the angle of view of lenses with focal lengths from ultra wide-angle through to long telephoto. As you can see, the bigger the focal length, the narrower the angle of view. This allows you to be selective about what is included in your pictures.

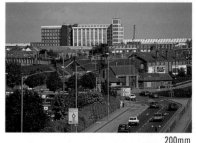

200mm

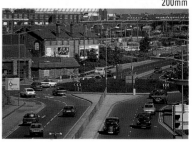

400mm

Here you can see how lenses with different focal lengths affect how much you can include in a photograph. Each shot was taken from exactly the same position.

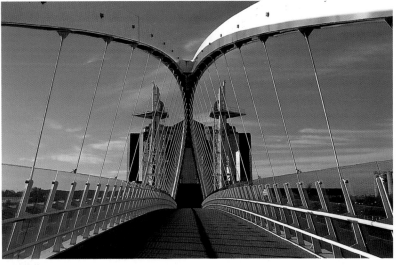

Salford Quays, Manchester, England
Wide-angle lenses are ideal for creating dynamic, sweeping compositions that stretch perspective, emphasize lines and allow you to include foreground interest. My favourite lens is a 28mm – a moderate focal length but wide enough to create powerful results.
Camera Nikon F5 Lens 28mm
Filter Polarizer Film Fujichrome Velvia 50

Q Standard lenses don't seem very popular these days. Are they still worth using?

Since zoom lenses have become so common the poor old standard 50mm lens has fallen out of fashion. However, it's a very useful lens and shouldn't be ignored. The optical quality is first rate, so you can produce pin-sharp results, and its angle of view is similar to the human eye so it's ideal for still lifes, landscapes and a whole host of other subjects.

Standard lenses also have a generously wide maximum aperture – usually f/1.8 or f/2, although f/1.4 and even f/1.2 models are available. Combine this with its small size and light weight and you have the perfect lens for taking handheld pictures in low light, so even if you have a zoom lens that offers a focal length of 50mm as part of its range, it's still worth buying a 50mm standard lens as well if you tend to take a lot of pictures handheld in low light.

Q How can I get the best results from my wide-angle lens?

The most obvious thing you'll notice when you fit a wide-angle lens to your camera is that it gives you the opportunity to capture much more on a single picture than can be seen with the naked eye – the shorter the focal length, the wider the angle of view. As a result, wide lenses are ideal for landscape, architecture and general scenic photography, or if in a confined space.

Wide-angle lenses also offer other benefits. Firstly, they appear to 'stretch' perspective so the features in a scene appear further apart than they really are, and tend to distort objects that are near to the edges of the picture area. This allows you to emphasize features by moving in close so they dominate the picture, or to exaggerate lines and foreground interest to produce powerful compositions.

Secondly, wide-angle lenses give extensive depth of field (the zone of sharp focus in a picture) at small apertures such as f/11 or f/16, so you can keep everything sharp, from the immediate foreground to the distant background.

Most photographers prefer a 28mm or 24mm wide lens for general use as either offers all the benefits without being tricky to use. You need to take care though, as it's still easy to end up with hopelessly boring compositions full of empty space.

Once your experience grows, you'll find the extra distortion of ultra wides (20mm or wider) ideal for producing strong images.

Q What is a mirror lens and what effect does it produce?

It's a specially designed compact telephoto that uses mirrors to fold the light back on itself. This allows a focal length of 500mm or 600mm to be achieved in a body that's only a fraction of the length and weight of a traditional telephoto lens.

Mirror lenses are handy if you need to travel light, and they're small enough to handhold. The main drawback is that they have a fixed aperture – usually f/8 – which limits your use of fast shutter speeds.

You can often tell if a picture has been taken with a mirror lens because out-of-focus highlights in the background record as doughnut-shaped rings. This effect can work really well on some shots, but if it appears on all your telephoto pictures it will quickly become repetitive and boring.

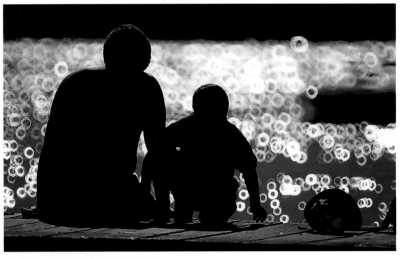

Windermere, Lake District, England
This shot illustrates the main characteristic of a mirror lens – the shimmering doughnut-shaped highlights in the background. The effect works well, but isn't always easy to achieve.
Camera Nikon F5 Lens 600mm mirror Film Fujichrome Velvia 50

Telephoto lenses basically do the opposite of wide-angles. Instead of including more in a shot they magnify your subject and include less. Instead of stretching perspective they compress it, so everything appears much closer together. And instead of giving extensive depth of field, they reduce it considerably, even at small apertures, so backgrounds are thrown out of focus and your main subject stands out. These characteristics become more evident as the focal length increases.

The most useful telephotos fall in the 85–300mm range. 85–105mm lenses are often referred to as 'portrait' lenses due to the way they flatter facial features. Slightly longer telephotos of 135–300mm are better suited to candid photography, or isolating small landscape and architectural details. The 300mm lens is a favourite among sport, action, press and nature photographers.

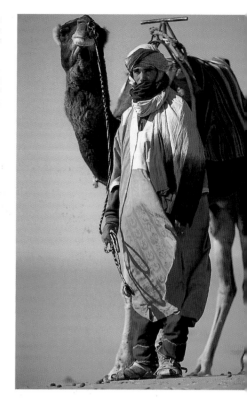

Sahara Desert, Morocco
Telephoto lenses allow you to magnify your subject, fill the frame and limit depth of field. The way elements are compressed together by tele lenses is also effective.
Camera Nikon F90x Lens 80–200mm zoom at 200mm Filter Polarizer Film Fujichrome Velvia 50

Beyond 300mm, the lenses begin to get much bigger, heavier and more expensive. This not only makes a tripod or monopod necessary to prevent camera shake, but the small maximum aperture tends to limit your use of fast shutter speeds in all but the brightest conditions, unless you use faster film or buy expensive faster lenses.

Long telephotos also need to be used with more care. Depth of field is severely limited, especially at wide apertures, so accurate focusing is crucial if your main subject is to be sharply recorded.

Saying that, if you're seriously interested in sport or nature photography, you'll soon discover that a 400mm, 500mm or even 600mm lens is necessary to take frame-filling pictures of distant subjects.

LENSES AND PERSPECTIVE

The angle of view of a lens not only determines how much it sees, but the way in which apparent perspective can be recorded as well.

If you capture the same scene from exactly the same position with a 28mm wide-angle lens, and then a 300mm telephoto, perspective will be exactly the same. This can be proven by enlarging a small section from the wide-angle shot that covers the same area as the telephoto shot.

However, by changing camera position, perspective can be altered for different results.

If you photograph a queue of people with a 28mm wide-angle lens, for example, the apparent distance between each person will be exaggerated. This is because wide-angle lenses stretch perspective. Now do the same with a 300mm lens, keeping the person at the front of the queue the same size in the frame – by moving much further back – and the people appear much closer together than

they are in reality. This is due to the way telephoto lenses compress perspective to give a 'stacking up' effect. When used creatively, these characteristics can produce stunning results.

This set of pictures shows how different lenses are able to alter perspective when one element in a scene is kept the same size in the frame.

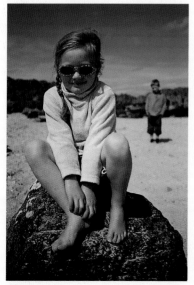

28mm

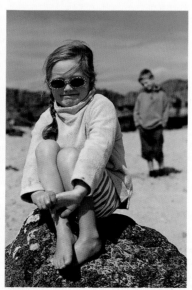

50mm

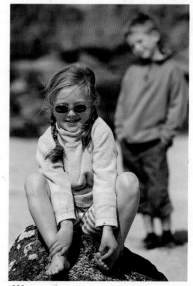

200mm

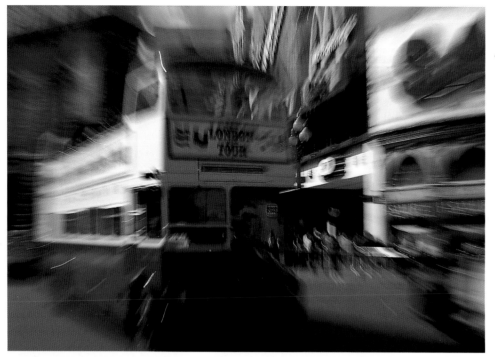

*Piccadilly Circus,
London, England
Here's a classic example
of a zoomed picture.
It was taken using a
standard zoom lens at a
shutter speed of 1/8sec.*
Camera Olympus OM4-Ti
Lens 35–70mm
Film Fujichrome RFP50

 Are zoom lenses better than fixed focal length lenses?

For most photographers, zooms are a firm favourite because they reduce the number of lenses that need to be carried and they allow you to adjust focal length precisely so your pictures are perfectly composed.

There are drawbacks to zooms though. For starters, the maximum aperture is usually a stop or two slower than on prime lenses in the same focal length range. This means in identical conditions you'd be forced to use slower shutter speeds or faster film with a zoom. The smaller aperture also gives a darker viewfinder image, which can make focusing trickier in low light. Fast zooms are available with a wide maximum aperture – such as 80–200mm f/2.8 – but they're more expensive and also bigger and heavier.

Secondly, zooms of any type are often heavier than their prime counterparts. Usually this isn't a problem, but it means that you need to use faster shutter speeds when handholding, to avoid camera shake.

Finally, though the optical quality of zoom lenses is better than ever, some photographers feel that prime lenses are still sharper. Though not always the case, this is true if you buy zoom lenses at the budget end of the market, so it's worth spending as much as you can afford to get the very best quality.

What's the easiest way to take 'zoomed' pictures?

Any type of zoom covering any focal length range can be used for this popular technique. The effect is created simply by zooming the lens through its focal length range during a longish exposure, so your subject records as a dynamic explosion of colourful streaks.

For the best results, choose a simple, bold subject so it will stand out in the final image. People, buildings, trees, flowers and statues are all ideal. You should also use a shutter speed of 1/8sec or slower, so you've got enough time to zoom through the full range before the shutter closes at the end of the exposure.

All you have to do then is focus on your subject with the zoom set at one extreme of its focal length range, and just as you're about to trip the shutter release, start zooming quickly and evenly through the focal length range. Continue zooming after the shutter has closed, for a smooth effect.

BUILDING A SYSTEM

With so many different types of lens to choose from, deciding which you'll need for your own brand of picture-taking will be a subject of much personal debate.

Until a decade or so ago, it was fairly traditional to start out with a 50mm lens, then, once funds allowed it, add a 28mm wide-angle and a 135mm telephoto. Today, zoom lenses have changed things considerably and it's now common practice to buy an SLR body with a 28–80mm or 35–70mm zoom then invest in a 70–210mm or 80–200mm telezoom later.

Whichever route you take, these initial investments will provide a good system for all-round use, and you'll find that lenses from 28–200mm will cover perhaps 90 per cent of your picture-taking needs. Any further additions can then be made once you begin to specialize in certain subjects.

If you're interested in sport or wildlife photography, for example, a 300mm, 400mm or 500mm lens will be invaluable for capturing distant subjects. Many photographers cover this range by purchasing a 300mm lens and a good quality 1.4x or 2x teleconverter to provide extra power when required.

For landscape, architecture and general scenic photography, wide-angle lenses from 20–35mm are more useful. So you may decide to cover that whole range with a 20–35mm zoom, or to purchase a single ultra-wide lens such as a 20mm, for example, to complement your standard 28–80mm zoom.

The main thing to bear in mind is that the lenses you use have a major influence on the quality of your pictures, so always buy the best you can afford.

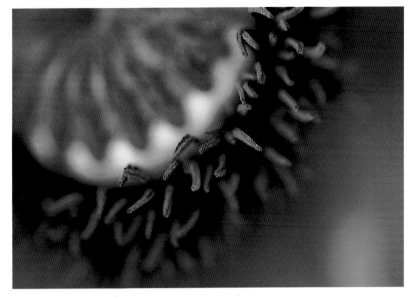

Californian Poppy
This close-up was taken
using a 1:1 macro lens at
full power to fill the frame
with colour and detail.
Camera Nikon F90x
Lens 105mm macro
Film Fujichrome Velvia 50

Q What does a shift lens do?

Shift lenses, also known as 'perspective
control' or PC lenses, are designed to
correct the converging verticals caused
when you have to tilt the camera back to
photograph a tall building or other
structure. This is made possible by
adjustable elements that can be moved up
and down, so you can include the top of the
building in the frame while keeping the
camera perfectly square.

Shift lenses for 35mm SLRs usually have
a focal length of 28mm or 35mm, although
there are one or two 24mm versions and a
90mm model from Canon. A high price tag
tends to restrict use to professionals only
(see Architecture, page 128).

Q Can you buy special lenses for close-up photography?

Yes. Many manufacturers produce a range
of lenses that are designed to give
optimum image quality when used at close
focusing distances. Most offer half lifesize
reproduction (1:2), while some allow you to
take lifesize (1:1) pictures either with or
without further attachments.

The focal lengths of macro lenses can be
divided into two main groups: 50/55mm
and 90/100/105mm lenses. The shorter
models are smaller and lighter and usually
offer 1:2 reproduction, but the longer lenses
allow you to work at greater focusing
distances, so the risk of scaring timid
subjects is reduced, and tend to give 1:1
reproduction. The focal length is also ideal
for portraiture. See Nature and close-ups
(page 123) for more details.

Q What are teleconverters used for?

A teleconverter is an optical accessory that
fits between your camera body and lens
and increases the focal length of that lens.

The most common type is a 2x converter
that doubles the focal length, turning a
200mm lens into a 400mm, or a 70–210mm
zoom into a 140–420mm. You can also buy
1.4x converters, which increase focal length
by 40 per cent.

The main advantage of teleconverters is
that they increase the optical scope of your
existing lens collection and reduce the
number of lenses you need to carry. Instead
of buying an expensive 400mm telephoto
lens, for example, you could buy a 2x
converter for a fraction of the cost and use
it on your 200mm lens.

Unfortunately, teleconverters do have
drawbacks. For a start you lose two stops
of light with a 2x model (one stop with a
1.4x), which can restrict your use of fast
shutter speeds, and make the camera's

viewfinder rather dark. They also reduce
the optical quality of the lens they're used
on, particularly zooms, so your pictures may
not appear quite as sharp – particularly at
the edges. To minimize this, buy a seven-
element converter.

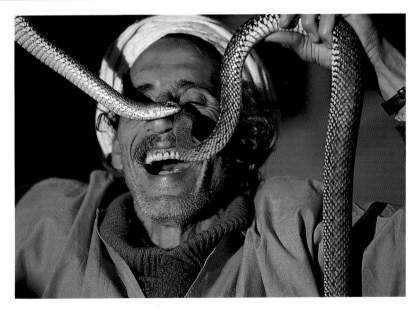

Snake charmer, Marrakech, Morocco
Teleconverters are ideal for travel
photography as they allow you to increase
the power of your lenses with only a minimal
addition to the weight of your kit.
Camera Nikon F90x Lens 80–200mm with 1.4x
teleconverter Film Fujichrome Sensia II 100

Filters

Professional photographers have been using filters almost since the birth of photography, but it's only in the last decade or so that their popularity has really taken off among enthusiasts. Today you can choose from hundreds of different types, all of which allow you to manipulate the image seen through your camera's viewfinder.

Filters are invaluable for controlling colour balance and contrast, so your pictures are as close to reality as possible. This is often necessary as what the eye sees isn't always the same as what the film or sensor in your camera records. You can also use filters to intentionally distort reality or to add a range of special effects. Whatever your reason for using them, all filters have one thing in common – they're an indispensable aid to creative photography.

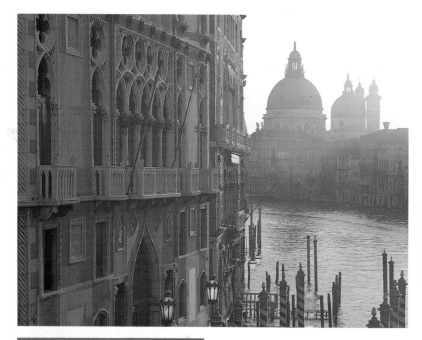

Santa Maria Della Salute, Venice, Italy
The key to success when using filters is to produce photographs that don't necessarily look as though they have been filtered. In this case I chose an 81D warm-up to enhance the naturally warm light of a Venetian dawn.
Camera Pentax 67 Lens 165mm
Filter 81D warm-up
Film Fujichrome Velvia 50

Q I'm about to start building up a filter collection, but can't decide which system to invest in. What do you recommend?

Q Square filters come in different sizes. Does it matter which type I buy?

Yes. The smaller square filters, measuring 64mm, are fine for use with 35mm SLR lenses as wide as 28mm. However, for wider lenses you will need to use a larger system of 84mm or 100mm filters, otherwise the lens will 'see' the edges of the filter holder and cause vignetting. A larger filter system will also be required if you use long telephoto lenses or medium-format lenses, simply because they have huge filter threads.

In terms of cost versus quality, the Cokin P system is the best available – the holders and adaptor rings are inexpensive; you can fit the holder to lenses with a thread size up to 82mm; and the system contains literally hundreds of different filters.

However, if you want optimum image quality and versatility, a 100mm system like the one from Lee Filters will be better, even if it does cost considerably more.

Square slot-in filter systems are the most versatile as you can use the same set of filters on all your lenses just by changing the adaptor ring.

There are two basic types of filter available: the round type that screws directly to the front of your lens, and the square type that slots into a special holder.

In terms of flexibility, the square systems are a better choice. All you need is one holder and a selection of adaptor rings, and you can use the same set of filters on lenses with different screw thread sizes. You can also use three or four filters in the holder at once to combine effects.

Round filters are designed to fit lenses with a specific filter thread, and come in all standard sizes. They're fine if all your lenses have the same thread size, but most don't, especially if your system contains both wide-angles and telephotos.

To use round filters on larger or smaller lenses you'll need step-up or step-down rings, which are fiddly and slow to use. The depth of the filter mount also means that if you use two or more together there's a risk of vignetting (see Problem solving, page 89).

Q Could you explain what a polarizing filter does, and when it should be used?

When light rays strike a surface, some of them are scattered in all directions and become polarized. This creates glare and specular reflections that weaken the colours in a scene.

Polarizing filters work by preventing that polarized light from entering your lens, and in doing so they provide several benefits. Blue sky contains a lot of polarized light, so if you photograph it through a polarizer its blue colour will be deepened considerably. Polarizers also reduce glare on non-metallic surfaces such as foliage and paintwork, so colours look far richer, and eliminate reflections in water and glass, so you can see into rivers and through windows.

For the best results, use your polarizer in bright, sunny weather. The effect can be gauged simply by rotating it in the mount or holder while peering through your camera's viewfinder. When you're happy with what you see, stop rotating and fire away.

When shooting blue sky, keep the sun at right-angles to the camera so you're aiming at the area of sky where polarization is maximized. Take care when using wide-angle lenses though – polarization is uneven across the sky, so you can very easily end up with a darker band on one side of your picture.

Similarly, when eliminating reflections, you'll get the best results if your lens is at an angle of about 30 degrees to the surface

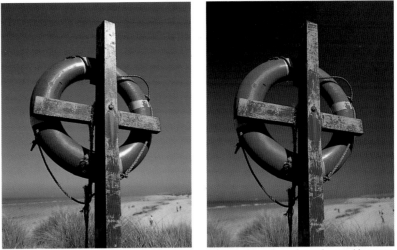

When used correctly, a polarizing filter can deepen blue sky, reduce glare and increase colour saturation – the difference between these two pictures is significant.

being photographed. You can find this by adjusting your camera position slightly and checking the effect. A polarizer can also be used to enhance attractive reflections in water. If you rotate it slowly the annoying surface reflections and glare will be removed to reveal the true reflections.

Finally, though it gives the best effect in sunny conditions, a polarizer can also be used in dull weather to remove glare and increase colour saturation – especially on woodland scenes.

Firostephani, Santorini, Greek Island
Polarizing filters come into their own for deepening blue sky, increasing colour saturation and improving clarity – here's an example of the results.
Camera Nikon F90x Lens 80–200mm zoom
Filters Polarizer Film Fujichrome Velvia 50

FILTERS AND EXPOSURE

Many filters reduce the amount of light that enters your lens, so you may need to compensate the exposure when using them to prevent your pictures from coming out too dark.

Each filter is given a 'filter factor' that indicates by how many times the initial exposure needs to be multiplied to make up for this loss of light. A factor of x2 indicates an exposure increase of one stop, x4 two stops, x8 three stops and so on. The filter factor is usually printed on the filter mount or box.

If your camera has TTL (through-the-lens) metering and you meter with the filter in place, any light loss will be taken into account automatically, so you needn't worry about it. However, if you meter without the filter in place, or use a handheld meter, you must increase the exposure accordingly based on the filter factor. The table shows the filter factors for some common filters.

Filter	Filter factor	Exposure increase
Red	x8	3 stops
Polarizer	x4	2 stops
Blue 80A	x4	2 stops
Orange	x4	2 stops
Orange 85B	x3	1⅔ stops
Yellow	x2	1 stop
81A warm-up	x1⅓	⅓ stop
Skylight	x1	none
Diffuser	x1	none

Q Which type of polarizer should I buy: circular or linear?

If your camera has a beam splitter or semi-silvered mirror you'll need a circular polarizer, otherwise exposure error will result due to polarized light being created inside the camera. This group includes all AF SLRs, plus those with spot metering.

If your camera doesn't fall into one of these categories, a linear polarizer will be fine, and as linear polarizers cost less than circular versions, it makes sense to find out which type you need.

Q I've heard that graduated filters
are used by many landscape
photographers. What exactly
do they do?

If you take a meter reading from the ground
and the sky when shooting landscapes,
you'll find there's a big difference between
the two – often two or three stops. This
means that if you set an exposure that's
correct for the sky, the landscape itself
will come out too dark, but if you correctly
expose the landscape the sky will come out
too light and lose most of its colour.

The easiest way to avoid this is by using
graduated filters, which are clear on the
bottom half and coloured across the top
half. By positioning the filter in its holder
you can darken down the sky so its
brightness is similar to the landscape and
both areas come out correctly exposed
when you meter for the landscape.

There are two types of graduated filter
currently available: coloured and neutral
density (ND). Coloured grads such as pink,
tobacco, blue and mauve can add life to a
dull, grey sky, and the warmer colours are
ideal for enhancing the sky at sunrise and
sunset. The effect they give can easily look
false though, so they must be used with
care. ND filters are designed to darken
down the sky without changing its colour,
so they're preferred by photographers who
want to produce natural-looking results.
They also come in different densities for
more precise control – a 0.3 ND grad
darkens the sky by one stop, 0.6 by two
stops and 0.9 by three stops. If you buy
0.3 and 0.6 grads, you can use them
individually or together to achieve a three-
stop reduction, the same as a 0.9 grad.

When using a graduated filter be sure to
align it carefully so you don't darken part
of the foreground as well. Pressing your
camera's depth-of-field preview while
adjusting the filter will help you to
determine its position.

As the filter is only affecting part of the
picture you don't need to adjust the
exposure. Modern metering systems should
be able to give correct exposure with the
grad filter in place, because by toning down
the sky with the grad you're actually
making the scene easier for your camera
to interpret. Alternatively, take a meter
reading without the grad in place and then
use the exposure once the filter has been
fitted to your lens.

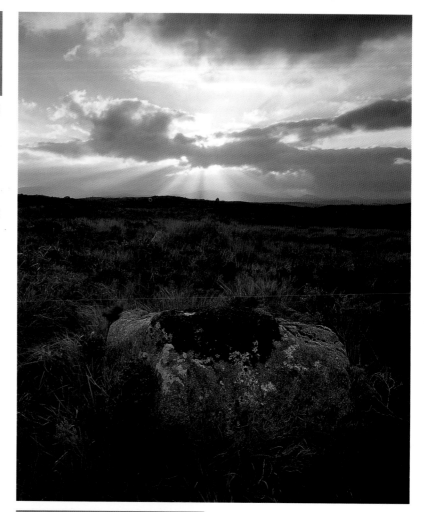

Rannoch Moor, Scotland
Neutral density graduated filters are
invaluable for toning down bright sky so
it doesn't overexpose when you meter for
the landscape – here I used a 0.9 density
grad, darkening the sky by three stops.
Camera Pentax 67 Lens 55mm
Filters 0.9 ND grad and 81C warm-up
Film Fujichrome Velvia 50

Q I hear it's a good idea to keep a
clear filter fitted to my lenses so
the front element is protected.
Which type should I use?

You can use either a skylight or ultraviolet
filter to protect your lenses. The UV filter is
designed mainly to cut through atmospheric
haze and to reduce the slight blue cast in
the light at high altitudes. The skylight filter
does the same, but also warms up the light
a little as well.

Using either of these filters reduces the
risk of you damaging the front element of
the lens – a damaged filter is cheaper to
replace than a whole lens. However,
remember that the more filters you use on
your lenses at the same time, the more
image quality will be degraded. Vignetting
is also more likely if you fit other filters on
top of the skylight or UV, especially with
wide-angle lenses, so it's a good idea to
remove your protective filter when using
other filters on the lens.

This is a common problem with screw-on
filters, and can cause great frustration. The
key is to apply even pressure around the
filter mount, so it doesn't buckle and grip
the lens even tighter. Your local camera
dealer may stock a purpose-made filter
wrench. Failing that, wrap a length of
electrical flex or a cable release around the
mount and twist to loosen the grip – or
lightly grip the filter mount with your finger
tips and try to loosen the filter. The worst
thing you can do is grip the mount tightly.

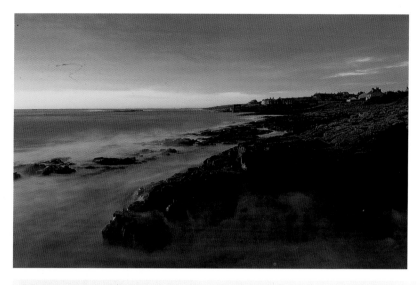

*Craster, Northumberland, England
Sunset graduated filters are ideal for
landscapes and seascapes shot at dawn
and dusk. The top half of the filter gives a
stronger effect than the bottom to enhance
and tone down the sky and the effect can
look superb on the right scene.*
Camera Pentax 67 Lens 45mm
Filter Cokin Sunset 1
Film Fujichrome Velvia 50

FILTERS FOR SPECIAL EFFECTS

Filters are mainly used to control contrast and lighting balance, but there's also a range available that allows you to create eye-catching special effects.

The starburst, or cross-screen, is probably the most common. This is simply a clear filter with fine lines etched into the surface, which turns bright points of light into twinkling stars – you can choose from two-, four-, six-, eight- and sixteen-point stars.

Starbursts are ideal for transforming night-time scenes, or for making the highlights on water shimmer. They can also be combined with coloured filters for more eye-catching results.

Taking the starburst idea one step further are diffraction filters, which break up bright points of light into the colours of the spectrum to create brilliantly coloured highlights. A variety of stunning effects are possible, particularly on silhouettes or night shots. Multiple-image filters work by surrounding your subject with anything from three to twenty-five repeated images of itself, depending upon the number of facets on the filter.

*An eight-point starburst filter was
used on this shot, turning the bright lights on the Christmas tree into stars.*

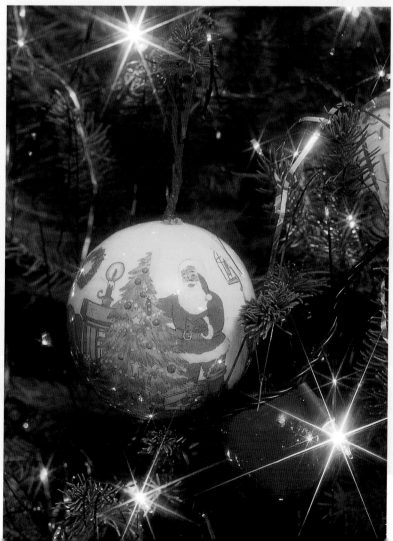

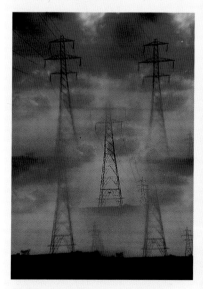

*Multiple image filters work well on a
variety of subjects from portraits to
buildings – here a multi-image 5 filter
was combined with a deep orange.*

Q My photos often come out with colour casts, and shots taken in tungsten lighting look yellow. Which filters will correct this?

There are two main groups of filters that are designed to balance colour deficiencies in the light, be they natural or artificially created. They're known as colour-correction and colour-conversion filters, and the type you need will depend upon the strength of colour cast produced.

Colour-correction filters comprise the 81-series of straw-coloured 'warm-ups' (81A, B, C, D and EF) and the 82-series of pale blue 'cool' filters (82A, B and C). With warm-ups the 81A is the weakest and 81EF the strongest. The 82-series work the opposite way, with the 82A being the strongest and 82C the weakest.

Warm-up filters are ideal for balancing the blue bias found in the light in dull, cloudy weather, in the shade or in really bright sunlight. They can also be used to enhance warm sunlight early or late in the day, and to make skin tones more attractive when shooting portraits. An 81B or 81C is best for general use, while the others are reserved for stronger colour casts or to give a more obvious warming effect. The 82-series of pale blue filters cool down the light. In this respect they have limited use, because it's rare that you would want to cool down natural daylight, and they're not strong enough to have a noticeable effect on artificial lighting. However, they can be used to give your pictures a cool cast – this looks effective when shooting in foggy or stormy weather, or at night.

Colour-conversion filters again come in two colours – the blue 80-series and orange 85-series – but their colour density is much deeper so they're able to balance stronger colour casts.

The blue 80-series is mainly used to neutralize the yellow/orange cast created if you take pictures in tungsten light on daylight-balanced film. A blue 80A filter (the strongest) should be used with household tungsten lights, a blue 80B for tungsten photoflood studio lights and a blue 80C for tungsten photopearl studio lights. You can also use these filters to give pictures shot in daylight a blue cast.

An orange 85B filter allows you to obtain natural results if you use tungsten-balanced film in daylight, or to lose the strong blue cast if you're shooting in dull weather. However, they're more commonly used creatively to add a warm glow to portraits and landscapes. See Lighting (page 57).

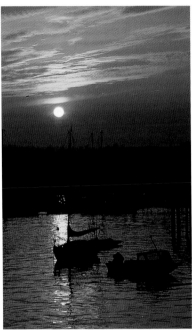

Torquay, Devon, England
The 81-series warm-up filters are invaluable for scenic photography as they allow you to enhance natural daylight. In this case an 81D filter was used to make the sunset even more sumptuous.
Camera Olympus OM1n Lens 50mm
Filter 81D warm-up Film Fujichrome RFP50

Q Can you explain what colour-compensation filters are?

These fall into another group of colour-balancing filters that tend to be used by professional photographers to control colour deficiencies in the light.

Kodak makes the most extensive series, known as Wratten filters. They're available in a variety of colours and strengths measured in colour correction (CC) values.

Usually a special colour-temperature meter is used to measure the colour temperature of the light and indicate which filters are required to balance out the casts. A combination of the required filters is then fitted to the lens.

The most common is C30 magenta, which balances the green cast that is caused by fluorescent lighting. An FL-D filter also does the same.

Alnwick, Northumberland, England
Stronger colour conversion filters can be used to give your pictures a deep colour cast. Here I used a blue 80A to cool down this misty river scene and add a sense of mystery to it.
Camera Pentax 67 Lens 45mm
Filter Blue 80A Film Fujichrome Velvia 50

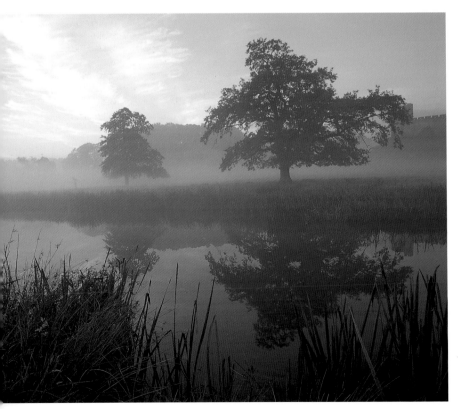

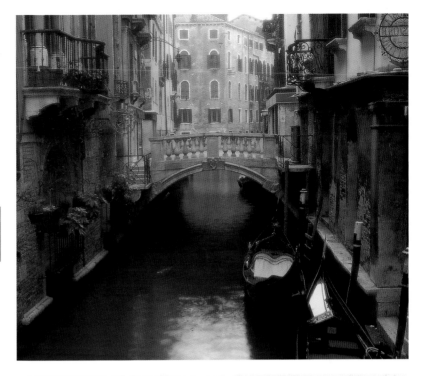

Venice, Italy
Soft-focus filters are ideal for adding mood and atmosphere to your photographs and suit scenic views as well as portraits or still lifes.
Camera Pentax 67 Lens 105mm
Filters Cokin Diffuser and 81B warm-up
Film Fujichrome Velvia 50

 How can I get the best results from soft-focus filters?

Soft-focus filters are perfect for injecting a touch of atmosphere into portraits, landscapes and still lifes. They work by bleeding the highlights (the lightest parts of the scene) into the shadows, so fine details are suppressed, colour saturation is reduced and your subject is surrounded by a delicate glow.

The effect obtained depends upon the make of the filter. Some filters add a lot of diffusion, while others are more subtle. There are also several variations on the diffuser theme available. Pastel filters, for example, add a haze that softens colours.

Whichever type you use, for the best results photograph subjects that are either backlit or against a dark background. Any lens can be used successfully, and you can control the level of diffusion by adjusting the lens aperture. Wide apertures give a strong effect, while small apertures reduce the level of diffusion.

FILTERS FOR BLACK AND WHITE

It may seem strange using colour filters for black-and-white photography, but they serve a very important purpose. The problem is that while all colours appear different to the naked eye, some record as very similar grey tones. Red and green are common examples.

To overcome this, photographers use strong-coloured filters to alter the tonal balance in a scene and to control contrast. These filters mainly work by lightening their own colour and darkening their complementary colour, but other effects are also produced.

Yellow	Slightly darkens blue sky so white clouds stand out. Lightens skin tones and helps to hide skin blemishes.
Orange	Noticeable darkening of blue sky in sunny weather so white clouds stand out strongly. Also helps to reduce haze, hide freckles and increases contrast. Ideal for general use.
Green	Good separation of green tones makes this filter ideal for landscape, garden and woodland photography. It also darkens red.
Red	Blue sky goes almost black, clouds stand out starkly and a dramatic increase in contrast allows you to create powerful pictures. Darkens greens considerably and can be used with mono infrared film. Needs care in sunny weather.
Blue	Increases the effects of haze but lightens blue sky. Also brings out details in the face and strengthens skin tones, so it can be used for portraits of men.

Alnmouth, Northumberland, England
An orange or red filter is ideal for emphasizing dramatic skies – especially in sunny weather.
Camera Nikon F90x Lens 20mm
Filter Red Film Ilford FP4 Plus

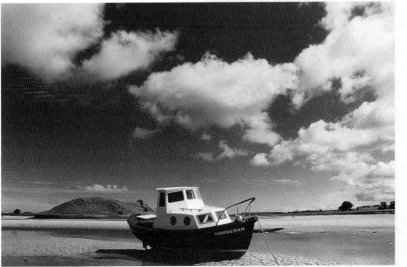

Film

With well over 150 different types of film available today, all capable of producing excellent results, photographers are spoilt for choice. Walk into a well-stocked photographic shop and you'll be confronted by thousands of yellow, green, blue and orange boxes, all seeming to shout out 'buy me, buy me!'

So which one do you buy? Is Kodak film better than Fuji, Konica, Ilford or Agfa? Should you use print or slide film? Do you need slow film, or will something faster be better? Throughout this chapter you'll find answers to these questions, and many more besides...

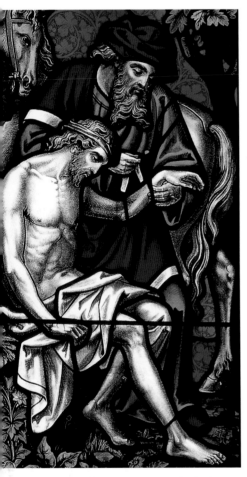

Barnwell, Northamptonshire, England
Although all colour films are capable of superb quality, they do vary from brand to brand so it's worth experimenting with a few to see which you prefer. My favourite, and that of many other photographers, is Fujichrome Velvia 50, a film renowned for its vibrant colours and fine grain.
Camera Olympus OM4-Ti Lens 135mm
Film Fujichrome Velvia 50

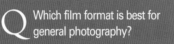

Q Which film format is best for general photography?

The most popular format is 35mm, mainly because it offers a good compromise between size, cost and quality. The film is still small enough to keep the camera size down to a manageable level, but image quality is of a high enough standard to make enlargements of 16x12in or 16x20in if slow film and good-quality lenses are used. You also get up to 36 shots on a roll, and the cost per shot is very reasonable.

Where greater image quality is required, medium-format cameras are favoured, for the simple reason that the bigger the original image is, the less it needs to be enlarged. The rollfilm used in medium-format cameras comes in two lengths – 120 or 220 – and gives a number of image sizes depending upon the camera type. The most popular sizes are 6x4.5cm, 6x6cm and 6x7cm, while some models offer 6x8cm or 6x9cm – these are commonly used for landscape photography.

Finally, when nothing but the best will do, 5x4in and 10x8in sheet film is used in large-format cameras. These formats are often used by professional advertising and architectural photographers, but the costs of material and equipment are generally far too expensive for the majority of amateur budgets to accommodate.

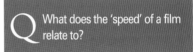

Q What does the 'speed' of a film relate to?

Film speed is a means of quantifying a film's sensitivity to light or, in other words, how much exposure the film requires to produce a correctly exposed image.

The ISO (International Standards Organization) scale is used to measure film speed. Film with a low ISO number – 50 or less – is said to be 'slow' because it isn't very sensitive to light and therefore needs to be exposed for longer. Film with an ISO of 100–200 is termed 'medium speed' and is ideal for general use, while film with a high ISO such as 400, 1000 or 1600 is considered 'fast' because it's more sensitive to light, and needs much less exposure than slow film.

Remember that every time you halve the speed of a film it needs to be exposed for twice as long, and vice versa.

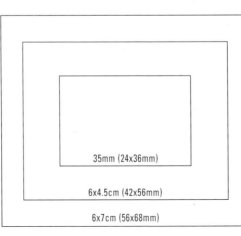

35mm (24x36mm)

6x4.5cm (42x56mm)

6x7cm (56x68mm)

This illustration shows the actual image sizes obtained using film formats from 35mm to 6x7cm.

Q How do I know which speed of film to use for different subjects?

The light levels you'll be working in will partly determine which speed of film you should be using, and also the type of subject you are photographing. Slow film is ideal in bright conditions, for example, because there's plenty of light around to allow decent exposures, but faster film is more convenient if you want to take handheld pictures in lower light, especially when fast shutter speeds are required to freeze movement.

However, film speed is also directly related to image quality, so you need to consider this factor as well.

Slow films offer fine grain, rich colour saturation and superb sharpness, but as the film speed increases quality begins to tail off. Grain becomes coarser, which leads to a reduction in sharpness and resolving power, shadow density is reduced and colours become weaker.

The ideal compromise is to use the slowest film you can, so you gain maximum benefits on both counts.

Q Which type of film is best for amateur photographers: colour print or colour slide?

If convenience is important, print film wins every time. To show family and friends your latest pictures all you have to do is pass around a photo album, or a pile of enprints. There are also thousands of high street labs where you can drop off your print films and pick up the results an hour or two later.

Another great benefit of print film is its tolerance to exposure error – known as exposure latitude. You can accidentally under- or overexpose a picture by at least three stops, and still obtain an acceptable result because any error can be corrected at the printing stage. Unfortunately, slide film has no more than half a stop of latitude, so you need to get the exposures spot-on when using it.

Of course, there are benefits to using slide film. For a start, image quality is superior because there's no intermediate printing stage, where problems can occur with colour balance and contrast. If you intend to sell your work you will also need to shoot slide film, as few publishers and picture buyers will accept colour prints.

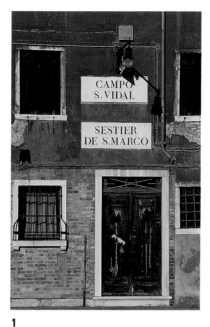

1

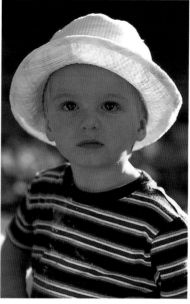

2

1 Slow film (ISO50 or below) This is the ideal choice when you require optimum image quality for subjects such as landscapes, architecture and still lifes. The lack of speed means you'll need to use a tripod in all but the brightest conditions, but the superb sharpness, perfect colours and almost invisible grain allow you to make big enlargements without sacrificing too much detail.

2 Medium film (ISO100–200) A good speed for all subjects, and the standard choice for most photographers. Image quality is still superb, with excellent colour saturation, sharpness and fine grain, but the extra speed means you can get decent exposures in normal conditions. You'll still need to use a tripod in low light though.

3 Fast film (ISO400–1000) The quality of fast film has improved dramatically in recent years so it needn't be considered a last resort any more. Grain is coarser and colours less saturated than ISO50 or ISO100 film, but it's invaluable if you need to use fast shutter speeds in dull light, or you want to take handheld pictures indoors without flash.

4 Ultra-fast film (ISO1000 and over) These films are designed for taking handheld pictures outdoors in low light, or photographing indoor subjects such as sport and stage plays. Grain is much coarser and colours are rather weak, but considering the speed, image quality is

excellent. You can also use the film's characteristics to add atmosphere to your photographs – in fact more ultra-fast film is used in this way than for the extra speed that it offers.

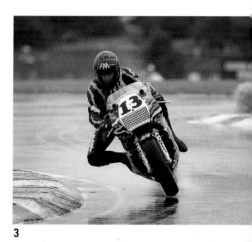

3

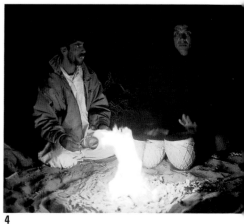

4

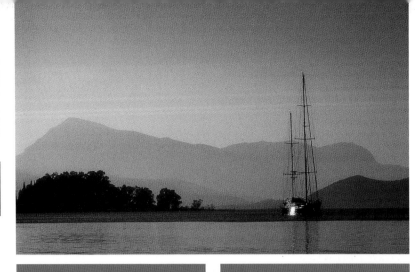

Poros, Greece
To increase the grain and contrast of this atmospheric picture, I uprated ISO400 colour slide film to ISO1600 then had it push-processed by two stops.
Camera Olympus OM4-Ti Lens 200mm
Film Fujichrome RHP400

Q My camera has DX-coding. What exactly does this do?

DX-coding allows film speed to be set by your camera automatically. This is possible because film is now manufactured with a chequered pattern of black and silver squares on the side of the cassette – a DX-coding pattern – which indicates its ISO rating. Most modern SLRs and compacts have DX-coding pins inside the film chamber, so when you load a roll of DX-coded film the pins read the pattern and the correct film speed is set.

The advantage of DX-coding is that it prevents you from accidentally setting the wrong film speed, which would lead to incorrectly exposed pictures. Unfortunately, it can also cause problems if you want to rate the film at a different speed.

Some SLRs give you the option of setting film speed manually, as well as using DX-coding. The alternative is to buy DX-coding labels, which you can stick on non-DX-coded films so the correct film speed is set or you can alter film speed.

Q Do films differ from brand to brand?

The differences between colour print films aren't so obvious because much depends upon the quality of the printing. However, slide films differ considerably in terms of colour saturation, contrast and sharpness.

Fujichrome Velvia slide film, for example, is known for its vivid colours and punchy contrast, whereas Agfachrome or Kodachrome slide films reproduce colours more faithfully. So Fujichrome is ideal if you want contrasty, well-saturated slides, but for portraits a film with more natural rendition may be chosen instead.

Experiment with a range of films, then pick and choose specific brands for different subjects or situations.

Q Can film be used at a different ISO rating than recommended?

Yes. Occasionally you may find the film isn't fast enough for you. If this happens you can improvise by rating the film at a higher ISO, known as 'uprating'. By rating a roll of ISO100 film at ISO400, for example, you can use faster shutter speeds or smaller apertures. By uprating film you're effectively underexposing it, so it is developed for longer, or 'push-processed', to compensate. If you uprate ISO100 film to ISO200 you need to push it by one stop; if you rate it at ISO400 you need to push it by two stops, and so on.

The drawback is that it causes an increase in contrast and grain, but when used creatively this can look highly effective.

Q Do I need to use a special film when taking pictures in tungsten lighting?

You can use normal daylight-balanced film in tungsten lighting, but a blue 80A or 80B filter must be fitted to your lens to counteract the yellow/orange cast (see Filters, page 26).

The alternative is to use tungsten-balanced film instead, which is designed to record colours naturally in tungsten light without the need for filters. There are several types of tungsten slide film available, including Fujichrome 64T and Kodak Ektachrome 64T for high-quality work, and Kodak Ektachrome 160T and 320T when you need extra speed. Tungsten-balanced colour negative film is also available now – Kodak Portra 100T and Fuji NPL 160L. These are mainly used by professional photographers.

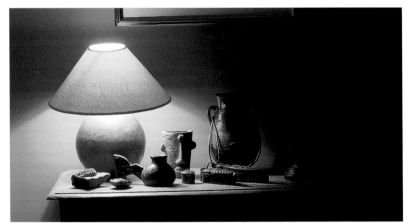

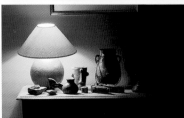

African artefacts
These pictures show how you can cool down the orange colour cast created when normal daylight balanced film is used under tungsten lighting. The bigger shot was taken using a blue 80A filter, while the smaller shot is unfiltered and much warmer.
Camera Nikon F90x Lens 50mm
Filter Blue 80A Film Fujichrome Velvia 50

Q Could you give me some advice on how to use infrared film – both colour and mono?

The main attraction of infrared film is that it records the world differently to the way our eyes see it. Mono infrared film turns blue sky black and foliage white, while colour infrared turns grass and foliage a deep crimson.

There are three main types of mono infrared film available: Kodak High Speed, Konica 750 and Ilford SFX.

The Kodak version is the most sensitive to infrared light, so it must be loaded and unloaded in complete darkness. It's also the fastest, grainiest and most dramatic. Konica 750 doesn't give such a strong infrared effect but it's very sharp and fine-grained, while Ilford SFX is the least sensitive and falls between the other two in terms of image quality. Konica and Ilford infrared film can be handled in subdued light, so you can load and unload with the camera under a jacket. Infrared film works best in bright, sunny weather.

All three films should be exposed through a deep red filter or a visually opaque infrared filter (Kodak Wratten 87 or 88A).

If you use a red filter, rate Kodak infrared at ISO50 and take a meter reading without the filter in place, or rate it at ISO400 and meter through the filter. For Konica, rate it at ISO6 if you meter without a filter, or ISO50 if you meter through it, and Ilford SFX at ISO25 without the filter in place, or ISO200 if you meter through it.

Getting the exposure correct can be tricky. To be on the safe side, take several shots at different exposures – metered, +1 stop, +2 stops and -1 stop. Do this using your camera's exposure compensation facility.

Finally, infrared film focuses on a different point to visible light, so you must focus as normal, then adjust the distance on the lens so it falls opposite the IR focusing index – usually a small red mark.

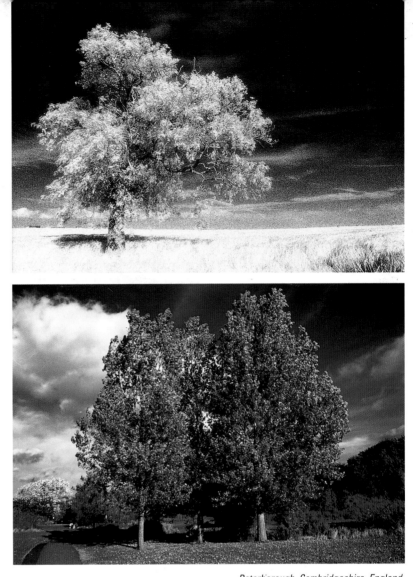

Peterborough, Cambridgeshire, England
Scenes containing lots of foliage show the effects of infrared film the best – with mono infrared film it goes a ghostly white tone, while colour infrared turns it a deep red.
Camera Nikon F90x Lens 28mm Filters Red for mono shot, yellow for colour
Film Kodak HIE Infrared for mono and Kodak Ektachrome EIR for colour

The only exception is if you're using a wide-angle lens set to a small aperture, in which case there will be sufficient depth of field to take in this difference and you can focus normally.

Kodak EIR colour infrared film must also be loaded and unloaded in complete darkness and exposed through a yellow filter – though it's worth trying red, orange and polarizing filters as well. Rate it at ISO640 and meter with the yellow filter on your lens, bracketing exposures up to two stops over and under the metered exposure, in half- or third-stop increments.

CARING FOR YOUR FILM

1. Keep unused film in its plastic tub or special film storage boxes. If grit gathers on the felt light trap it could scratch the whole roll of film when you use it.
2. If your film is going to remain unused for several weeks or more, store it in an airtight container inside your refrigerator. When you need to use some, allow it to warm up to room temperature for a few hours before removing it from the tub. Storing film at a low temperature will extend its life so you can use it a year or more after the expiry date with no ill-effects.
3. Never leave film in direct sunlight or warm places. High temperatures cause colour shifts that spoil your pictures.
4. Never buy film that has been stored on a shelf in direct sunlight for long periods. Professional film should always be stored in a refrigerator in the shop, not stocked on the shelves.
5. Process exposed film as soon as possible after you use it. This will ensure you get the best possible results.

Digital capture

The advent of digital technology means that you no longer need to use film to record photographic images. This process can now be done using cameras that contain light-sensitive chips to record information. Instead of carrying rolls of film and incurring expensive processing bills, all you need are special memory cards and a computer to download the images.

Q Film comes in different speeds – what's the digital equivalent?

You can vary what's known as the 'chip' speed, which, like film, uses the ISO scale. If you want optimum image quality you would set the chip sensitivity to its slowest speed of ISO50 or 100, but in low light you could increase it to ISO400 or 800 – some digital SLRs go as high as ISO6400.

The benefit of this over film is that you can change the chip speed as and when required, which can sometimes be difficult with film. The downside is that at higher speed settings digital images often suffer from 'noise', which is caused by brightly-coloured pixels being formed by mistake in shadow areas.

To avoid this, always keep your chip speed to the lowest setting you can possibly manage.

Q How can I store digital images as I'm taking them?

Early digital cameras stored images in their internal memory, so once the memory was full you had to download the images onto a computer before taking further pictures. However, these days, removable memory cards are standard issue, so when one card is full you simply replace it with an empty one, just like you would load an unexposed roll of film.

The two types of memory card available are SmartMedia and the more popular CompactFlash. Memory size varies – some digital cameras come supplied with a card offering 16MB or 32MB of storage, but resolution is so high now, even on digital compacts, that 256MB storage cards are the smallest you should consider otherwise you will quickly run out of card space. If you use a digital SLR, 1GB or bigger makes sense because large file sizes use a lot of memory. The largest memory cards available at the time of writing are 4GB.

Ideally, you need more than one card so you don't run out of memory before you download the images and wipe the cards for reuse. This is especially true if you're away travelling or on holiday.

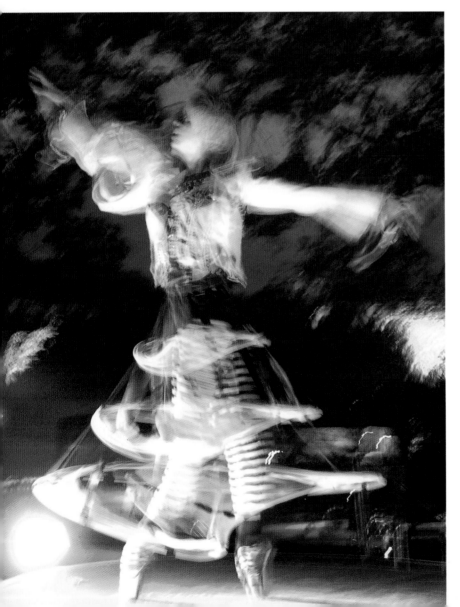

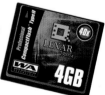

CompactFlash cards are the most popular type of memory card for use in digital cameras – and 4GB is currently the biggest storage capacity available.

Dancer, Alnwick, Northumberland, England Adjusting the sensitivity of the CCD allows you to cope with different light levels and maintain reasonable exposures – I set the highest speed of ISO400 for this handheld shot taken at night.
Camera Nikon Coolpix 4300
Lens 38–114mm zoom

What resolution should I set my digital camera to?

The higher you set the resolution, the better image quality will be so you can make bigger prints from the files. At the same time, each image will use more memory so you'll get fewer pictures on your memory card before it needs to be emptied.

Ideally, it makes more sense to always use your camera at its highest resolution and simply buy more or bigger memory cards. You can always resize the images as required later on the computer if you want to email them or put them on a website, but a small image file can't be increased if you decide to make a big print. At the end of the day, there's no point spending money on a high-quality camera then not using it to its full potential.

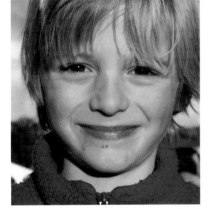

Maximum resolution (2272x1704 pixels)

Normal resolution (1280x960 pixels)

Basic resolution (640x480 pixels)

This set of pictures shows how the quality of your digital images is affected by the resolution at which you take them. The main shot is a portrait of my son, Noah. I took this shot at three different settings to demonstrate the differing quality, as shown in the details of his left eye.

How do I know what the maximum size of print I can make from a digital file is?

The quality of a digital image is determined by the number of pixels it contains – the more it has, the bigger the image can be output.

Your camera's instruction book will tell you what the pixel dimensions are at the highest quality setting, and from that you can work out maximum print size.

To achieve photo-quality resolution you need to print at at least 200 pixels per inch (ppi, also known as dots per inch or dpi) so that individual pixels aren't visible to the naked eye. So, for example, if your camera's maximum resolution is 2272x1704, at an output of 200dpi maximum print size will be just over 28x21cm (11x8½in).

How can I download images off my memory cards without carrying a computer with me?

There are two options. One is to buy a portable hard disk so you can store images off your memory cards until you have access to a computer. Storage capacity varies but can be as high as 80GB – which will hold a lot of material. The other is to buy a portable CD writer, which allows you to archive images from your digital memory cards direct to recordable CDs (CD-R) without the need for a computer. This means that you could spend months away from a computer and never run out of storage space for images – providing you can get hold of recordable CDs.

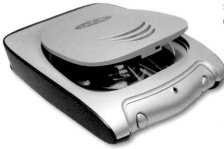

Portable CD writers allow you to copy digital images straight from your digital camera to CD-R without the need for a computer.

How do I transfer images from memory cards to my computer?

In most cases you can connect the camera direct to your computer via a Universal Serial Bus (USB) or FireWire lead and download the images off the memory card inside the camera onto the computer.

Alternatively, you can buy a card reader, which is a small, inexpensive drive that plugs into your computer. The cards are then slotted into the reader so you can download the images and wipe the card clean, ready for reuse.

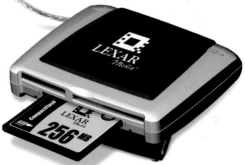

A card reader provides a quick and easy way of downloading images from a memory card to your computer.

What's the most cost-effective way to store digital images?

CD-Rs are still the best way to archive and store digital images because they are inexpensive and each one will hold 650MB of memory. Re-recordable CDs (CD-RW) are becoming more popular now as well. CD-RW are more efficient because you can reuse them time after time, whereas CD-R can only be used once.

Another storage medium to consider is recordable DVD (DVD-R). Each disk will hold 3.9GB, so they're ideal if you want to archive collections or store lots of big image files.

When I download images to my PC they are saved as JPEGs. Should I leave them like that?

No. JPEGs are compressed files so as you re-save them, image quality is lost. To prevent this, save them as TIFF or PSD (Photoshop Document) files before you start working on them, so you don't lose quality.

Flash

Flash photography is a subject that causes great confusion and frustration among enthusiast photographers. Just about everyone buys a flashgun at an early stage in their hobby, but few ever get to grips with it. As a result, for most of the year it lies in the bottom of a gadget bag gathering dust, only to make the odd fleeting appearance at parties or family get-togethers.

However, the humble flashgun is an invaluable piece of equipment that can create stunning results. As well as being a handy source of extra illumination in low-light situations, it's also ideal for a range of creative techniques and offers endless scope for experimentation.

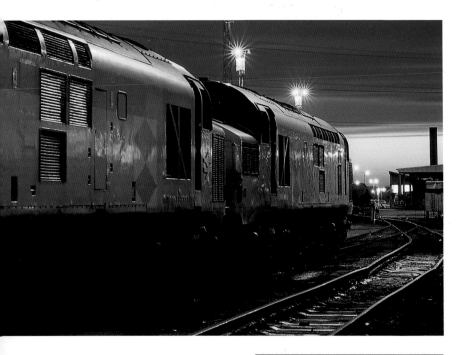

Goods train
Once you've mastered the basic techniques, your portable flashgun can be used to create all kinds of eye-catching effects. In this case, I used a fairly basic flashgun to paint the side of the train with light by walking alongside it and firing the flash several times while my camera's shutter was locked open on B (bulb) during a 60-second exposure.
Camera Olympus OM4-Ti Lens 50mm
Film Fujichrome Velvia 50

Q What features should I look out for when buying a flashgun?

Flashguns vary enormously in size, shape and price, but most models offer a range of similar features. Here's a basic rundown of what they are and what they do, using a typical dedicated flashgun as an example (see page 35).

Hot shoe This is the part of the flashgun that connects to the camera. It includes electrical contacts that ensure flash synchronization occurs when you take a picture and that the flash communicates with the camera's metering system so that correct exposure is achieved automatically. You need to make sure that the gun you buy is compatible with your camera, as each make differs.

Bounce/swivel head Allows you to angle the head of the flashgun and bounce the light off a wall, ceiling or reflector to make the light more attractive and prevent red eye (see page 38).

Zoom head Allows you to adjust the angle of coverage of the flash to give even illumination for lenses with different focal lengths – usually from 24–105mm. Clip-on diffusers are often available to extend the coverage for lenses as wide as 17mm. Some expensive flashguns adjust automatically as you zoom your lens, or you can dial in the required focal length using controls on the gun.

LCD This is the heart of a modern dedicated flashgun as it displays all the information you need and allows you to set things like lens focal length, film speed, aperture, flash power output and numerous other features.

Test button Allows you to fire the flash without taking a picture, to ensure correct exposure will be obtained. This button is also handy when you want to fire the flash several times during a single exposure – when painting with light, for example.

Variable power output Allows you to set the power output of the gun to 1/2, 1/4, 1/8, 1/16 etc so that you can balance flash and ambient light and avoid the flash dominating the picture – this is especially handy for fill-in and slow sync flash techniques (see pages 36 and 38).

Strobe mode Some flashguns can be programmed to fire a rapid sequence of flash bursts automatically, allowing you to create multiple exposures of moving subjects – such as a golfer taking a swing.

Flash exposure compensation Allows you to force the flashgun to give more or less light than it would if left to its own devices. This enables you to overcome exposure error when faced with a really light or dark subject, or for creative effect – in the same way you would use your camera's exposure compensation facility.

Focus sensor The majority of modern flashguns have an AF illuminator that shines a beam of light onto your subject when you're shooting in low light so the lens can focus. This makes it possible to shoot in complete darkness.

Sync socket This is where you plug a sync lead into the flash if you decide you want to use it off the camera and still have full dedicated control.

Wireless sensor Some of the more expensive dedicated flashguns have a special sensor that allows them to be used off the camera without the need for sync leads – when you press the camera's shutter release to take a picture the flashgun is triggered remotely. Several guns can be used together in this way.

Q I have seen flashguns with a guide number. What is this?

The guide number (GN) of a flashgun gives an indication of its maximum power output, and the distance it will be effective over – the bigger the number the greater the output, and vice versa. All GNs are stated in metres, for ISO100 film.

The integral flashgun found on compacts and many SLRs has a relatively small GN – usually 10 to 14 – so they're only effective over a shorter distance. Press photographers, on the other hand, tend to favour large hammerhead flashguns with a GN as big as 60, as they can be used to capture long-range subjects.

For general use, a flashgun with a GN of 30–40 is powerful enough, allowing you to photograph subjects that are a reasonable distance away or use small apertures for close-range subjects.

By dividing the GN by the flash-to-subject distance (in metres), you can calculate the aperture required for correct exposure (for ISO100 film). If the GN is 30 and your subject is 2m away, the aperture needed is 30/2=15 or, when rounded up, f/16.

These photographs of a Nikon Speedlite SB-80DX give you an idea of the features found on a modern dedicated flashgun.

Bounce/swivel head
Zoom head
Focus sensor
Sync socket
Hot shoe

Film speed setting
LCD
Auto distance range
Focal length setting
Aperture setting
Flash mode button
On/Off button
Test button
Flash ready light

FLASH SYNCHRONIZATION

Back in Cameras (page 11) we looked at how the focal plane shutter in an SLR works. When you trip the shutter release, the first blade in the shutter moves away so light can reach the film, then soon after, the second blade follows to cover the film again. At fast shutter speeds this action is like a narrow slit moving across the film in a fraction of a second.

If you use flash with fast shutter speeds, part of your subject will be obscured by the shutter blade when the flash fires, resulting in a section of the picture being blacked out. To prevent this, cameras have a 'flash sync speed' – usually 1/125sec, although a growing number have a faster sync speed of 1/250sec. This is the fastest shutter speed you should use when working with flash to ensure a successful result. Slower shutter speeds can be used, but nothing faster.

The only exceptions to this are certain SLR and flashgun combinations, which allow flash synchronization to occur at all shutter speeds – even 1/1000 or 1/2000sec!

FILL-IN FLASH

Fill-in flash is a technique used to soften harsh shadows and lower contrast when you're shooting portraits against the light or in bright sunlight. An added benefit is that the flash also puts attractive catchlights into your subject's eyes.

The basic idea is to combine a controlled burst of flash with the daylight exposure, so the flash has the desired effect without dominating the photograph. This is done by setting your flashgun to fire at half or quarter power, rather than at full power.

If your flashgun has a variable power output you can do this by simply setting 1/2 or 1/4 and the rest will be done automatically. If not, you have to fool it into delivering less light. This is easiest to achieve with automatic guns.

- First you need to take a meter reading for the daylight (ambient light) and set it on your camera, remembering that the shutter speed used must be no faster than your camera's flash sync speed. Let's say this is 1/125sec at f/11.

- Using the flash on quarter power to give a flash-to-daylight ratio of 1:4 tends to give the most attractive results. This is achieved by setting your flashgun to an auto-aperture setting that's two stops wider than the aperture you're going to use on the lens – in this case the flash should be set to f/5.6.

- If the light is really harsh and you need more flash, a stronger effect can be produced by setting the flash to an aperture one stop wider than the one you're using, so a ratio of 1:2 is obtained. With the lens set to f/11, for example, you should set the auto aperture on the flash to f/8.

- If you need only a weak burst of light, set the auto aperture on the flash to a setting three stops wider – in this case f/4.

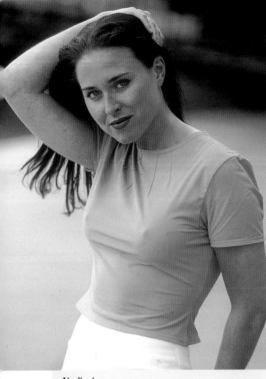

No flash

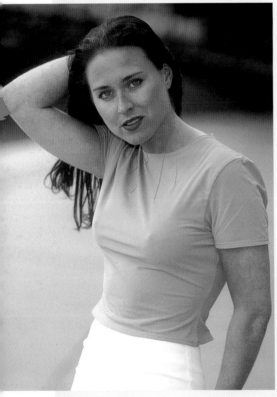

Flash to daylight ratio of 1:4

Fill-in flash
Here you can see how a controlled burst of fill-in flash can improve portraits shot outdoors in harsh light. A flash-to-daylight ratio of 1:4 usually gives the most flattering results.
Camera Canon EOS 1N Lens 70–210mm
Flash Canon Speedlite 540EZ Film Kodak Ektachrome E100SW

The main difference between these types of flashgun is the amount of control they give you. Price is also a factor – the more features and automation a gun has, the more it tends to cost.

Manual flashguns are the simplest type, with the power output usually fixed at maximum so the amount of light delivered is always the same. A table on the back of the gun tells you which aperture to set to give correct exposure for different flash-to-subject distances and film speeds. If you need to use a different aperture you must change the flash-to-subject distance or use faster/slower film.

Automatic flashguns use a series of automatic aperture settings that allow correctly exposed pictures to be taken over a specified flash-to-subject distance range – the extremes of which are indicated by a scale on the gun.

You set the flashgun and lens to the same aperture, then when the flash fires, a sensor on the front of the gun measures the light reflecting back from your subject, and once sufficient light has been delivered it quenches the flash to ensure a correctly exposed picture is obtained.

The number of auto-aperture settings varies, but the more a gun has the better because it gives you greater flexibility over aperture choice.

Dedicated flashguns work in conjunction with the metering system of a specific SLR model to guarantee perfect exposures. All you have to do with dedicated flashguns is to switch the gun on, fire away and everything else is set automatically, including the correct sync speed and the lens aperture.

Levels of dedication vary. Some models are totally automated, so you can't override them at all, while others have both automatic and manual modes, plus a range of other features that may include variable power output, strobe flash, multiple flash and much more (see page 35). Obviously, the more features on offer, the more expensive the gun, and you may find that the weight increases too.

The main reason photographers use bounced flash is that it gives much more flattering results than using direct flash. If you point a flashgun straight at your subject, the light produced is very harsh and casts dense shadows on the background; by bouncing the light off a wall or ceiling first, it's softened considerably and shadows are weakened.

If your flashgun has a bounce/swivel head you can simply tilt it in the right direction while it's still attached to your camera's hot shoe. If not, take the gun off the camera and point the whole gun towards the bouncing surface. To do this you'll need a flash sync lead, so the gun can be connected to your camera.

For the best results, bounce the flash off a white wall, ceiling or reflector. High ceilings are of no use as they spread the light over too wide an area to be effective, and coloured surfaces should be avoided because they give the flash a colour cast that will spoil your pictures.

Some flashguns have a secondary flash unit, fitted below the main tube, that can be used to soften the shadows created by bouncing. Alternatively, place a white reflector beneath your subject's chin if you're bouncing from a ceiling, or on one side of their face if you're bouncing from a wall to put light into the shadows.

Finally, bouncing causes a light loss. Automatic and dedicated guns make up for this loss by increasing the light output, but if you're using a manual gun the lens aperture must be opened up by one-and-a-half- to two-stops for correct exposure.

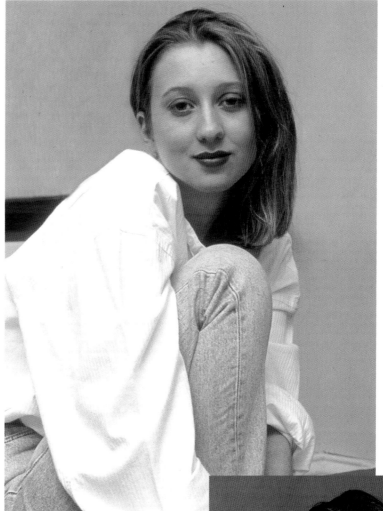

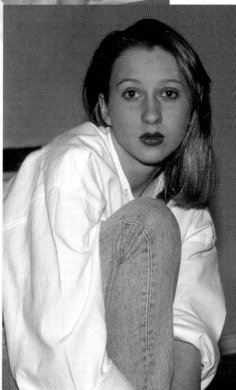

Bounced flash
Bouncing flash (above) produces more flattering light than direct flash (right). Today's dedicated flashguns make it easy to achieve perfectly exposed results because any light loss is compensated for automatically.
Camera Canon EOS 1N Lens 70–210mm
Flash Canon Speedlite 540EZ
Film Kodak Ektachrome E100SW

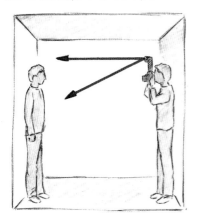

Direct flash

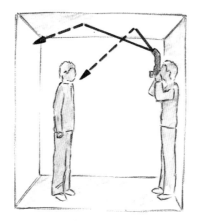

Flash bounced off ceiling

Red eye is caused by light reflecting back off the retinas in your subject's eyes, and usually occurs when a flashgun is positioned too close to the lens axis and fired directly at your subject.

Cameras using an integral flash are the biggest culprits because the position of the flash can't be altered. To combat this, many models use a red-eye reducing flash, which fires one or more weak preflashes to reduce the size of the subject's pupils before the main flash fires – with varying degrees of success.

If your camera doesn't have a red-eye reduction facility, or you're using a hot shoe-mounted flashgun, here are a few tips on how to banish red eye:

- Ask your subject to look to one side of the camera instead of straight at it.
- Ask your subject to look towards a room light or stand near a window for a couple of minutes, so their pupils reduce in size.
- Fire the test button on your flashgun before taking the final picture.

- Bounce the light off a wall or ceiling so it isn't hitting your subject directly.
- Take the flashgun off your camera's hot shoe and either hold it to one side or place it on a flash bracket.

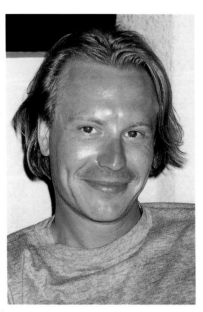

Although this is a common problem when using direct flash, red eye can be avoided with a little care.

Using a flashgun off your camera is indeed possible, and opens up a whole new avenue of creativity because you can vary the position of the gun around your subject to control the lighting effect obtained, instead of being limited to just frontal light.

Place the gun at 90 degrees to your subject, for example, and you'll create strong side-lighting, with half their face lit and the other half in shadow. Alternatively, by holding the flashgun at an angle of 45 degrees you can mimic traditional three-quarter lighting.

To use off-camera flash you'll need to buy a flash sync lead, which allows you to connect the gun to the camera.

Ideally, go for a cable that's several metres long, so you can vary the flash-to-subject distance. If your camera doesn't have a flash sync socket you'll also need a co-axial adaptor; this slots onto the camera's hot shoe and provides a socket into which you can plug one end of the sync cable to ensure that you get correct flash syncronization.

SLOW-SYNC FLASH

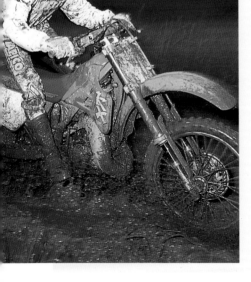

This technique is often used by sports photographers, but it can be used on any moving subject that's close to the camera. All you do is combine a burst of flash with a slow shutter speed, so your subject is frozen by the flash but blurred by the ambient exposure. Many compact cameras have a 'flash-on' or 'slow-sync' mode that automatically combines flash and a slow shutter speed in low light, but an SLR with a flashgun mounted on the hotshoe gives better results.

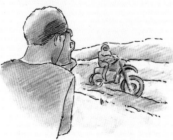

For this shot I combined a burst of flash with a slow shutter speed (1/4sec) to both freeze and blur my subject as he raced by.
Camera Olympus OM4-Ti Lens 28mm
Flash Olympus T45 Film Fujichrome Velvia 50

- Start by taking a meter reading for the ambient (available) light and setting this on your camera. Use your camera in aperture-priority mode so you can set the aperture, which is important for control of the flash exposure, while the shutter speed is set automatically.
- Use a shutter speed of 1/15sec or slower to get sufficient blur in the picture. Using slow film and stopping your lens down to f/11 or f/16 will help if light levels are quite high.
- To make your flashlit subject stand out, underexpose the background by one stop. This is achieved by setting the exposure compensation facility on your camera to -1. The shutter speed will be altered, not the aperture.
- To balance the flash with the ambient light you also need to underexpose the flash by one stop. To do this with a dedicated gun, set the flash exposure compensation to -1 stop or the output to 1/2. With automatic guns, set your flashgun to an auto-aperture setting that is one stop wider than the aperture you are using on the lens – f/8 instead of f/11, say.

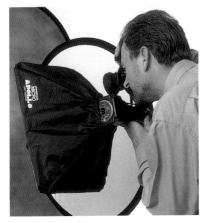

Flash attachments such as the Lastolite Micro Apollo softbox shown here are ideal for improving the quality of light from your portable flashgun.

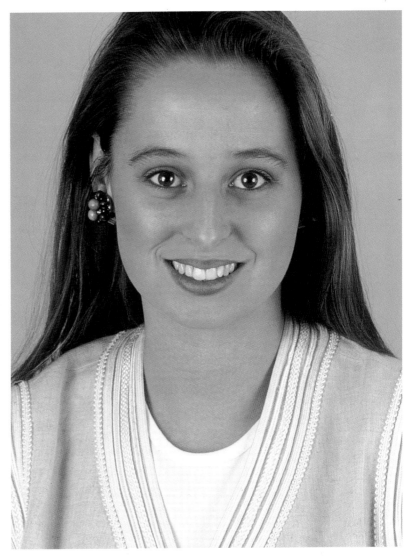

Q Are there any other ways of improving the light from a portable flashgun?

There are various accessories available from manufacturers such as Lastolite and Stophen that are designed for use with portable flashguns. A special attachment allows you to fit a portable flashgun to a lighting stand so it can be positioned anywhere in relation to your subject, while softboxes or flash brollies are used to soften and spread the light.

The only drawback with using these attachments is that they lose up to three stops of light, so you need fairly powerful flashguns to make up for this and allow you to work at an aperture of f/8 or f/11 with slow- or medium-speed film.

It's also a good idea to use dedicated flashguns with a sync lead so all exposure calculations will be dealt with automatically.

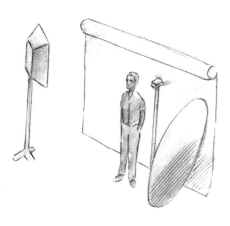

Combining two or three flashguns with a reflector makes studio-style lighting possible.

Q What about if I want to use more than one flashgun at the same time?

Using two, three, four or more flashguns for the same shot, along with some of the accessories described above, is a great way to produce professional-quality lighting.

All you need is some means of ensuring that the flashguns fire at the same time. You could do this by purchasing a multi-socket attachment that allows several guns to be connected to your camera at once via flash sync leads. However, a much better way is to connect just one gun to the camera then

Here the photographer used two flashguns, each bounced off large white reflector boards, to produce studio-quality lighting. The guns were positioned at 45 degrees to the model, one either side of the camera.
Camera Canon T90 Lens 90mm
Flash Canon Speedlites
Film Fujichrome RDP100

fit the others with a slave unit – a small electronic eye that triggers the gun it's attached to at the same time as the main flash fires. That way, you won't have cables trailing everywhere.

As for the position of each gun, that's entirely up to you. Shown here is just one example, but there's an endless number of lighting set-ups possible – all you need is a little imagination.

Try placing one light behind your subject, aimed back at the camera, with two others directed on your subject's face.

Accessories

As well as cameras and lenses there are several other items worth considering as you build a system of photographic equipment. Some, such as tripods and gadget bags, are essential, while others are designed to make your life easier.

The key when buying accessories is to decide which you really need for your own brand of picture-taking. As with all hobbies, photography is inundated with gizmos that promise miracles but rarely deliver, and if you get bitten by the gadget bug you could find yourself spending large amounts of money on things that just aren't necessary.

> **Q** I'm thinking of buying a tripod. What features should I look out for when choosing a model?

The main aim of a tripod is to provide a stable support for your camera, so you can use slow shutter speeds without having to worry about camera shake spoiling your pictures. This allows you to load up with the slowest films for optimum image quality, stop your lenses down to small apertures to maximize depth of field, and use exposures of many seconds, even minutes, to capture low-light scenes.

When choosing a tripod the first factor to consider is its weight. A big, heavy model may keep your camera rock-steady in a hurricane, but you won't want to carry it long distances. Similarly, a small, lightweight tripod may be highly portable, but if it's unsteady your pictures will suffer – especially in windy conditions.

The solution is to find a model that offers the ideal compromise between weight, height and stability – and cost. This is possible with traditional alloy tripods – professional manufacturers such as Manfrotto and Gitzo offer a whole range of models to suit every possible need. In recent years, carbon-fibre tripods have also become popular because they offer all the stability of alloy but are at least 30 per cent lighter. That said, they're also two or three times more expensive.

The main thing to remember is that a good tripod can last a lifetime, so it's worth investing more in a model that's going to work for you rather than compromising and regretting it.

Having decided between alloy or carbon fibre, there are some other factors to consider.

Height Ideally you need a model that can be extended to eye-level – 1.5–1.8m (5–6ft) is about right – without needing the centre column. If the tripod is too low at maximum extension it will be uncomfortable to use, but equally there's little point having a tripod that extends to 2.5m (8ft) when you don't need such height – it will only make the tripod heavier than necessary.

Legs All tripod legs are broken down into sections so they can be tucked away for carrying. Generally, the fewer leg sections there are, the sturdier the tripod – three is an ideal number. Tubular legs are stronger than open-section legs.

Leg locks These need to be robust if they're to withstand regular use and spare parts should be readily available. Quick-release locks are the most common, but make sure they're strong enough – metal is preferable to plastic.

Feet The choice is basically between spikes for soft surfaces and flat rubber feet for harder terrain, with the latter being better for general use.

Centre column A common feature that provides extra height. It tends to be the most unstable part of the tripod though, and should only be used when absolutely necessary.

Head The type of head you use is as important as the tripod itself, so don't automatically accept the head supplied with the legs – if you're buying a professional model you will be able to choose your own head.

The most common type is a pan-and-tilt head which allows you to adjust the camera position up and down, around 360 degrees and turn it on its side. These adjustments are made independently using separate control arms.

An alternative is a ball-and-socket head which allows you to move the camera in any direction then lock it in position. These are quicker to use and more compact.

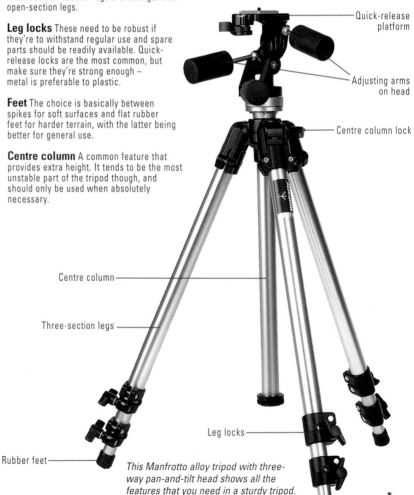

Quick-release platform

Adjusting arms on head

Centre column lock

Centre column

Three-section legs

Leg locks

Rubber feet

This Manfrotto alloy tripod with three-way pan-and-tilt head shows all the features that you need in a sturdy tripod.

Yes. If you shop around you'll find all sorts of different supports for use in every conceivable situation.

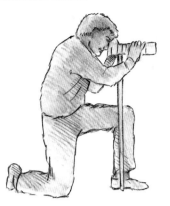

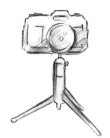

Pocket tripods are ideal when you need to travel light or in situations where a full-sized model isn't permitted. They can be rested on a wall, pillar, car bonnet or other support to provide the necessary height.

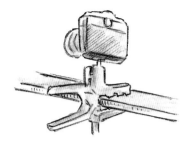

Where support is required but you don't have room for a tripod you could use a **clamp**, **spike** or **suction pod** to fit your camera to fences, railings, table tops, shelves, window ledges and so on.

Monopods are a popular alternative to tripods. They're basically a telescopic tube, just like a single tripod leg, and are used in conjunction with your body weight to keep the camera steady.

Sports photographers prefer monopods because they provide plenty of support for heavy lenses but still give freedom of movement. They're also ideal when you need to use slowish shutter speeds.

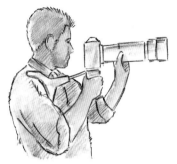

Chestpods and **pistol grips** can be used to support long lenses or prevent camera shake when using slow shutter speeds, but they don't provide the same level of stability and require a steady hand.

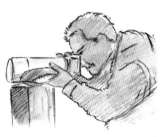

Finally, for uneven surfaces, you can rest your camera on a beanbag, which will turn walls, fence posts, car bonnets, rocks, tree stumps and all sorts of other things into impromptu supports.

You need a small spirit level that can be slipped onto your camera's hot shoe to let you know if the camera is perfectly square. Most levels have bubbles that allow you to check for horizontal and vertical accuracy, but your camera must be on a tripod for this to work properly.

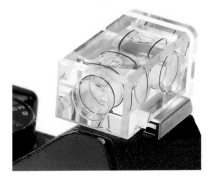

USING LENS HOODS

When shooting towards the light, or taking pictures with a bright light source just out of frame, you may notice strange ghostly patterns in your camera's viewfinder. This is known as flare, and it ruins pictures by lowering contrast and reducing colour saturation to produce washed-out images.

To prevent flare you should fit your lenses with lens hoods when shooting in bright conditions, so the front element is protected from stray light. Many telephoto and zoom lenses have a sliding lens hood built in, but with others you'll need to buy hoods that can be screwed onto the end.

Make sure the hoods you buy are designed to be used with a specific focal length, otherwise they won't work properly. This is particularly important with wide-angle lenses, as a hood that's too narrow will cause vignetting (see Problem solving, page 89).

An alternative to a lens hood is some kind of lens shade. Often your hand can do the trick - position it to keep light off the front of the lens - or a sheet of card. Handy gadgets known as 'flare busters' are also available - they use a flexible arm that clips onto the camera's hot shoe at one end and holds a piece of card or a shading disc in a clip at the other. You can adjust the arm so the card/shade shields the lens and prevents flare.

Flare can ruin a potentially great picture, but using a lens hood will prevent it by protecting the front element of the lens from stray light.

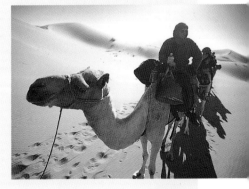

BAGS AND CASES

Photographic bags and cases are designed to serve three main functions: to make carrying your equipment as easy and comfortable as possible; to protect that equipment from damage; and to provide easy access to the contents. When choosing a bag or a case you also need to consider the amount of equipment you normally carry and the type of conditions you expect to be taking pictures in.

Traditional shoulder bags were first choice for a long time, but photographic backpacks have now taken over. The main benefit of a backpack is that it distributes the weight of the contents evenly across your back instead of putting it all on one shoulder – this makes a big difference when you're carrying a heavy load all day and is much safer on uneven ground because you will be more balanced, as well as having both hands free to aid balance.

There are many backpacks now available, in sizes to suit all needs. Lowe Pro is the best-known brand, though Tenba and Tamrac are worth considering.

Key considerations are:
- Ideally that the outer shell is weatherproof – some models have a pullout waterproof cover that can be placed over the pack if you get caught in the rain.
- Capacious pockets on the outside of the main compartment to store clothing and accessories.
- Lots of padding inside with adjustable dividers so you can customise the interior to suit your needs.
- Not too big that you have lots of empty space – items will rattle around if you do – but not so small that you struggle to fit your equipment in.
- A well-designed harness for carrying in comfort.
- The option to add accessories such as side pockets to increase storage space.

Shoulder bags are ideal if you need rapid access to your equipment, but they make carrying heavy loads uncomfortable. Photographic backpacks like the Lowe Pro Photo Trekker AW II (left) solve this problem and are fast growing in popularity among landscape, travel and nature photographers, while hard cases offer ultimate protection but are the least practical.

Q Could you recommend a selection of items for cleaning my cameras, lenses and filters?

It makes sense to put together a cleaning kit, so you've always got the necessary items to hand should you need them in an emergency. The following bits and pieces should cover your needs:

- Stiff brush to clean camera bodies and lens barrels.
- Anti-static or blower brush to remove dust and hairs from lenses and filters.
- Microfibre cloth to remove marks and smears from lenses and filters.
- Cleaning solution – to aid removal of marks and smears without damaging delicate lens elements or filters.
- Jet-air duster – handy for blasting away dust and dirt, but take care on lenses and filters as a liquid residue is often emitted.

Microfibre cloths and anti-static brushes are the most useful accessories for keeping your cameras, lenses and filters clean.

Q What's the purpose of a cable release?

Cable releases allow you to take a picture without touching your camera's shutter release. This is handy when the camera is on a tripod and you're using long exposures or long telephoto lenses, as pressing the shutter release with your finger can cause vibrations which lead to camera shake. There may also be occasions when you need to take pictures at a distance from the camera – when photographing timid animals and birds, or shooting self-portraits, for example.

The most common type of cable release these days is an electronic lead that plugs into the camera body of modern SLRs and fires the shutter at the press of a button. More traditional cable releases screw into the camera's shutter release and are operated by pressing a plunger on the end. Finally, pneumatic releases consist of a thin plastic tube – usually around 6m (20ft) long – with a plunger on one end and a rubber bulb on the other. A photograph is taken by squeezing the bulb. If your camera doesn't have a cable release socket – and don't be surprised if your modern SLR doesn't – you can buy an attachment that allows a release to be fitted.

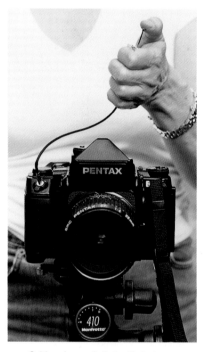

Cable releases help to eliminate camera shake by allowing you to trip your camera's shutter without touching it.

part two
techniques

Depth of field

Whenever you take a picture, an area extending in front of and behind the point on which you focus the lens also comes out acceptably sharp. This area is known as the 'depth of field', and being able to control it is a vitally important part of photography. When shooting landscapes, for example, it is common practice to keep everything in the scene sharply focused, so depth of field needs to be as big as possible. However, when shooting portraits you usually want minimal depth of field so your main subject stands out against the background.

Q What are the factors controlling depth of field?

There are three factors you can use to control depth of field: the size of the lens aperture used; the focal length of the lens; and the camera-to-subject distance.

For any lens, wide lens apertures, such as f/2.8 or f/4, give limited depth of field, whereas small lens apertures, such as f/11 and f/16, give much greater depth of field. The smaller the f/number, the more limited depth of field will be and the bigger the f/number the more depth of field you get.

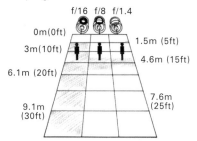

At any given lens aperture, depth of field becomes less as focal length increases. A 28mm wide-angle lens set to f/16 will record everything sharply from about 2m (6½ft) from the camera to infinity, for example, but the depth of field from a 300mm set to f/16 will only extend a few metres either side of the point you focus on.

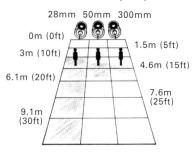

The closer you are to your subject, the less depth of field there will be for any lens or aperture. So if you use a 50mm lens set to f/16 and focus on 2m (6½ft) there will be far less depth of field than if you focus

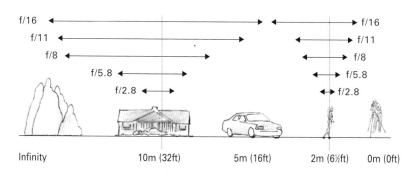

the same lens on 10m (32ft) and shoot at the same aperture. This makes accurate focusing essential when working at close range – especially if you are shooting close-up or macro images.

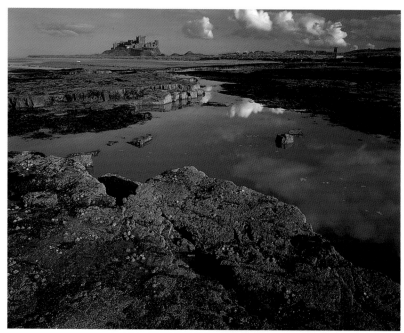

Bamburgh Castle, Northumberland, England
Wide-angle lenses such as a 28mm or 24mm combined with a small aperture of f/16 or f/22 will allow you to keep everything in sharp focus from the immediate foreground to infinity.
Camera Walker Titan 5x4in Lens 90mm
Filter Polarizer Film Fujichrome Velvia 50

Being able to assess depth of field is important, because often you will need to know roughly what is going to be in and out of focus in the final picture.

Looking through your SLR's viewfinder is no help unless you intend shooting at the widest aperture setting (smallest f/number) because your lens is always set to maximum aperture for viewing purposes and what you see in the viewfinder is depth of field at its minimum.

The easiest way to assess depth of field is by using your camera's stopdown or depth of field preview button. If you press it, the lens iris will close down to the aperture set to give you a rough idea of what will be in focus and what will be out of focus. The main drawback with this method is that when using small apertures such as f/16 or f/22, the viewfinder goes very dim, so you can't see very clearly – which is a problem because it's usually when you're shooting at small apertures that you need to check depth of field.

The second method is to use the depth of field scale on your lens, which appears either side of the main focusing index – though many modern AF lenses and most zooms don't have such a scale. All you do is focus on your subject, then read off the distances that fall opposite the aperture you are using on the depth of field scale – as shown in the diagram below. These distances indicate the nearest and furthest points of sharp focus.

If you need greater depth of field, set the lens to a smaller aperture; if you need less, set the lens to a wider aperture.

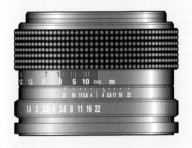

From this illustration you can see that with the lens focused on 5m (16ft) and set to f/22, depth of field extends from roughly 2m (6½ft) to infinity.

MAXIMIZING DEPTH OF FIELD

One of the problems of trying to obtain maximum depth of field is knowing exactly what to focus on, especially if you are using a wide-angle lens to capture a sweeping view. As a rough guide, you could work on the basis that depth of field extends twice as far behind the point of focus as it does in front and focus roughly one-third into the scene, but this is not very accurate. The alternative is to employ a technique known as hyperfocal focusing. To do this, focus your lens on infinity and check the depth of field scale to see what the nearest point of sharp focus will be at the aperture you are going to use. This distance is known as the hyperfocal distance. Now refocus your lens on the hyperfocal distance, and depth of field will extend from half the hyperfocal distance to infinity.

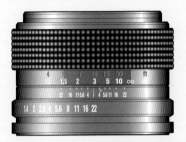

Here you can see that with the lens focused on infinity and set to f/22, the hyperfocal distance is 3m (10ft).

By refocusing the lens on 3m (10ft), the hyperfocal distance, depth of field now extends from 1.5m (5ft) to infinity.

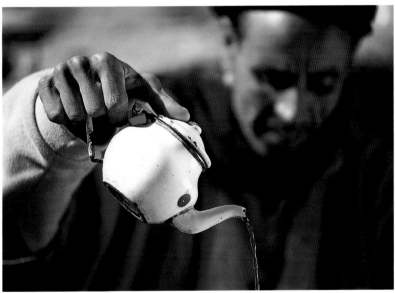

Ait Benhaddoi, Morocco
Use a telephoto lens set to its widest aperture to minimize depth of field.
Camera Nikon F90X Lens 80–200mm
Film Fujichrome Velvia 50

Yes, that's why you should think carefully about the lens and aperture you're using. Pictures taken with a wide-angle lens with everything sharply recorded can look stunning. But that impact will be diluted if the background or foreground comes out blurred because you didn't set an aperture that was small enough to provide sufficient depth of field.

Similarly, a simple subject can be made to look strongly three-dimensional if you restrict depth of field so much that it's the only sharp thing in the picture. However, the effect will be ruined if you give too much depth of field so that other elements in the scene begin to compete for attention, such as a cluttered background that's sharply focused in a portrait shot.

Exposure

Exposure is without doubt the most crucial aspect of photography, because unless you know how to get the right amount of light to the film in your camera, everything else pales into insignificance. Fortunately, modern cameras have taken much of the guesswork out of getting the exposure right, and can be relied upon to come up with the goods 95 per cent of the time. But that still leaves a crucial 5 per cent of situations where, unless you have a thorough understanding of exposure theory, you'll end up with badly exposed pictures. Ironically, it's those very situations that tend to generate the most exciting pictures, so knowing how to deal with them is vitally important if you don't want to miss out.

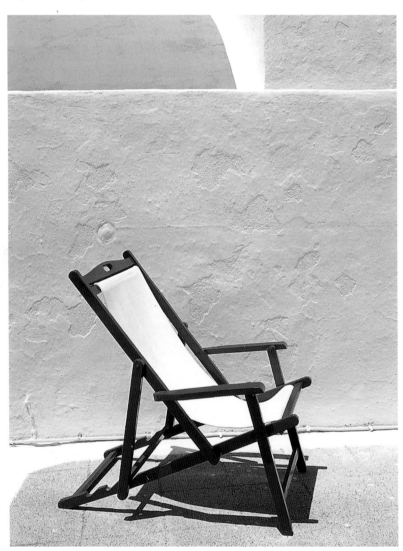

Santorini, Greece
A thorough understanding of metering and exposure is important if you want to produce perfectly exposed pictures in tricky lighting conditions. The extreme brightness of this scene, for example, would almost certainly fool the metering system of the most sophisticated SLR, so to prevent this I used a handheld lightmeter to take an incident light reading that wasn't influenced by the reflectancy of the white walls.
Camera Nikon F5 Lens 28mm Filter Polarizer
Meter Minolta Autometer IVF Film Fujichrome Velvia 50

Q I am confused about exposure – how do apertures and shutter speeds relate to each other?

The basic aim of exposure is to get exactly the right amount of light onto the film in your camera so an acceptable image is created on its light-sensitive emulsion.

To do this, the correct film speed (ISO) is first set on the camera, so the meter is calibrated to the right sensitivity. Next, a meter reading is taken to measure the light levels and to establish how much exposure the film needs.

To achieve that exposure (and get just the right amount of light to the film) you have two controls: the lens aperture, which regulates how much light passes through the lens; and the shutter speed, which determines how long that light is allowed to expose the film for. You can use different combinations of aperture and shutter speed to achieve exactly the same exposure – if the aperture is small, the shutter must stay open for longer to allow the required amount of light to expose the film, whereas if the aperture is wide, the shutter doesn't need to be open for as long.

To understand how this works, imagine you're filling a kettle. The amount of water required is the exposure, the size of the tap is the lens aperture, and the length of time the tap is left running is the shutter speed.

If you use a large tap (wide lens aperture), you only need to turn it on for a short time (use a fast shutter speed). But if the tap is narrow (small lens aperture), it must be left running for much longer (slow shutter speed) to get exactly the same amount of water into the kettle.

Now apply this theory to exposure. Each time you set your lens to the next biggest

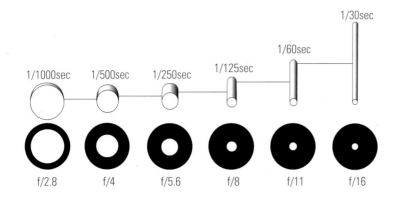

1/1000sec	1/500sec	1/250sec	1/125sec	1/60sec	1/30sec
f/2.8	f/4	f/5.6	f/8	f/11	f/16

f/number, the size of the aperture is halved, so the shutter speed must be doubled to ensure that the same amount of light reaches the film. If your camera suggests an exposure of 1/250sec at f/5.6, for example, any of the combinations shown in the diagram above could be used to achieve exactly the same exposure.

The combination you choose will depend on what your subject is. For sport and action a fast shutter speed is usually required to freeze movement, so 1/1000sec at f/2.8 would be ideal, whereas for landscapes a small aperture is more important as you need maximum depth of field, so 1/30sec at f/16 would be better, or 1/15sec at f/22.

Venice, Italy
Backlit scenes can fool your camera into causing underexposure because the brightness of the background influences the exposure set, irrespective of its importance. If your camera has a backlight button it can be used to prevent this, or you can simply increase the exposure by 1.5–2 stops using the exposure compensation facility, as I did here.
Camera Nikon F90x Lens 28mm Filter 81EF Film Fujichrome Velvia 50

Q How does my camera measure the light and calculate the correct exposure?

All cameras with an integral meter use a system known as TTL (through-the-lens) metering to measure the light passing through the lens. This means that if you place a filter or any other attachment on the front of the lens, any light reduction will automatically be taken into account.

The light measured is that being reflected back from your subject, so the reflectance of the subject, and light or dark areas in the scene, can influence the reading obtained. This is covered in more detail later.

Q My camera has a backlight button. How does it work?

This handy feature is designed to help prevent underexposure when your subject is backlit by the sun. If you press it just before taking the picture it will increase the exposure set by about 1½ stops. It's fine in most situations, but in very bright conditions the increase may not be enough.

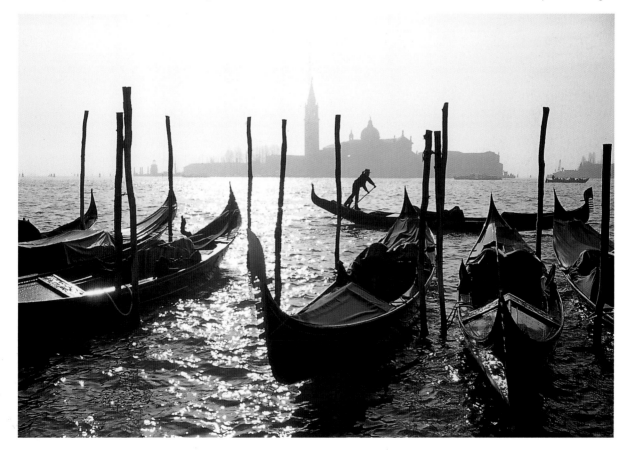

The job of any camera is to ensure that the correct amount of light reaches the film inside it to produce a well-exposed picture. However, different cameras do this in different ways using a variety of modes, which vary the degree of control you have over the exposure set. Most compact cameras use just one fully automatic exposure mode, but SLRs tend to give you the choice of one, two, three or more so you can pick and choose the mode to suit different subjects. Here's a description of the most common and how they work.

Program mode This is a fully automatic mode which sets both the aperture and shutter speed, usually displaying them in an LCD panel on the top plate. The choice made is based on data programmed into the camera's memory, so you have no control over it. Fortunately, most SLRs now have a Program Shift facility, so you can alter the aperture and shutter speed combination if the one selected isn't suitable – selecting a smaller aperture (and slower shutter speed) or wider aperture (and faster shutter speed).

Program is a quick mode to use so it's ideal when you need to respond instantly to a photo opportunity. Without Program Shift, however, it offers the photographer no creative control.

Specialist program modes Some SLRs use program modes that are tailored for more specific use.

Program Depth, or Program Low, for example, is designed to set the smallest practicable aperture to give maximum depth of field. In doing so it also gives slow shutter speeds. Program High, or High-Speed Program, sets a fast shutter speed to freeze action. As a result it's handy when using telephoto lenses, as the fast shutter speed helps to prevent camera shake. A wide aperture is also set, so it can be used if you need to throw the background out of focus to make your subject stand out.

Pictograms Taking the specialist program mode idea one step further, some SLRs use a series of subject-based modes that set not only the exposure controls, but the

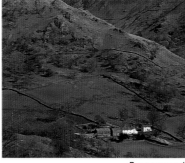
Program mode

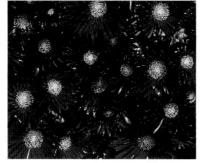
Specialist program modes

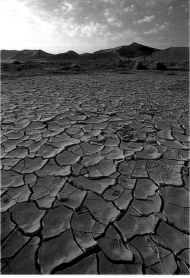
Aperture priority AE

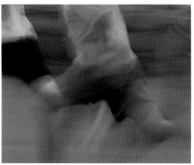
Shutter priority

autofocusing, flash, film advance and various other camera functions to suit specific subjects, such as portraits, landscapes, action and close-up. The idea of this is to give novice photographers the opportunity to capture a range of different subjects without any prior knowledge of the settings required. The modes offer no control, but as your experience grows you can switch to other modes that only handle the exposure.

Aperture priority AE In this mode you set the lens aperture and the camera automatically selects a shutter speed to ensure the correct exposure. It's one of the most common and popular modes, and is ideal for subjects such as landscape photography, where control over depth of field is important. It also enables you to use the camera's long exposure capability when taking pictures at night, but you will need to use a tripod to avoid camera shake.

Pictograms

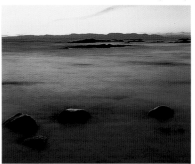
Metered manual

Shutter priority This time you set the shutter speed and the camera sets an aperture to give correct exposure. Again, it's a relatively quick mode to use, and ideal for subjects such as sport and action, where control over the shutter speed set is more important than the aperture.

Metered manual The simplest and most basic exposure mode available. After taking an exposure reading, you set both the aperture and shutter speed required. It's relatively slow to use, but offers total control and allows you to work in conjunction with a handheld light meter.

Q Do I need to expose differently when using colour slide instead of colour print film?

The basic rule with colour slide film is to expose for the highlights and leave the shadows to their own devices. This is because the slides themselves are just pieces of processed film, so what you record on that film is what you end up with, and well-exposed highlights – even if the shadows come out very dark – are preferable to well exposed shadows but overexposed highlights. Exposure accuracy is also far more important with colour slide film, as it can only tolerate half a stop of over- or underexposure before a picture is fit for nothing but the bin.

With negative film, the opposite applies. You should expose to record some detail in the shadows and not worry too much about the highlights because they can always be toned down to show detail at the printing stage. Print film also has much wider latitude. You can under- or overexpose by at least three stops and still obtain an acceptable result, as any error can be corrected at the printing stage.

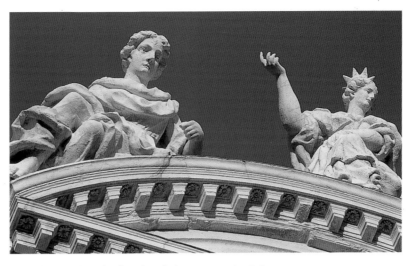

Venice, Italy
Slight underexposure of colour slide film can increase colour saturation, but take care because if you go too far, the image will be dark and the colours muddy.
Camera Olympus OM4-Ti Lens 135mm
Film Fujichrome Velvia 50

METERING PATTERNS

When you use your camera to take an exposure reading, the light entering the lens is measured using a metering pattern.

These days, intelligent multi-zone or multi-pattern metering systems are the most common, though most 35mm SLRs give you a choice of patterns so you can pick and choose, depending upon the subject you're shooting.

Here are the most common patterns, and how they work.

Centre-weighted average Used to be the standard metering pattern and is still featured in many SLRs. It works by taking a light reading from the whole of the viewfinder, but pays particular attention to the central 40–60 per cent because that's where the main subject tends to be positioned. In normal conditions it gives accurate results but can be fooled by tricky lighting such as a really bright sky.

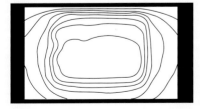

Partial metering Takes a light reading from a smaller central area of the viewfinder, which varies in size from 6–15 per cent of the total image area. This allows you to meter from a more specific part of the scene so surrounding light or dark areas don't influence the reading obtained. More accurate than centre-weighted in tricky light.

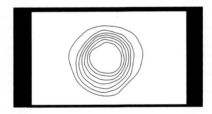

Multi-zone/multi-pattern metering Now standard issue in the vast majority of 35mm SLRs, these 'intelligent' metering systems are designed to reduce exposure error by recognizing tricky situations.

This is achieved by taking individual light readings from different parts of the scene – anything up to 14 – to assess the contrast and brightness. This information is then compared to lighting situations built into the memory. They're reliable, but far from foolproof, though the more segments the pattern has, the more accurate it is.

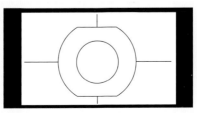

Spot metering With this pattern a light reading is taken from a tiny spot in the centre of the viewfinder – usually covering only 1 per cent of the total image area. This allows you to take readings from a very specific part of the scene and obtain perfect exposures in the trickiest conditions. In experienced hands it's the most accurate system available, but it can take some getting used to.

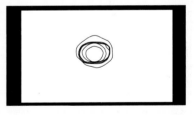

Multi-spot metering Works in the same way as spot metering, but allows you to take several different spot readings from the scene, store them in the camera's memory, then average them out to obtain the correct exposure. Many cameras with spot metering give you this option.

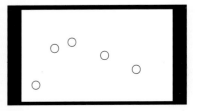

Q Whenever I shoot against a light or dark background, the pictures always come out either too light or too dark. Why is this?

You've discovered a problem that many photographers fail to realize even exists — namely that no matter how modern or sophisticated your camera is, it isn't totally foolproof and can still get the exposure wrong in certain situations.

There are two reasons for this. Firstly, your camera's metering system measures reflected light — the light bouncing back off your subject. However, some colours and surfaces reflect more light than others and this can fool your camera — in exactly the same lighting conditions, a white surface will reflect much more light than a black surface, for example.

Secondly, and most importantly, your camera's metering system is calibrated to record everything as a mid-tone. Visually this can be represented as a mid-grey colour, technically known as 18 per cent grey because it reflects 18 per cent of the light falling on it.

No matter what you photograph, your camera always tries to record it as a mid-tone. Most of the things we photograph are 'average' in their tonal balance, so your camera can usually be relied upon to give correctly exposed results. However, when you try to photograph something that isn't average, your camera still tries its best to record it as if it were, and that's when exposure error occurs.

Below is a list of the most common causes of exposure error, and advise on how to deal with them. In just about all cases you can obtain an accurate exposure reading by using a handheld light meter or taking a substitute meter reading from a smaller part of the scene. Where this isn't practical or possible, just adjust the exposure your camera suggests by the amount shown below.

Subject against a light background

This is one of the most common tricky lighting situations. Examples include a person against a white wall, sky, water or snow. The high reflectance or brightness of the background fools your camera's meter into underexposing, so your main subject comes out too dark.
Solution: Increase the exposure by 1½ to 2 stops.

Subject against a dark background

This is the exact opposite of the problem described above, and again usually occurs when you photograph someone or something against a dark, shady backdrop. Your camera tries to record the background as grey, so it overexposes and your main subject comes out too light.
Solution: Reduce the exposure by 1½ to 2 stops.

Bright subject The most common example is a snow scene, but a bride in her wedding dress, an animal with white fur or any other light-coloured subject can cause the same

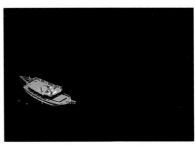
Subject against dark background

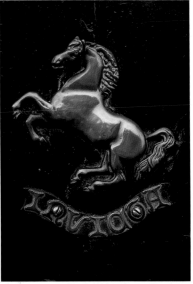
Dark subject/low reflectancy

problem. Again, your camera meter treats the subject as average, so underexposure occurs and it comes out grey.
Solution: Increase the exposure by 2 to 2½ stops.

Dark subject This time it's the proverbial black cat in a coal cellar, or any other dark subject including people dressed in black clothing. Your camera meter again treats the subject as average, so overexposure occurs and everything comes out grey.
Solution: Reduce the exposure by 2 to 2½ stops.

Shooting into the light This situation covers any subject where a bright light source, like the sun for example, is in the shot, and includes backlit portraits. The bright background influences the exposure set and your main subject will either be grossly underexposed or will record as a silhouette. Sometimes that approach can give stunning results, but usually only when it's done intentionally.
Solution: Increase the exposure by 1–3 stops, depending upon the brightness of the background.

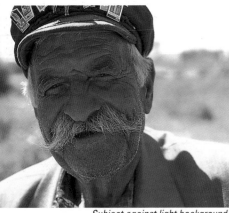
Subject against light background

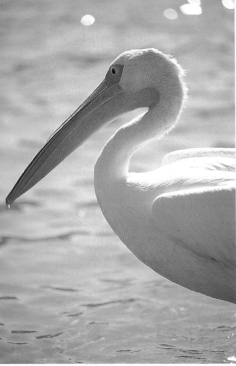
Bright/highly reflective subject

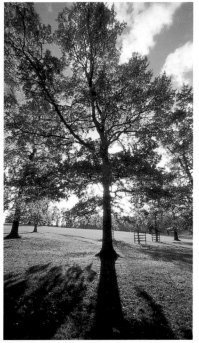

Bright sky in shot The sky is generally much brighter than the ground, so if you include a large area of it in your pictures it tends to influence your camera's meter and cause underexposure of the landscape. This is easily overcome by tilting your camera down to exclude the sky, so you're metering from the foreground alone.

Solution: Increase the exposure by 1–3 stops, depending upon the brightness of the sky, and use a neutral density (ND) graduated filter to prevent the sky from overexposing (see Filters, page 24).

High-contrast scene Colour slide film is able to record a brightness range of about 5 stops, while colour negative film can record a range up to 7 stops. Unfortunately, in really bright, sunny weather, the brightness range of a scene can be as much as 9 or 10 stops, so something has to give and detail must be sacrificed in either the highlights or the shadows.

If you leave the decision to your camera, underexposure will probably result, so decide what the most important part of the scene is and meter directly for that – for the picture below I took a spot reading from the bottom stair and used this exposure for the final picture.

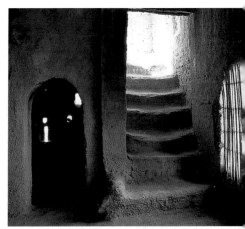

Shooting into the light

High contrast

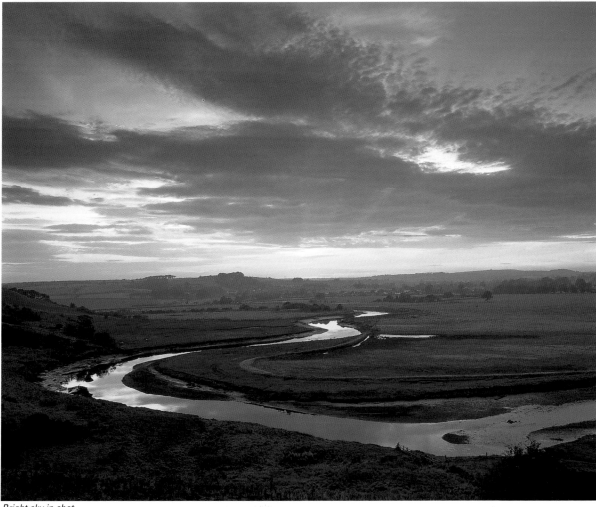

Bright sky in shot

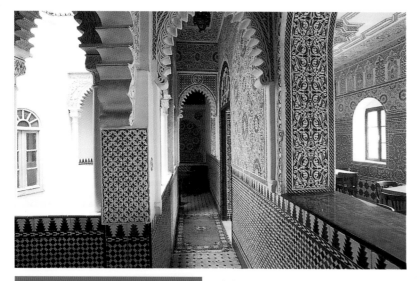

Hotel Continental, Tangier, Morocco
A handheld meter allows you to obtain
accurate exposure readings no matter how
tricky the subject or lighting is – in this case
I used an incident light meter to measure
the light falling onto the walls so their high
reflectancy didn't cause underexposure.
Camera Nikon F90x Lens 20mm
Film Fujichrome Velvia 50

Q What does the exposure compensation facility do, and when should I use it?

This allows you to override the exposure set by your camera when it's set to an automatic exposure mode such as aperture priority, and tends to be used when you're photographing a non-average subject that may fool the integral light meter into setting the wrong exposure (see page 46).

Most SLRs have some kind of exposure compensation facility that allows you to increase or reduce the exposure set by anything up to three stops, in third-, half- or full-stop increments.

If your camera lacks such a facility, you can still override the meter by switching to manual exposure mode and adjusting the aperture or shutter speed after setting the suggested exposure.

Q Do handheld meters offer any advantages over the light meter built into my camera?

Yes, they do. The main benefit of using a handheld light meter is that it gives you the option to take incident readings of the light falling onto your subject, rather than the light being reflected back. As a result, the reading obtained isn't influenced by the reflectance of your subject, or light and dark areas in the scene, so you can obtain perfect exposures in the trickiest lighting.

To use a handheld meter, hold it in front of your subject so the white invercone is pointing back towards the camera. If you're unable to get close to your subject, simply hold it up and point the invercone over your shoulder, so it's in the same light that's falling on your subject.

The meter reading obtained can then be set on your camera, which should be switched to manual exposure mode.

Q Can I obtain accurate exposures when photographing non-average subjects if I don't have a handheld meter?

There are various methods of doing this. One way is to take a normal meter reading, then increase or reduce the exposure suggested by an amount you think is correct. However, this is rather hit and miss, because no two situations are the same.

A much better method is to take a substitute meter reading from something that's similar in tone to 18 per cent grey and won't confuse your camera's meter. All sorts of things are suitable, such as green grass or foliage, concrete, roof slates, stone or bricks, grey clothing and so on. Or you could buy an 18 per cent grey card and meter from that.

Alternatively, take a reading from your hand or your subject's skin, and then increase the exposure. Caucasian skin is roughly one stop brighter than 18 per cent grey, so you would need to increase the exposure by a stop.

If your camera has a spot or partial metering facility you can use that to take a substitute reading. If not, fit a telephoto lens to your camera and isolate a suitable area, or where possible, move in close to take the reading.

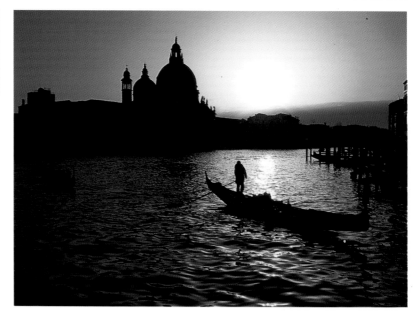

Grand Canal, Venice, Italy
This shot was taken just before sunset.
I intentionally let the camera underexpose it
to add drama and ensure that the buildings
and gondolas recorded as silhouettes.
Camera Nikon F90x Lens 28mm
Filter 81D warm-up Film Fujichrome Velvia 50

Q Do I always need to use the exposure my light meter sets, even if I know it's correct?

Not at all. The 'correct' exposure isn't necessarily the exposure that will get sufficient light to the film to produce a technically perfect image, but the exposure you think will record your subject in the way you want to see it.

That's why it's so important to have a thorough understanding of the factors influencing exposure, and how your camera will respond in different situations. Once you know all the technical tricks you can then commit them to your subconscious and let your imagination take over. Creative photography isn't about doing everything by the book, but following your instincts.

Imagine you're photographing a landscape in very stormy weather. Once you know which exposure will record the scene as you see it, there's nothing to stop you intentionally underexposing by half or even a full stop, so the tones are darkened down. Similarly, you can overexpose slightly when shooting portraits or nudes in soft lighting, to lighten the tones and create a dreamy, high-key effect.

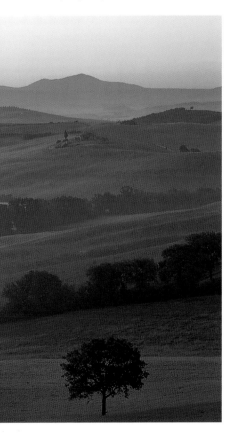

BRACKETING

If you're ever unsure which exposure will give the best result when shooting in tricky lighting, then you can resort to a technique known as bracketing.

This basically involves taking a picture at the exposure your camera sets, then further pictures at exposures over and under this, to make sure that at least one frame is perfectly exposed.

The amount that you need to bracket by will depend on the type of film you're using and how difficult the conditions are. Slide film demands great exposure accuracy, so bracketing in one-third or half-stop increments is advised. Negative film has far more latitude to exposure error however, so bracketing in full stops will be sufficient. In some situations you may only bracket half a stop over and under, while in others a two-stop bracket either way will be required.

If you know that the subject you're photographing is likely to cause underexposure then you may also limit the bracket to just overexposure, rather than wasting film by going both ways.

Some modern SLRs have an auto bracketing facility which fires off three or five frames in quick succession using the bracket set. But most photographers bracket by using their camera's exposure compensation facility and taking each picture in turn.

This set of pictures shows the effect that bracketing has on colour slide film. Notice how only a small amount of over- or underexposure can totally transform the picture.

Exposure is very subjective to the individual photographer and is open to endless personal interpretation, so never be afraid to experiment.

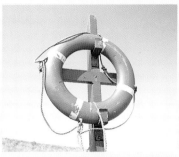

+2 stops

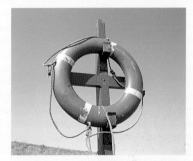

+1 stop

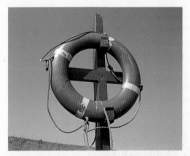

Metered exposure

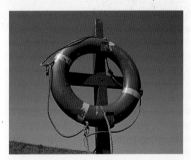

-1 stop

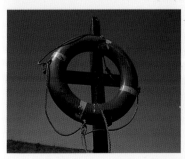

-2 stops

*Val d'Orcia
Tuscany, Italy
Spot metering is the most accurate of all metering methods as you can measure light levels in just a tiny area. In this case I metered from the field behind the tree so the bright sky didn't influence the exposure.*
Camera Pentax 67 Lens 200mm
Filter 0.6 ND graduate Meter Pentax digital
spotmeter (shown) Film Fujichrome Velvia 50

Lighting

Light is the single most important ingredient in photography. Without it we couldn't take pictures in the first place, but there's much more to it than that. Light changes considerably in colour, harshness, intensity and direction, and all these factors influence the success of our photos.

As the earth rotates each day, we on the ground experience the light as constantly changing and constantly moving. You can't control the light in any way, but you can exploit it by timing your shoot carefully to capture the best conditions, and by changing camera or subject angle.

In other words, to make the most of daylight you must accept the limitations it imposes and work within them. Once you're able to do that you'll discover that God is the best lighting cameraman in the world, and anything is possible with a little patience.

Q What's the main factor affecting the quality of daylight?

The time of day is the chief factor that will affect the light. Throughout every 24-hour period the sun travels in an arc across the sky, and as it does so the colour and intensity of the light changes from one hour to the next.

The most attractive periods for outdoor photography are early morning and late afternoon, when the sun is low in the sky. During these periods the light has a beautiful warm quality that makes everything look photogenic and its intensity is reduced due to the sun's rays passing through a denser atmosphere when it's closer to the horizon. Long, raking shadows are also cast at these times, revealing texture and modelling (the interplay of light and shadow that gives objects depth in a two-dimensional photograph) in even the flattest subjects.

In the hours between, the sun is relatively high in the sky – especially during the summer months. Many photographers naturally consider this to be the best time to shoot as there's lots of activity going on and high levels of light allow you to use fast shutter speeds and small apertures.

However, at these times the light is extremely harsh, creating high contrast, and with the sun almost overhead, shadows are very short and dense. As a result, the landscape can tend to look rather flat and uninspiring, while glare reduces colour saturation and prevents you from getting any really good results.

If you're forced to shoot in these conditions, choose your subject and camera angle carefully – the middle of the day is more suited to graphic and abstract subjects that don't require as much subtlety.

I also recommend that you use a polarizing filter to maximize colour saturation, while an 81A or 81B warm-up filter will help to balance the slight blue cast that is present in the light. Portraits are best taken in the shade, where contrast is lower and the light is much softer.

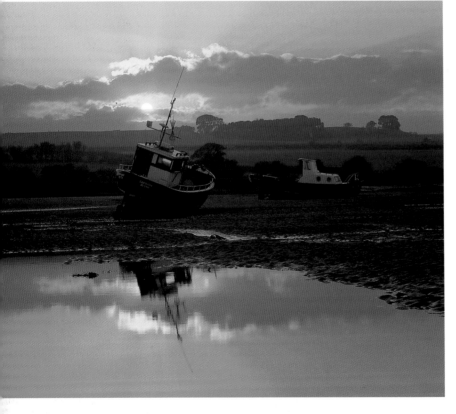

Alnmouth, Northumberland, England
This photograph, and the one of La Digue in the Seychelles (above right) show how dramatically the light changes throughout the day – this shot was taken at sunset. Both images work well, but they're worlds apart in terms of mood.
Camera Pentax 67 Lens 165mm
Filter 81D warm-up Film Fujichrome Velvia 50

Most definitely – in some cases more so than the time of day. If a cloud obscures the sun, for example, the intensity of the light is immediately reduced and shadows are weakened. You can see this clearly in windy weather, when the sun is forever dipping in and out, but you need to take care with the exposure as the light levels can fluctuate by several stops.

Replace that cloud with a grey, overcast blanket and the effect is even stronger. Light levels fall dramatically, shadows almost disappear, and the sky acts like an enormous diffuser. The soft light of an overcast day is ideal for portraiture, fashion, outdoor glamour, and, to a certain extent, architectural and landscape photography. Colours take on a delicate, pastel appearance, fine detail is obscured and visibility is reduced to create very moody lighting conditions.

These effects are increased by mist and fog. Early morning mist gives scenes a flat, monochromatic feel that makes for very atmospheric pictures. Fog is less photogenic because it reduces visibility, weakens colours and makes everything appear very flat. The all-encompassing greyness can also be rather depressing to look at.

To make the most of fog, try to include one or two dominant shapes such as buildings or trees rising out of the gloom, and ideally a splash of bright colour to provide a focal point. The effect of both mist and fog can be emphasized using a telephoto lens.

Dull, rainy weather is less inviting, but you can produce successful pictures in heavy downpours. Try using a slow shutter speed to blur the rain so it records like mist, or shoot against a dark background so the raindrops are clearly visible.

Stormy weather can also be very rewarding. If the sun breaks through against a dark, stormy sky the contrast creates wonderfully dramatic conditions for landscape and architectural photography. If you're lucky you may even have the chance to capture a rainbow, or bolts of lightning. Predicting such phenomena is almost impossible though, so you simply have to brave the elements and hope for the best.

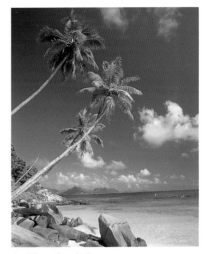

La Digue, Seychelles
Compare this shot, which was taken in the middle of the day with the shot of Alnmouth (below left). Camera Pentax 67 Lens 45mm Filter polarizer Film Fujichrome Velvia 50

Grimspound, Dartmoor, England
Shooting in stormy weather is always a risky business, but sudden changes in the light can create magical conditions for so it's worth taking the risk!
Camera Pentax 67 Lens 55mm Filter 0.6ND grad Film Fujichrome Velvia 50

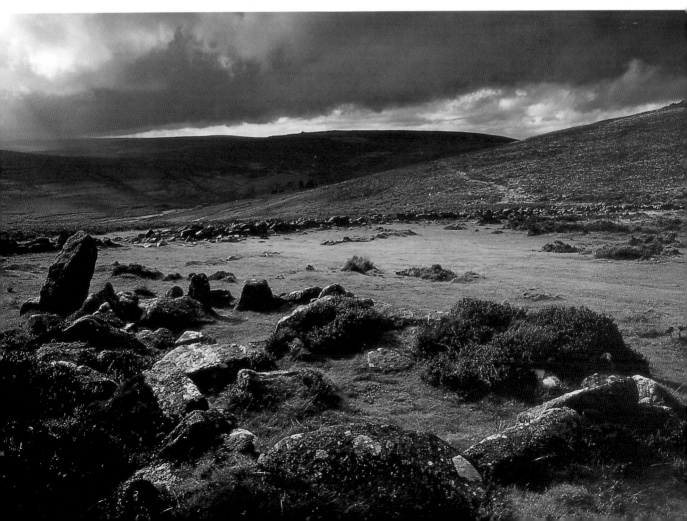

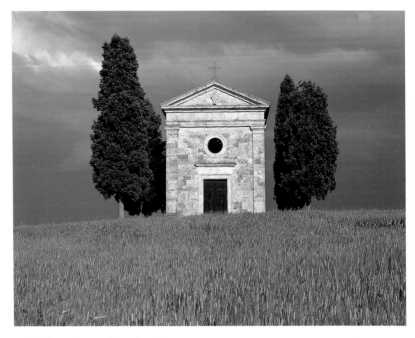

Church, Tuscany, Italy
Though dramatic storm light makes this
picture a success, because the scene is
being lit frontally, no shadows are visible
and it appears flat and two-dimensional.
Camera Pentax 67 Lens 55mm
Film Fujichrome Velvia 50

Q Does it matter where the sun is in relation to my main subject when I'm taking a picture?

Lighting direction is just as important as the intensity and colour of light, because it has a great effect on the appearance of your subject.

Most photographers still follow the old adage of keeping the sun over their shoulder when taking a picture. This is fine if the light has an attractive warm cast that makes everything glow. The downside is that shadows are cast behind your subject, so the results have a tendency to look rather flat. When the sun is low in the sky you may also have problems excluding your own shadow, especially when using a wide-angle lens.

A much better approach is to keep the sun on one side of the camera, or at least at an angle. That way, shadows are cast across your subject and help to reveal texture and form to give a strong three-dimensional effect. This works particularly well during early morning or late afternoon, when shadows are long and the warm light glances across surfaces.

Dramatic images can also be created by shooting into the light. If you leave the exposure to your camera, any solid foreground features will record as strong silhouettes. Alternatively, meter carefully for your main subject, and either let the background burn out or tone it down with a graduated filter.

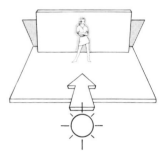

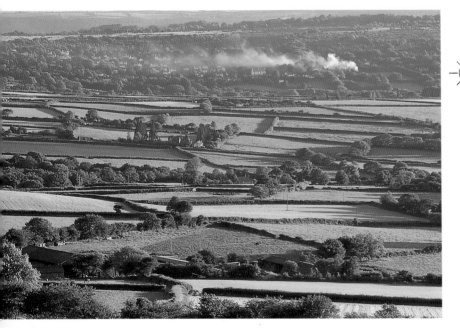

Walkhampton Common, Dartmoor, England
Side-lighting is best for landscape photography to reveal texture and depth.
Camera Nikon F90x Lens 80–200mm zoom
Filters 81C warm-up and polarizer Film Fujichrome Velvia 50

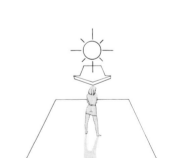

The direction from which light strikes your subject can have a powerful influence on its appearance. In the illustrations above you can see how frontal, side and back lighting alter the way shadows are cast.

Photographers often consider sunrise and sunset as more or less the same thing, but although both create beautiful conditions for photography, they're very different.

When the sun comes up at the start of the day it's rising over a cold earth and into an atmosphere that has been cleansed during the night, so while the first rays of sunlight may be very warm, shadows are blue and the landscape has a very cool, eerie feel. The weather also plays a key role. On a clear summer's morning the sun's intensity tends to be very high as soon as it peeps over the horizon – often too intense to include in a shot without causing flare. But in autumn and winter the sun is usually obscured by light mist or haze, so you can photograph its beautiful orange orb without any problems.

At sunset, conditions are rather different. The earth is much warmer, the atmosphere is thicker due to dust and pollution, and the light rays from the sun are scattered. This increases the warmth of the light considerably, and during the last hour before sunset it appears almost golden. The sun's orb also tends to look bigger because the light has to cut through the thicker atmosphere.

To exaggerate the size of the sun's orb, use a telephoto lens of 200mm or longer – but never look directly at the sun through your viewfinder if it's bright, as you could cause permanent damage to your eyesight.

At sunrise, contrast tends to be quite low, unless you're shooting in clear, summer weather, so you can usually obtain a well-exposed foreground without burning out the sun itself. When this seems unlikely, use a strong neutral density graduated filter (0.6 or 0.9 density) to darken the sun and sky so its brightness is toned down to match that of the landscape.

At sunset, the light is often stronger and contrast is higher, so the usual approach is to create silhouettes of key foreground details such as buildings, trees and people. This can usually be done by firing away with your camera on automatic, but in very bright conditions you should take a meter reading from an area of sky on one side of the sun, to prevent the sun's intensity underexposing the whole scene.

COLOUR TEMPERATURE

Yet another factor you need to consider is the colour of light. At sunrise and sunset daylight is much warmer than around midday, or in dull weather. Artificial light sources such as tungsten also have their own colour. These variations are measured using a colour temperature scale, and expressed using a unit known as Kelvin. Warm light has a low colour temperature; cool light has a high colour temperature.

Our eyes can adapt to changes in colour temperature automatically, so any type of light looks more or less white. Unfortunately, film can't do this. It records colour temperature as it really is, so if you take pictures in light that's too warm or too cold, your pictures will have a colour cast.

Normal daylight-balanced film is balanced for light with a colour temperature of 5,500K. This is usually found around midday in sunny weather, and is known as 'mean noon daylight'. At sunset, however, the colour temperature can be as low as 3,000K, so pictures will come out much warmer than the original scene. Similarly, in intense sunlight under a clear blue sky the colour temperature can be as high as 10,000K, so pictures take on an obvious blue cast.

When accurate colour balance is required these casts can be corrected using filters. The table below shows the recommended filtration for a range of common situations captured on daylight-balanced film.

Source	Colour temp (k)	Filter
Blue sky	10,000	Orange 85B
Open shade in summer sun	7,500	81B + 81C warm-ups
Overcast weather	6,500	81C warm-up
Slightly overcast weather	6,000	81A warm-up
Average noon daylight	5,500	none
Electronic flash	5,500	none
Early morn/eve sunlight	4,000	blue 82C
Hour before sunset	3,500	blue 80C
Tungsten photopearl bulbs	3,400	blue 80B
Tungsten photoflood bulbs	3,200	blue 80A
Sunset	3,000	blue 80A
Domestic tungsten	2,800	blue 80A + 82C
Candle flame	2,000	blue 80A + 80C

Embleton Bay, Northumberland, England
Scenes containing water always make great locations at sunrise and sunset as the water mirrors the rich colour of the sky. Here the sandy beach was still wet enough after the tide had retreated to reflect the warm light.
Camera Pentax 67 Lens 55mm Filter 81D warm-up Film Fujichrome Velvia 50

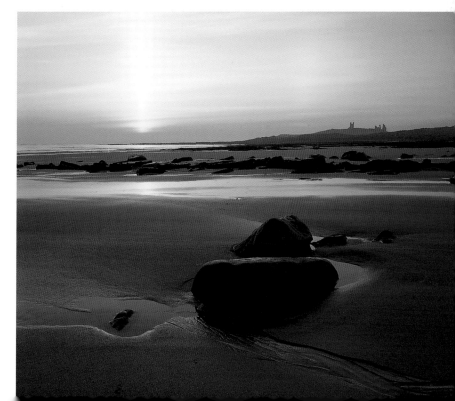

Composition

Painters have a distinct advantage over photographers when it comes to composition. Their canvas is empty, and they can arrange the elements in a scene as they wish. Unfortunately, you don't have the same freedom. Your canvas is already full, so in order to create a successful composition you first have to decide which part of the scene you want to capture, then arrange the elements contained in it so they form a visually pleasing whole.

To help you do this there are many different tools at your disposal – lenses, choice of viewpoint, the quality of light; there are even rules and formulas to help improve your compositional skills.

In the beginning you'll use all these things at different times. However, as your skills, confidence and experience grow, the act of composition will become an intuitive response.

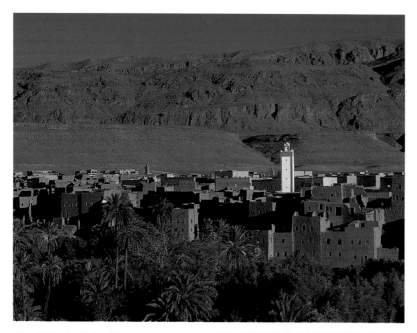

Tinerhir, Dades Valley, Morocco
Composition is a diverse subject that's influenced by our individual way of seeing the world and aesthetic style – which is why no two photographers shoot things in exactly the same way. The success of this composition can be attributed to the white minaret. Because it's brighter and taller than the other buildings, it stands out boldly and acts as the main focal point – as well as adding scale. To see just how effective this tiny element is, cover it with your finger and notice how different the composition appears.
Camera Pentax 67 Lens 165mm
Filter Polarizer Film Fujichrome Velvia 50

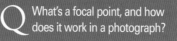 **What's a focal point, and how does it work in a photograph?**

The focal point is the main point of interest in a picture, to which the eye is naturally drawn. Often that will be your main subject, as in the case of portraits. However, with scenic subjects, particularly landscapes, a focal point is usually included to add visual balance and give the viewer's eye something to settle upon – like a hiker on a hillside, or a barn in a field. Brightly coloured and easily identifiable objects make ideal focal points because they stand out, even when only very small in the frame. Where more than one focal point is included, the way you arrange them in the viewfinder can alter the compositional balance. A group portrait

of three people will work better if the sitters are arranged in such a way that their heads form a triangle, for example, rather than a straight line, as the triangle is a very strong shape.

 Does the viewpoint I shoot from make a difference to the composition of a picture?

Many photographers have a habit of taking pictures from the first viewpoint they come across, but by exploring your subject from different angles and positions you'll often come up with a far better composition.

First of all, always make sure you're close enough to your main subject. Nine times out of ten a picture can be improved simply by taking a few paces forward so the overall composition is tightened up and unwanted detail is omitted from the frame – as the late photojournalist Robert Capa used to say, 'If a picture's not good enough, you weren't close enough.'

Secondly, notice how changing camera-to-subject distance alters the relationship between foreground and background. The closer to your subject you are the more it will dominate the shot, whereas if you move further away it becomes smaller in the frame and has less emphasis.

With static subjects like landscapes and architecture it's always a good idea to have a stroll around for a few minutes before taking any pictures. That way you can find the best angle, locate suitable foreground interest, and observe the way your subject's appearance changes with the light falling from different directions.

Finally, never be afraid to try shooting from unusual viewpoints. We're all used

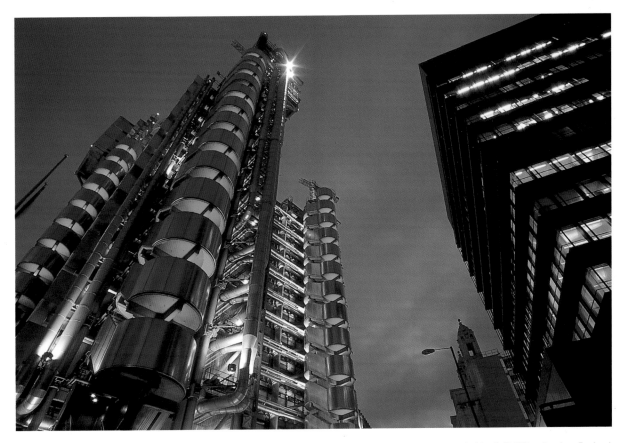

Lloyds Building, London, England
Shooting from high or low viewpoints can produce exciting, dramatic images because it gives us an unusual glimpse of the world that stimulates the senses.
Camera Nikon F90x Lens 20mm Film Fujichrome Velvia 50

to seeing the world from eye-level, so by intentionally raising or lowering the camera you'll immediately produce an unusual and more striking image.

High viewpoints offer a much clearer view and allow you to see further into the distance. You can discover this by standing on a wall or stepladder. Scale is also changed, and the higher you go the more dramatic it becomes. If you look down from a tall building or bridge, for example, people appear like small dots, dwarfed against much bigger structures. This in itself is enough to produce superb images if you home in on part of the scene with a telephoto lens, and can make the ordinary appear extraordinary.

Shooting from a low position to capture a worm's eye view of the world has the opposite effect. Smaller objects appear much larger in relation to their surroundings, so you can make people seem as tall as office blocks and create dramatic results in the most everyday locations. Subjects that are close to the camera also dominate the whole composition. When shooting landscapes, for example, you can make a relatively small object fill the whole foreground by crouching down and moving in close to it.

THE RULE OF THIRDS

This is by far the most common compositional rule used by photographers, and it's intended as a means of achieving visual balance in a picture.

All you do is divide up your camera's viewfinder into sections using horizontal and vertical lines a third of the way in from each corner. Your main subject or focal point should then be positioned on one of the four intersection points created.

The rule of thirds won't work for every single picture that you take. However, for pictures that include a small focal point, it can make all the difference.

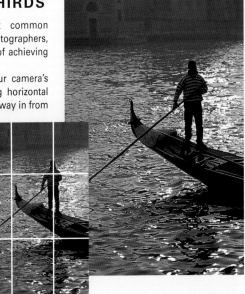

Venice, Italy
This shot was composed in accordance with the rule of thirds. Had the gondolier been in the centre, the composition wouldn't have been so effective.
Camera Nikon F90x Lens 80–200mm zoom Filter 81C warm-up Film Fujichrome Velvia 50

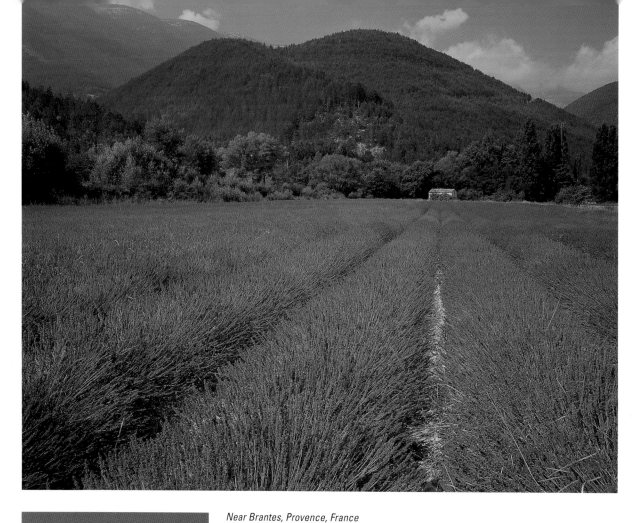

Near Brantes, Provence, France
Converging lines carry the eye through a scene as they taper away into the distance, and in doing so create a sense of depth. Here the rows of lavender create lines that carry the eye to the barn on the horizon.
Camera Pentax 67 Lens 55mm Filter Polarizer Film Fujichrome Velvia 50

Q How can lines be used to improve the composition of a picture?

Lines serve three important purposes in a composition. First, they help to carry the viewer's eye through the picture to the horizon or focal point. Second, they can create a strong feeling of depth and make that picture appear three-dimensional. Third, they can effectively divide a picture into well-defined areas, and help concentrate attention on the most important subject matter.

All sorts of man-made and natural elements form powerful lines, for example roads, walls, hedges, rivers, paths and fences. The furrows created by a plough or the shadows cast by lamp posts and trees also work well.

Wide-angle lenses are ideal for emphasizing lines because the way they stretch perspective exaggerates the effect. If you stand in the middle of a road and look down it through a 28mm lens, for example, the lines created will converge dramatically into the distance.

At the other extreme, a telephoto lens will allow you to make a feature of lines that would be lost in a wider view, such as the strong vertical lines created by tree trunks or other upright structures.

Different types of lines also create a different feel. Horizontal lines are restful and easy to look at, carrying the eye from left to right. Vertical lines, on the other hand, are more powerful because their upward movement suggests urgency – especially if you compose the picture with your camera in portrait format.

Diagonal lines cover more ground, so they're ideal for carrying the eye through a picture from the foreground to the background, while converging lines are the most powerful of all because they add a strong impression of depth.

Finally, assumed lines can work as well as real lines. The line of a person's gaze will attract just as much attention as a road cutting across a scene, for example.

Q Does a picture look better if it's framed by something, like the overhanging branches of a tree?

Using natural or man-made frames in a picture can work wonders, because as well as tightening up the overall composition they also direct attention on the main subject and get rid of unwanted space. The overhanging branches of a tree make an excellent frame that hides dull, empty sky for example, while doorways, gateways and windows also work well because they create a 'keyhole' effect that the eye can't resist looking through.

Wide-angle lenses are ideal for exploiting frames because their angle of view allows you to juggle with the relationship between the elements in a scene. To make sure both the frame and your subject are in sharp focus, set a small aperture of f/11 or f/16 so there's plenty of depth of field.

USING PERSPECTIVE

One of the biggest problems with photography is that you're recording three-dimensional subjects in two dimensions. The third dimension – depth – is missing. To give your pictures a feeling of depth you must therefore include visual clues that suggest it, and by far the easiest way to do this is by using perspective creatively.

If you capture a scene that contains rows of similar-sized features, such as lamp posts, trees or buildings, for example, they appear to get smaller as their distance from the camera increases. This is known as diminishing perspective, and it's a common way of showing depth. In the same way, parallel lines created by roads, railway tracks and ploughed furrows suggest depth because they converge into the distance. This is linear perspective. For the strongest effect, include the vanishing point where the lines appear to meet, and use a wide-angle lens for emphasis.

Other forms of perspective include aerial and tonal. Aerial perspective occurs when contrast, colour and tone are reduced with distance due to atmospheric haze. You can show this by taking telephoto shots of mountains or hills – each layer of the scene will appear lighter than the one in front. Tonal perspective is based on the fact that light or warm colours are said to 'advance' while darker or cooler colours 'recede'. If you photograph an orange subject against a blue background, tonal perspective will create a feeling of depth and distance.

Finally, lenses allow you to control perspective. If you take a picture through a telephoto lens the elements in a scene appear crowded together, while wide-angle lenses space everything further apart.

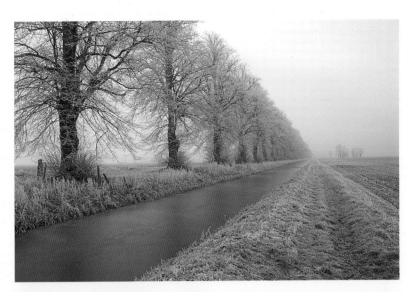

Fenland drain, Cambridgeshire, England
Linear, diminishing, tonal and aerial perspective are all evident in this scene and combine to create a strong three-dimensional effect.
Camera Olympus OM4-Ti Lens 21mm
Film Kodachrome 25

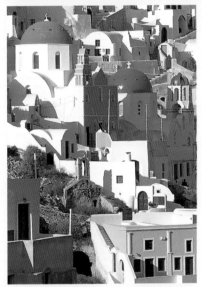
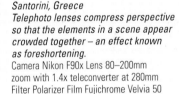

Santorini, Greece
Telephoto lenses compress perspective so that the elements in a scene appear crowded together – an effect known as foreshortening.
Camera Nikon F90x Lens 80–200mm
zoom with 1.4x teleconverter at 280mm
Filter Polarizer Film Fujichrome Velvia 50

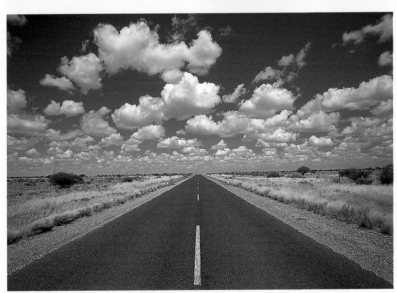

Near Mariental, Namibia
Diminishing perspective is created by converging lines – you can emphasize the effect with a wide-angle lens.
Camera Nikon F90x Lens 18–35mm
zoom at 18mm Filter Polarizer
Film Fujichrome Velvia 50

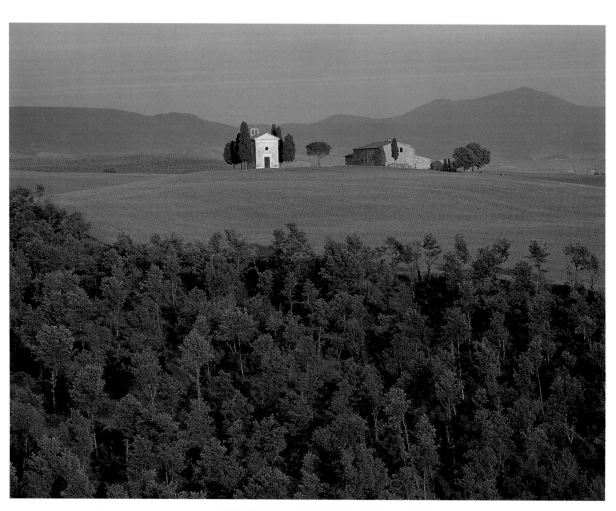

Near San Quirico d'Orcia, Tuscany, Italy
The best place to position the horizon
is one-third down from the top of the
frame – in this case it helps to balance
the composition and produces a
tranquil effect.
Camera Pentax 67 Lens 200mm
Filters Polarizer and 81D warm-up
Film Fujichrome Velvia 50

USING PATTERNS

We've already seen how the repetition formed by trees, lamp posts and other features have a role to play in emphasizing depth through perspective. However, when approached in a different way they can create eye-catching, abstract compositions for no other reason than that a pattern or rhythm is formed.

If you stand in line with a row of electricity pylons and peer through them, for instance, the repetition of bold lines and shapes produced looks stunning. Looking down a row of trees or architectural columns gives a similar result, which can be emphasized by using a telephoto lens to exclude all other elements from the shot.

If you keep your eyes peeled when you're out and about you'll also see patterns emerge in other ways. Crowds at a soccer match, cars in a congested car park, apples in a grocer's shop window, goods on a market stall and piles of bricks or timber on a construction site are just a few of the most common examples.

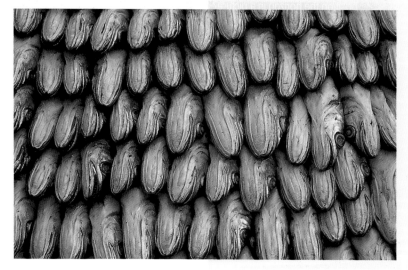

Essaouira, Morocco
I noticed this crate of fish while strolling
through the market in Essaouira – the
tightly packed heads created a fascinating
pattern that I emphasized by moving
in close to fill the frame.
Camera Nikon F90x Lens 50mm
Film Fujichrome Velvia 50

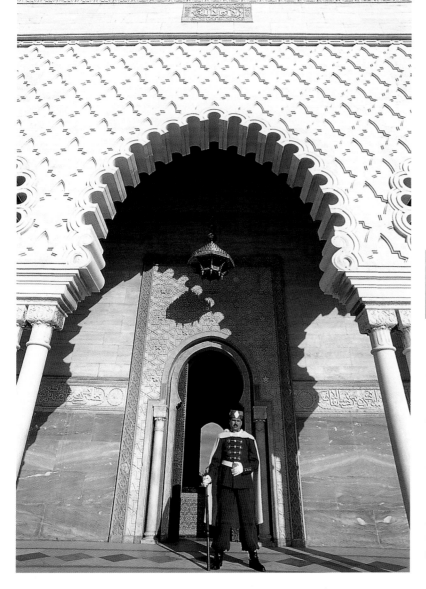

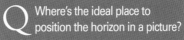

Rabat, Morocco
The strong vertical elements in this scene naturally lent themselves to an upright composition – had I shot in landscape format the result wouldn't be as dynamic.
Camera Nikon F90x Lens 20mm Filter Polarizer Film Fujichrome Velvia 50

Q Is it best to use the camera horizontally or upright when taking pictures?

That really depends upon what you're photographing, and what kind of 'feel' you're trying to create. The horizontal format creates a restful, soothing composition because it suggests repose, and echoes the horizon. That's why it tends to be used for landscape photography. Upright pictures are more energetic and powerful, suggesting motion and vertical direction, so this format is preferred for strongly vertical subjects such as tall buildings and trees.

There are no hard-and-fast rules about when to use each format, but both should be considered because the one you choose can make a big difference to the visual impact of the shot.

Q Will using a tripod help improve the composition of my pictures?

One advantage of using a tripod is that it slows down the whole picture-taking process and forces you to think more carefully about everything that you're doing. You can spend as much time as you like fine-tuning a composition until it's perfect, then leave the camera in position until you're ready to shoot.

From a purely technical point of view, a tripod also allows you to work at slow shutter speeds and small apertures, so you can take control over depth of field or take pictures in low light without having to worry about camera shake. This in turn maximizes your options and makes composition easier.

Q Where's the ideal place to position the horizon in a picture?

Many photographers have a habit of placing the horizon across the centre of the frame, but more often than not this is the worst place because you end up with a static, lifeless image. Generally you should position the horizon a third up from the bottom or a third down from the top of a shot, so the other two-thirds of the picture can be used to emphasize the foreground or sky. By positioning the horizon in this way you'll create a much more dynamic and visually pleasing composition. The only exception is if you want to produce a symmetrical picture of reflections – in a lake, for example. In those situations, a central horizon can work well.

Q Is it okay to break the 'rules' of composition?

Rules are made to be broken, and often doing so can lead to far more impressive results. There's nothing to stop you placing your main subject in the centre of the frame or cutting a picture in half with the horizon. Equally, no one says you have to produce logical, cohesive compositions.

Basically, when it comes to composition anything goes, but what you do must be intentional and considered if it is to produce successful work. And you must understand the 'rules' of composition before even thinking about abandoning them, because there's a big difference between a picture with a bad composition and one with an unusual composition.

Colour

Few photographers ever think about the colour content of a scene before committing it to film, but the way different colours relate can make a big difference to the success of a picture. Certain colours harmonize beautifully, for instance, while others clash. But unless you're aware of this you'll never be able to avoid or exploit it. Colour can also be controlled through the use of light, filters and film, giving you the opportunity to create an endless range of powerful effects.

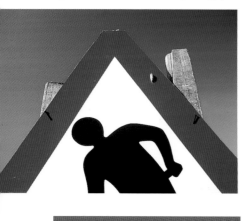

Northamptonshire, England
Colour is everywhere if you keep your eyes open for it. I noticed this Men At Work sign while driving past roadworks. It stood out brilliantly in the bright sunshine, and I emphasized the colour by shooting from a low viewpoint so the sign was captured against the sky.
Camera Olympus OM4-Ti Lens 28mm Filter Polarizer Film Fujichrome Velvia 50

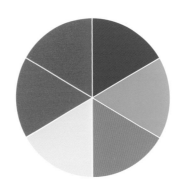

Q What are primary, secondary and complementary colours?

These three types of colour can be shown on a colour wheel that contains all the colours of the spectrum – like a rainbow. Primary colours in photography are red, green and blue. If you have a light source in each of these colours it's possible to create any other colour. If you combine all three the result is white light.

Complementary colours lie opposite each other on the colour wheel – cyan and red, magenta and green, and yellow and blue. If you mix a primary colour with its opposing complementary colour you get grey.

Secondary colours are formed by mixing two other colours together to form purple, orange and violet.

When you take a picture these colours are formed by the colour layers in the emulsion. Those layers comprise of cyan, magenta and yellow, which record the brightest because they require only one dye layer. Primary colours are formed by the combination of two layers – yellow and magenta form red, yellow and cyan form green, and magenta and cyan form blue – so a wide variety of shades is possible. The secondary colours are formed by a combination of all three layers, so their brightness is never as strong. They're also the most difficult to record.

The relationship between different colours can be seen by comparing them on a colour wheel representing the colours of the spectrum.

Q Is it okay to include contrasting colours in the same picture?

Use of contrasting colours in a picture is a powerful creative tool because it produces images that jar the senses and attract attention. Young people often choose to wear clothes that clash so that they stand out from the crowd, as you'll know only too well if you're old enough to remember the punk rock generation. Well, it's exactly the same in photography.

The strongest colour contrasts are formed if you combine a primary colour with its opposing complementary colour in equal strengths – see the colour wheel above. Yellow and blue are good examples. They clash violently when included in the same picture. The effect is weakened if one colour occupies more of the shot than the other, or if one colour is stronger.

Another factor to consider is the way different colours work on their own.

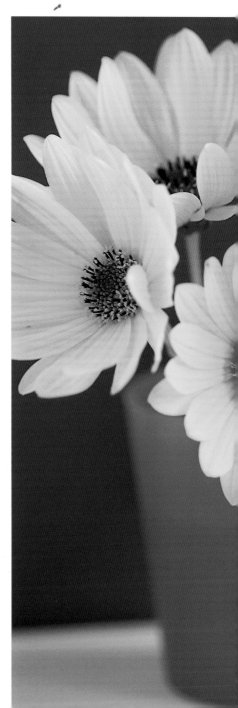

Warm colours such as red, yellow and orange are said to 'advance' because they stand out, while cool blues and greens 'recede' because they remind us of open space – the sea, sky and the countryside. So if you combine a warm colour with a cool colour, the warmer colour will always dominate the photograph, even if it only appears in small amounts, but the cooler colour will make an effective background.

Yellow flowers
This picture exploits the strongest colour contrast there is – between yellow and blue.
Camera Nikon F90x Lens 105mm macro
Film Fujichrome Sensia II 100

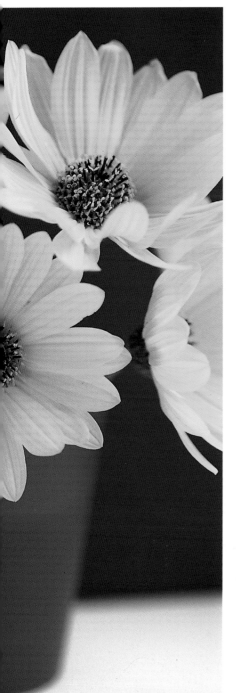

 How can I make sure the colours in a scene look as deeply saturated as possible?

There are three ways to maximize colour saturation. Firstly, film choice is important as colour rendition varies between brands. Fujichrome Velvia is renowned for its super-saturated colours, while Kodachrome 64 has a more neutral rendition.

Secondly, the quality of light can affect colour saturation. Colours tend to be at their strongest by bright sunlight during mid-morning and mid-afternoon, with the light striking your subject frontally.

Thirdly, you can use a polarizing filter to reduce glare on non-metallic surfaces and deepen blue sky, (see Filters, page 23).

If you're using slide film, underexpose your pictures by a third or half a stop.

Q Which colours harmonize the best?

Colours that are close to each other in the colour wheel produce a harmonious result – such as yellow and red, yellow and green, green and blue and so on. However, any colours will harmonize if they're weak.

Colour harmony is useful as it allows you to produce images that have a soothing effect on the viewer. Think of the colours of woodland in autumn, or the soft hues in a misty landscape You can also take superb pictures of scenes comprising just one colour, or the same colour in different shades. Soft, hazy light tends to create this effect in nature by bringing the colours closer together, but you'll also find man-made evidence of it too. The effect is known as monochromatic colour.

THE SYMBOLISM OF COLOUR

Colour has the power to evoke different reactions in the viewer due to the way we associate different colours with our moods and emotions.

Red is associated with blood, romance, evil, love, hate, danger and anger, and is often used as a warning due to its brightness and ability to attract attention. Orange and yellow are soothing, relaxing colours that remind us of the sun.

Of the colder colours, blue can suggest freedom and wide open spaces (the sky and sea), as well as being cold, lonely and sad. Finally, green is nature's own colour so it reminds us of the great outdoors, freshness, new birth and beauty.

You're not going to create these feelings simply by including a certain colour in your pictures, but it's worth bearing in mind this subliminal power when you take a picture. A fiery sunset enhanced by an orange filter will radiate warmth, for instance, while a picture taken on a cold, misty day with an overall blue cast will send a chill down the hardiest spine.

St Mark's Square, Venice, Italy
Blue can be both a positive colour and a negative one, depending on how it's depicted. Here I used a blue filter to add a cold cast to this misty dawn scene.
Camera Nikon F90x Lens 17–35mm zoom
Filter 80A Film Fujichrome Velvia 50

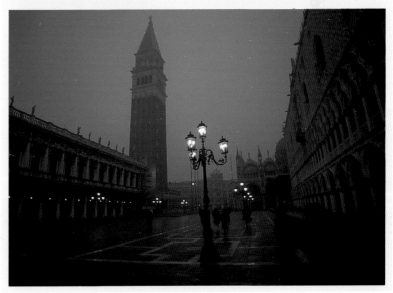

Processing

With processing labs in just about every high street around the country, processing your own films may seem like a waste of time. However, the advantage is that it puts you in control of yet another vital part of the photographic process. You can use materials that are intended for a specific brand of film, and vary processing times for film that has been up- or downrated so the best possible results are produced.

Processing black-and-white film involves just three chemicals – developer, fixer and stop bath, all of which can be purchased from your local camera shop.

Developer reacts with the silver halides in the film emulsion to reveal the image. Stop bath – a weak solution of acetic acid – is then used to arrest development by neutralizing the developer. Finally, fixer is used to clear the film and to make the image permanent.

Below is a list of the basic items of equipment that you will need to process your first film.

Having to work in complete darkness makes loading film tricky in the beginning, simply because you cannot see what you are doing. However, if you have a few practice runs with a blank roll of film, first in daylight, then in the dark, you will soon be able to find your way around by using touch alone.

To avoid problems, make sure the spiral is completely dry, as any moisture in the grooves will cause the film to jam. Blowing the spiral with a hairdryer for a few minutes should do the trick.

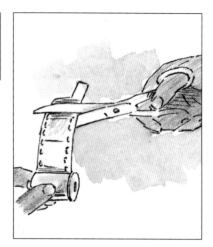

1. Cut off the film leader to create a straight line with curved corners.

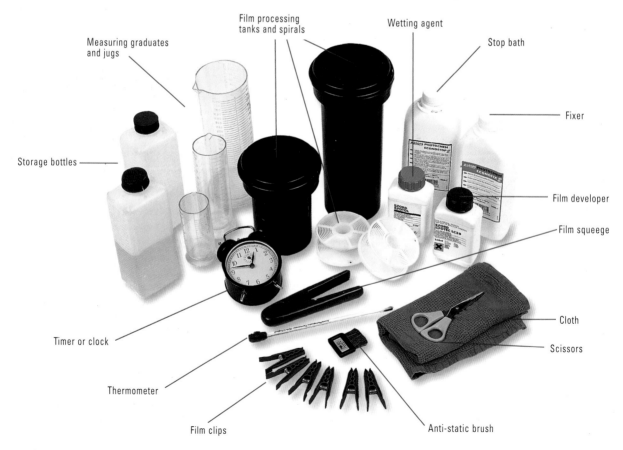

Measuring graduates and jugs

Film processing tanks and spirals

Wetting agent

Stop bath

Fixer

Storage bottles

Film developer

Film squeegee

Timer or clock

Cloth

Scissors

Thermometer

Film clips

Anti-static brush

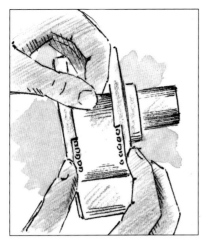

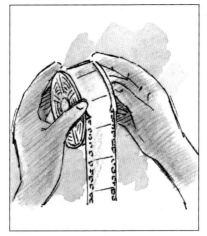

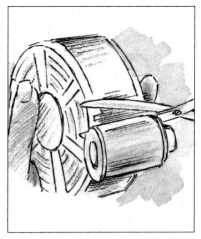

2. Feed the end of the film onto the spiral carefully, using your fingers to guide it into the grooves.

3. Pull out a length of film from the cassette, then carefully rack the sides of the spiral back and forth to feed it onto the grooves.

4. Once the film is fully loaded, cut off the spool with a pair of scissors.

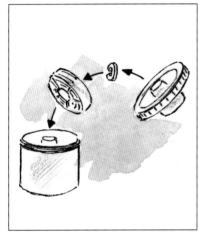

5. Pop the spiral into the tank and secure the lid. You can now switch the lights on and begin processing.

 How can I load film onto a spiral if I do not have access to a room that can be blacked out?

You need to buy a lightproof changing bag, which will allow you to load film onto the spiral in daylight. Alternatively, there are small dome tents available, such as the Harrison 'Pop' tent, which are designed so that photographers can load sheets of large-format film into darkslides while out shooting on location. They are more expensive, but they do work better than changing bags. The film, spiral and tank are placed inside the bag or tent, and you put your hands through two elasticated holes to do the loading.

Q What is the best way to store processing chemicals?

Once you open a bottle of developer or fixer it starts to oxidize due to exposure to the air, and eventually becomes exhausted. To prevent wastage, buy small quantities of liquid concentrate – 250ml (half a pint) bottles are ideal. Larger amounts are only worth buying if you process a lot of film.

Most film developers are known as 'one-shot'. This means you dilute the concentrate to produce the required amount, then discard it immediately after use. Diluter stop bath and fixer can be reused until they are exhausted.

Stop bath usually has an indicator dye in it that changes the colour of the solution from yellow to purple when it's exhausted, while you can test fixer by placing a small piece of undeveloped film into it (such as the leaders you cut off each roll of film prior to development). If the film clears in half the recommended fixing time, the fixer can still be used. If it doesn't, discard the solution and make a new batch.

Chemicals for reuse should be stored in full, tightly capped bottles. Plastic or glass drinks bottles are fine, although special concertina storage bottles are better because they can be squashed down to remove excess air. To remove air from partly used bottles of concentrate, either squeeze the sides of the bottle or drop glass marbles into them until the liquid reaches the top of the neck.

Q Is liquid developer better than powder?

Both work equally well. Liquid concentrates are convenient because you just dilute the amount required. Powder developers have to be mixed with water first, then you can either use the stock to develop several batches of film, or dilute a small amount of it to produce a one-shot working solution.

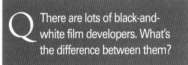 **There are lots of black-and-white film developers. What's the difference between them?**

Most of the time a general purpose developer is the best choice because it offers the ideal compromise between image contrast, sharpness and grain size. However, there are other types available that have certain characteristics that you may find useful.

If you uprate a film to a higher ISO, for example, you'll need to use a 'compensating' developer that's designed for push-processing. You can also buy developers that give extra-fine grain, increase contrast to give sharper results, and developers that can be used in different dilutions to vary image contrast.

Once your experience grows you can choose developers to suit specific brands of film, different subjects and varying lighting conditions depending on the type of results you want to produce.

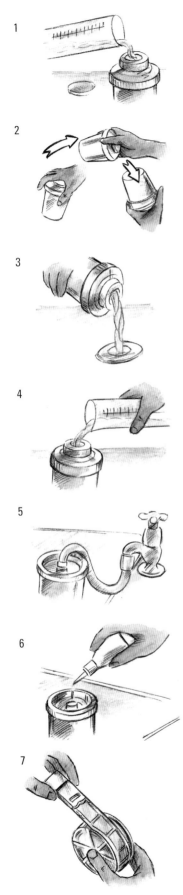

Once you've loaded the film into the processing tank, clear a suitable working area and get all your chemicals and equipment ready.

The chemicals should be mixed according to the manufacturer's instructions, using measuring graduates to get the quantities right, and clean water. Mark each graduate 'Dev', 'Stop' and 'Fix' so they don't get muddled up in the future.

The correct temperature for processing black-and-white film is 20°C (68°F). If the chemicals are too warm, place the graduates in a basin of cold water; if they're too cold, use warm water. Check the temperature with a thermometer, and remove them when they reach 20°C (68°F).

1 Pour the developer briskly into the tank and start the timer. Once all the developer has settled in the tank, place the lid on the tank then tap the tank base on a solid surface to dislodge any air bubbles on the film surface.

2 Agitate the film for 10 seconds by inverting a couple of times. This helps to ensure even development and should be repeated for 10 seconds every minute, or according to the manufacturer's specific instructions, should they differ.

3 Keep an eye on your clock or timer, and 10 seconds before the development period ends start pouring the solution out of the tank into a jug. Pour in the stop bath, agitate the tank continuously for about a minute, then return the stop bath to its storage bottle.

4 Pour in the fixer, agitate continuously for the first 15 seconds, then for 10 seconds every minute. Fixing usually takes two or three minutes, after which the solution can be returned to its storage bottle for future use.

5 Wash the film under running water for about 30 minutes to remove excess fixer. For the best results feed a hose from the tap into the tank to ensure thorough cleaning, and use a water filter if your local water supply contains particles that could stick to the film.

6 Before removing the film, place a couple of drops of wetting agent in the final rinse. This is a weak detergent that breaks down surface tension so excess water slides off the film and it dries quickly and evenly.

7 Pull a few inches of film from the spiral and attach a film clip to it, then draw out the rest.

8 Remove excess water with a squeegee – make sure the squeegee is clean, otherwise grit may scratch your film. Fit a weighted clip to the other end.

9 Hang the film up to dry in a clean, dust-free room for at least 12 hours – a shower cubicle in your bathroom is ideal. Once dry, cut the film into strips of five or six frames with a pair of scissors and place them in filing sheets for protection and storage.

Q How do I know if my negatives are correctly developed?

As long as you exposed the film correctly in the first place, and you then follow the manufacturer's recommended development time and keep the developer at 20°C (68°F), there is no reason why you shouldn't get perfect results.

The problem is that badly exposed negatives look similar to badly developed negatives, so if there is a fault you may not be able to identify the cause when you first start processing your own films. Following a set processing routine will make life easier, because if you develop the film correctly, any error can then be attributed to exposure; however if you use sloppy working practices you won't have a clue what went wrong in the process.

Once a roll of processed film has dried, examine the negatives on a lightbox and use the examples given here as a guide to check that yours are successful, or if not, where the error was created. Your aim should be to produce a correctly exposed and correctly developed negative that will print easily on normal grade 2 paper and produce a full range of tones from pure white to deep black.

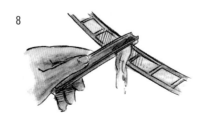

NEGATIVE FAULTS

Occasionally you may examine a newly processed roll of film and find some or all of the negatives ruined by various faults. To help you identify them, here is a rundown of the most common.

Clear film If the lettering on the film edge is visible, the film was grossly underexposed – probably due to taking a picture with the lens cap on – or you processed a roll of unexposed film. If the lettering is missing, fixer was poured into the tank before the developer.

Black film If the lettering on the frame edge is visible, the frame was grossly overexposed. If it is missing the film was badly fogged before or during development. To avoid this take care when loading/unloading film.

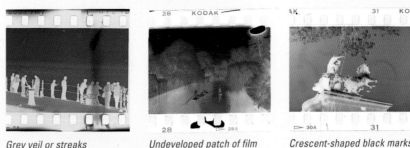
Grey veil or streaks

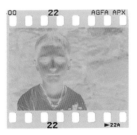
Undeveloped patch of film

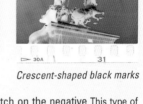
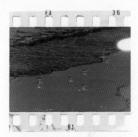
Crescent-shaped black marks

Grey veil or streaks These indicate the film was fogged before development – check your camera back or darkroom for a light leak. Grey fog and sprocket edge line indicate fogging during development.

Undeveloped patch on film This problem is caused by loops of film on the spiral touching, resulting in areas of the film not receiving developer and fixer. This is usually due to poor loading of the film.

Crescent-shaped black marks These are caused by the film being creased; this usually occurs during loading into the processing tank, so that the emulsion is damaged. Avoid by careful loading, and start again if the film jams, rather than forcing it.

Clear patch on the negative This type of fault indicates that the film was exposed to light before processing, probably by a light leak in the camera or developing tank. If the fault occurs on each negative in the same place it's probably the former.

Powdery stains These are caused by chemicals left on the film due to insufficient washing. Rewash the film to try and remove them. Water droplets left on the film as it dries can also cause drying marks that appear as circular patches.

Dense negs with yellow stains or grey streaks These usually indicate the developer was exhausted. Never use stock solution for more films than recommended, and store it in full, tightly capped bottles.

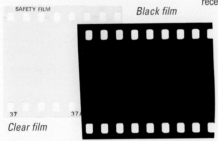
Black film

Clear film

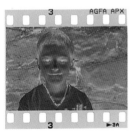

Exposure error
A correctly exposed negative shows a good balance of detail in both the highlights and shadows.

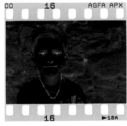

An overexposed negative appears dark and dense, with loss of the subtle highlight details and weak shadows.

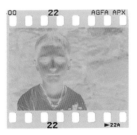

An underexposed negative has an overall light appearance, with low contrast and no visible shadow detail.

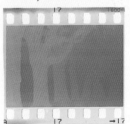
Clear patch on negative

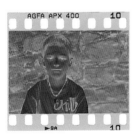

Development error
A well exposed and developed negative shows a good range of tones, with shadow detail.

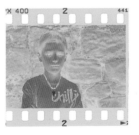

A correctly exposed but underdeveloped negative will exhibit low contrast, a poor range of tones and weak highlights.

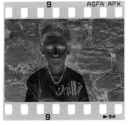

A correctly exposed but overdeveloped negative tends to look very dense and overly contrasty, with no real detail.

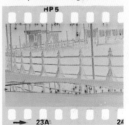
Powdery stains on film

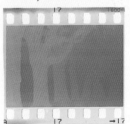
Dense negs with yellow stains

Darkroom printing

So you've processed your first film, produced a successful set of negatives, and now the time has arrived to make your first prints. Printing your very own pictures is an extremely rewarding experience that will amaze and delight you for many years to come.

The procedure involved in making black-and-white prints is relatively simple providing you follow a few guidelines, so there's no reason why you shouldn't get perfect results on your very first attempt. All you need to do then is practise, practise and practise some more.

The thing to remember with black-and-white photography is that half the work and most of the fun comes in the darkroom. Once you've gained a little experience, endless manipulations are possible and you can take complete control over the whole process.

Q: What equipment do I need to make black-and-white prints?

The basic equipment required to make enlargements from black-and-white negatives is relatively inexpensive. Most of the items you'll need can be picked up secondhand if you're working to a tight budget, and in some cases you can improvise by using things you already own.

1 Enlarger This forms the heart of any darkroom. It's also likely to be the most expensive item, so you should think long and hard before choosing a model. Most of the prints you make initially will probably be no bigger than 10x8in, but it's worth buying a model that allows enlargements up to 16x12in or even 16x20in. If you can afford the extra cost it's also a good idea to buy an enlarger with a colour filter head. This means you can make colour prints and use the

filters for variable-contrast (multigrade) black-and-white printing papers. Finally, go for an enlarger with a diffuser light source rather than one that uses condensers, as the latter produces much contrastier results and tends to show every speck of dust on the negative.

2 Enlarger lens The quality of your enlarger lens is of great importance because it determines the sharpness of your prints — especially once you start making big enlargements. Six-element lenses cost more than

four-element models, but they're sharper and worth paying the extra for. An illuminated aperture scale will also come in handy, plus a wide maximum aperture — f/2.8 is ideal — to aid focusing when you're printing from dense negatives. For prints from 35mm negs, use a 50mm lens; for 6x4.5cm, 6x6cm and 6x7cm use an 80mm lens.

3 Easel This is also known as a masking frame, holds your printing paper flat on the enlarger's baseboard during exposure. It can be adjusted to accept different sizes of printing paper, and allows you to create a white border around the print's edges. 16x12in is a good for general use.

You can put together a working darkroom for surprisingly little if you shop around and are prepared to buy secondhand. I am still using the same equipment that I purchased more than a decade ago.

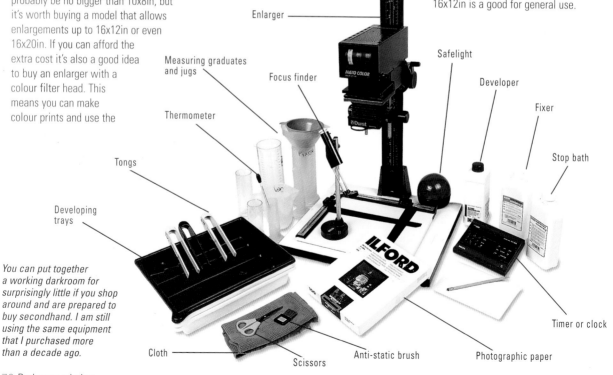

Enlarger · Measuring graduates and jugs · Focus finder · Safelight · Developer · Fixer · Thermometer · Stop bath · Tongs · Developing trays · Cloth · Scissors · Anti-static brush · Photographic paper · Timer or clock

4 Timer This is handy for giving precise control over print exposure times and consistency of results. The best timers are wired up to the enlarger, so all you do is set the required time, switch the enlarger on, then the timer switches it off at the end of the set time.

5 Safelight A low-powered light which provides enough visibility in the darkroom to see what you're doing, but won't fog printing paper. For standard printing paper a red light is used, but for variable-contrast papers a copper light is more suitable. The safelight colour required for a specific type of paper is usually printed on the packet or box.

6 Focus finder This handy accessory allows you to focus on the actual grain of the film to ensure perfect focus.

7 Developing trays Chemical-resistant plastic trays used to process the print. You need at least four: one for the developer, one for the stop bath, one for the fixer and one for water into which fixed prints can be placed until they're washed. They should be slightly bigger than the printing paper.

8 Jugs/graduates Accurate measuring of chemicals is essential for high-quality results, so equip yourself with a selection of measuring jugs and graduates. To prevent cross-contamination, mark each one using indelible marker pens.

9 Cleaning aids To minimize retouching, each negative should be carefully cleaned before printing using a blast of canned air, a blower brush or an antistatic brush.

10 Chemicals You need three: developer, stop bath and fixer. Different types of developer are available to give optimum results with certain printing papers, but you can produce acceptable results using one brand for all conventional papers. Stop bath and fixer can also be used with any paper type. Always mix according to the manufacturer's instructions, and discard when exhausted.

11 Accessories Among the accessories you may need are tongs to lift prints out from the developing trays, a cloth to wipe your hands and mop up chemical spills, scissors to cut paper and film, a thermometer to check the temperature of chemicas, and pad and pencil to note down exposure details.

12 Printing paper (see page 74).

 There isn't the space at home for a permanent darkroom. Where's the best place to print?

Most photographers are in the same situation, but they get around it by temporarily converting a room in their home. The bathroom, a spare bedroom, a cupboard under the stairs, even the garden shed will do providing it meets the following criteria:

- It can be blacked out easily to prevent the fogging of printing paper.
- You have sufficient space to position an enlarger and processing trays well apart, so there's no danger of liquids coming into contact with electricity.

- It has adequate ventilation and is warm.
- There's an accessible power point to plug in your enlarger and safelight.

Bathrooms are a favourite choice because running water is on hand. A sheet of plywood laid across the bath will create a surface for your trays, and you can stand the enlarger on a small table or cupboard. The drawback with bathrooms is they don't have socket outlets and you can guarantee that as soon as you start printing the whole family will want to pay a visit.

A spare bedroom is better, because you won't necessarily have to pack everything away after each session. The same applies with a garage, garden shed or cupboard under the stairs. Don't worry about running water – you can always put processed prints in a bucket or tray.

If all else fails, an empty cellar or loft with no windows would do. The only snag is that cellars tend to be damp, which can damage equipment and ruin printing paper, while lofts tend to be hot during the summer but freezing cold in winter.

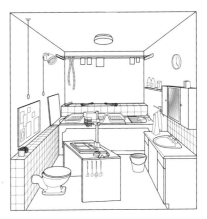

If you don't have the space for a permanent darkroom, your bathroom can be easily be converted for temporary use.

- Place a board over the bath for print trays
- Place processed prints in a tray in the bath
- Running water to wash prints
- Enlarger placed on cupboard
- Board over sink to hold paper and negatives
- Window blacked out with board
- Safelight

Got a vacant understairs cupboard? With a little planning it can easily be converted into a functional darkroom.

- Enlarger
- Printing paper
- Timer
- Safelight
- Storage shelves
- Bench for trays
- White light with pull-switch
- Socket outlet
- Paper storage
- Bucket for processed prints
- Cloth to dry hands
- Doorframe lined to give lightproof seal
- Louvre ventilation in door

Q **How do I know which negatives will make good prints after processing a roll of film?**

It is difficult to see what a picture is going to turn out like just by looking at the negative. So to make your life easier you can produce a contact sheet from the set of negatives. This is basically a print containing a small positive image of each shot from which you can choose the best for enlargement.

It's important that you make good-quality contact sheets as they will be filed away with your negatives and used for reference on many occasions when you want to make prints from a particular film. They can also be marked with cropping lines and other information as you decide on the best way in which to print individual frames. Before making the final contact sheet you first need to produce a test strip to determine the exposure required.

Because you're dealing with maybe 36 different images it's impossible to get the exposure for every one perfect on the same sheet, but by trying various exposures you can find the best compromise. The step-by-step guide below gives full details of how to make a test strip.

Once you know which exposure to use you can make the final contact sheet by laying the negatives out on a full sheet of printing paper, exposing it for the required time, and repeating the processing stages mentioned below. After washing and drying it you can then decide which shots to enlarge.

Don't expect every frame of film to be correctly exposed on the contact sheet. This is virtually impossible unless the whole roll of film was shot in very similar conditions, so a second contact sheet may be required for some frames if you want to see them all.

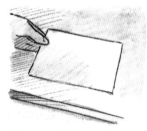

1 Under safelight conditions, place half a sheet of printing paper (10x4in) on the enlarger baseboard, emulsion side up. Cover the lens with a red safety filter, check light pool will cover the paper and set the lens aperture to f/8 or f/11.

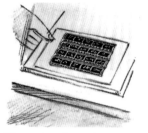

2 Lay strips of negatives, emulsion side down, on the printing paper until the sheet is full. Place a clean sheet of glass over the negatives to hold them flat, then cover two-thirds of the area with a piece of black card.

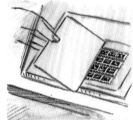

3 Switch on the enlarger and expose the area shown for five seconds. Uncover two-thirds of the printing paper and expose for a further five seconds, then remove the card completely and expose the final third for five seconds.

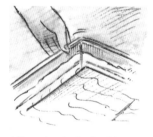

4 Your chemicals should already be mixed up and ready for use. You'll need a tray of developer, a tray of stop bath and a tray of fixer. Mix enough chemicals to half fill each tray, and make sure the developer is at roughly 20°C (68°F).

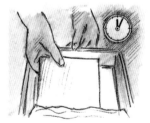

5 Place the test strip in a tray of print developer and start your timer or clock. Gently agitate the tray so developer washes over the print, and continue agitating until the end of the recommended development time – usually one-and-a-half minutes.

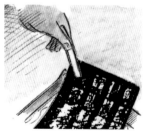

6 Lift the print from the tray and allow excess developer to drain off for a few seconds. Place it in a tray of stop bath and agitate the tray gently for about 30 seconds. Then lift the print from the tray with another pair of tongs and allow it to drain again.

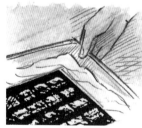

7 Place the print in a tray of fixer, face down, and agitate for about 20 seconds. Turn the print over, and continue to agitate the tray gently, then after one minute, turn the room lights back on and complete fixing. The contact test sheet is now complete.

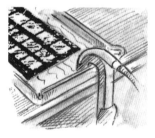

8 Remove the test sheet from the fixer, drain off excess chemicals then wash for five minutes under running water. Examine the test strip to see which exposure is required for the final contact sheet and make another one using a full sheet of paper.

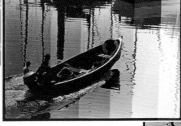

BELOW
This test strip was exposed in increments of two seconds, so the lightest strip received two seconds and the darkest 14 seconds. I chose an exposure of eight seconds for the final print shown.

Q How do I know how much exposure to give a print?

More often than not each negative you enlarge will require a different exposure due to variations in image density, the type of film and paper you use, plus the actual size of the enlargement made. To discover what this exposure is you need to make another test strip, this time using just the negative you want to print up.

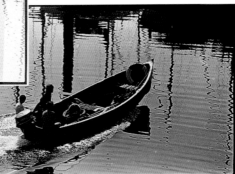

LEFT *A carefully made contact sheet will prove invaluable for assessing your work and deciding which frames to enlarge. Number each contact sheet and film so you know which goes with which.*

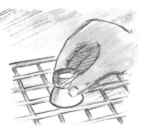

1 Select the negative you want to enlarge by examining the contact sheet you have already made. Clean the negative to remove any particles of dust, then place it in the negative carrier and slot the carrier into the enlarger.

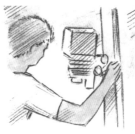

2 Switch off the room light, turn on the enlarger and set the enlarger lens to maximum aperture. Adjust the height of the enlarger head until the image it projects on the masking frame is the correct size for the final print.

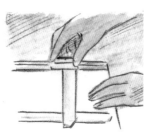

3 Place the masking frame on the enlarger baseboard and adjust the blades to hold the size of paper you want to work with. Remember to make provision for a neat white border around the edges of the print.

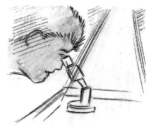

4 Focus the image on the masking frame by adjusting the focusing control on the enlarger head while looking through a focus finder placed on top of the masking frame. Set the enlarger lens aperture to f/5.6 or f/8.

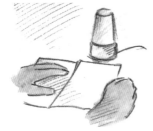

5 Switch off the enlarger, then under safelight conditions, cut a strip of printing paper about 12cm (3 or 4in) wide from a sheet of the same type and contrast grade you intend to use for the final print. Return the rest of the paper to its box to avoid fogging.

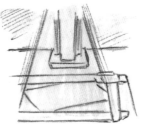

6 Place the strip of printing paper on the masking frame so it covers an area that's either representative of the whole picture area, or concentrates on the most important subject matter – like your subject's face in a portrait – so you can determine correct exposure.

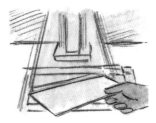

7 Hold a sheet of black card an inch above the masking frame so only one-fifth of the strip is revealed, switch on the enlarger and expose for five seconds. Repeat this procedure until the whole of the strip has been exposed a section at a time.

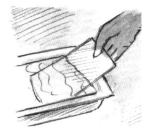

8 Remove the test strip from the masking frame and process it as you did the contact sheet. When fixing is complete, turn on the room light and check the strip to see which exposure you need to use for the final print or make a second test strip.

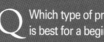

Q So how do I make the final enlargement?

With the test strip completed, the required exposure chosen and the enlarger already set up, you're almost there.

Now all that remains is to give the negative one last clean, make sure the chemicals and everything else you need is ready and waiting, then follow these steps.

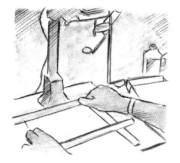

1 Set the required exposure on your enlarger timer, then turn on the enlarger so it projects the image of the shot onto the masking frame. Check to make sure it's still sharply focused.

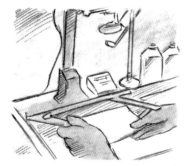

2 Switch off the enlarger, then under the safelight remove a full sheet of printing paper from its packet and place it in the masking frame. Expose the print for the required time.

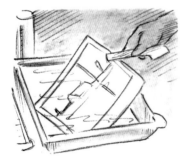

3 Develop, stop and fix the print as you did the contact sheet and test strip. Then turn on the light to assess your handiwork, then wash it under running water (five minutes for resin-coated paper; 30 minutes for fibre-based) before drying.

Q Which type of print developer is best for a beginner?

Any make of developer can be used with any conventional type of paper, so it doesn't really matter which one you go for. Standard brews, such as Ilford PQ Universal or Paterson Acuprint, are ideal if you intend to try using different types of paper, but there are also developers specially designed for variable-contrast papers, such as Ilford Multigrade.

Buy developer in small quantities as it begins to oxidize once the bottle has been opened and partly used – 250ml (half a pint) bottles of concentrate are a good size if you only print occasionally, while 500ml or 1 litre bottles (1 or 2 pints) will suit the more frequent darkroom worker. Alternatively, buy a bigger bottle but decant it into smaller bottles and use them one at a time.

Diluted print developer can be reused providing it's stored in full, tightly stoppered bottles, but you should discard it once the specified number of prints have been developed, otherwise it won't give top-quality results.

It's also vital that you leave prints in the developer for the recommended period – usually one to one-and-a-half minutes. If a print seems to be going very dark too soon it's tempting to 'snatch' it from the developer prematurely, but this doesn't solve the problem because that print won't exhibit a full range of tones – usually the highlights will look washed out.

If this occurs it's because the print has received too much exposure under the enlarger, so reduce the exposure and make another print. Similarly, if the print is too light after the recommended development time make another print but expose it for a longer period.

CHOOSING THE RIGHT PRINTING PAPER

With so many different brands to choose from, deciding which printing paper to use can cause great confusion. To make this decision easier, let's look at the factors you need to consider.

Firstly, most brands of paper come in two forms: resin-coated and fibre-based. Resin-coated paper is ideal for beginners as it has a plastic base that aids flat drying and it only needs to be washed for five minutes. Fibre-based paper gives a wider tonal range, so it's preferred by experienced printers, but it must be washed for at least 30 minutes to remove all traces of chemistry, and it curls while drying.

In terms of size, 10x8in is ideal for general use as it's fairly economical, while 16x12 or 16x20in is better for exhibition and portfolio prints. Glossy is the most popular surface finish because it gives very clean, crisp prints, but a matt or semi-matt finish may suit certain shots.

Finally, printing paper is made in different contrast grades, so you can produce the best prints from negatives with different contrast levels. These grades run from 1, which is known as 'soft' because it reduces contrast, to 5, known as 'hard' because it increases contrast to give stark prints with few mid-tones. A well-exposed negative with an average contrast range should print easily on grade 2 paper, so this is considered 'normal'.

To make life easier you can buy variable-contrast paper such as Ilford Multigrade III or Agfa Multicontrast, which allows you to obtain any contrast grade, from 0 to 5 in half-grade steps, from the same box of paper. This is achieved using filters that are fitted above or below the enlarging lens, or by dialling in the necessary filtration on your enlarger's colour head if it has one. The table shows the filtration values required to obtain different grades.

Contrast Grade	Filtration		
	Durst enlargers	De Vere enlargers	Kodak CC filters
0	110Y	170Y	80Y
1	70Y	115Y	30Y
2	none	none	none
2.5	30M	20M	25M
3	45M	70M	40M
4	95M	120M	100M
4.5	130M	200M	150M
5	150M	–	–

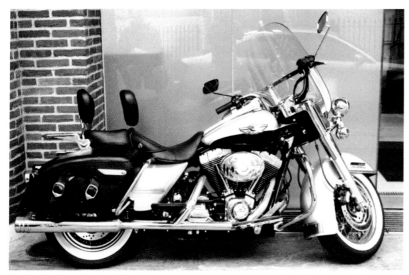

Harley Davidson, London, England
If everything has gone according to plan, you should have a successful print that shows a full range of tones from white through to black and is free of faults. But if you haven't, don't worry – just try again and eventually you will get there.
Camera Nikon F90x Lens 50mm Film Ilford HP5 Plus

Q What's the easiest way to get rid of the white marks caused by dust and hairs?

You'll need to buy a pack of special photo dyes such as Spotone and a fine sable brush – 00 and 0 sizes are ideal and should be available from all good art materials shops. Dilute a tiny amount of dye with water until its shade matches the tone of the area to be retouched, then cover the blemish by applying tiny spots of dye. With really bad marks, try building up the density of the dye gradually.

CHOOSING THE RIGHT CONTRAST GRADE

Deciding which grade of paper to use for a particular print can prove confusing to begin with, but as your experience grows you'll know exactly which one will give the best result just by looking at the negative.

As mentioned earlier, a negative with an average contrast range should print easily on grade 2 paper, providing it's well exposed and developed. However, a picture taken in dull, flat light may need to be printed on a harder grade, say 3 or 4, to boost contrast and produce a more punchy result. Similarly, a picture taken in harsh, contrasty light may need a softer grade such as 1 or 1.5 to produce the maximum tonal range, or detail will be lost on the print.

Different grades can also be used intentionally to create certain effects. Harder grades are ideal if you want bold, graphic prints, for example, because they produce deep blacks and crisp whites with far fewer mid-tones.

Printing the same negative on different grades of paper produces completely different results. Notice how contrast increases considerably as you move from grade 0 to 5 in this comparison, resulting in a loss of highlight and shadow detail. Grade 3 gives the best result.

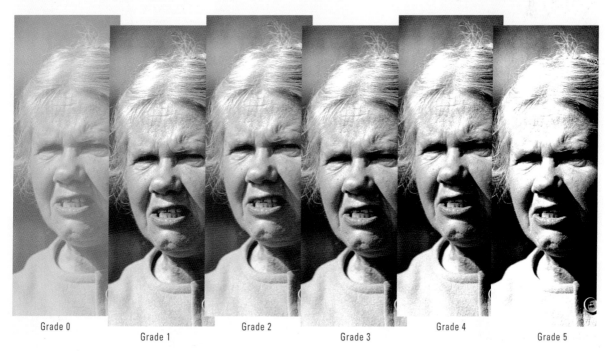

Grade 0 Grade 1 Grade 2 Grade 3 Grade 4 Grade 5

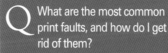

Q Is it possible to make a decent print from a badly exposed or poorly developed negative?

Q What are the most common print faults, and how do I get rid of them?

It is possible, but don't expect the same quality you'd get from a well-exposed and correctly developed negative. Underexposed or overdeveloped negatives appear rather thin and produce flat, grey prints. You may be able to rescue it by printing on a harder grade of paper – try 3 or 4. If a negative has been overexposed or underdeveloped it will be dark and dense and produce prints with plenty of shadow but burned-out highlights.

If you take your time when printing, and work with a well-exposed, correctly developed negative, there's no reason why your first prints shouldn't be perfect. However, more often than not, enlargement will reveal a number of flaws that will need to be remedied either by making another print or treating the one you've already made. Opposite I have outlined the most common faults and how to overcome them.

Uneven border This is caused by not putting the printing paper into the masking frame properly. Next time, make sure it aligns correctly with the guides on the frame so you get an even border.

White spots and lines Dust and hairs on the negative are responsible for this problem. Thorough cleaning of the negative before printing should prevent it from happening – try using a blast of canned air or an antistatic brush, both work effectively – but if the marks are too bad you can spot them out with dyes (see Dodging and burning-in below).

DODGING AND BURNING-IN

If you've done everything right, there's no reason why you shouldn't end up with a near-perfect print. However, because the brightness range that printing paper can record is smaller than the range a negative can record, you may find that some areas of the print are too light or too dark.

If you enlarge a landscape, for example, and print so the foreground is correctly exposed, more often than not the sky will be far too light. Similarly, if you correctly expose the highlights when making a print, the shadows may go too dark.

To solve this problem, two handy techniques known as dodging and burning-in are used. Dodging involves shading areas of the print during exposure so they receive less light and come out lighter, while with burning-in you expose selected areas of the print for longer so they go darker, while shading the rest of it.

The extent by which the exposure must be increased or reduced can be determined by analyzing the initial test strip, and where necessary making further test strips that concentrate on different areas of the image.

Burning-in

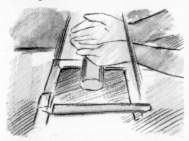

If large areas need burning-in, such as the sky in a landscape, you can use a sheet of card or your hand to cover the rest of the image while extra exposure is given. Take care not to cover areas that don't require burning-in.

Dodging

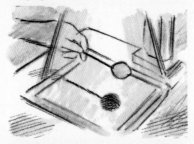

Small areas can be dodged by taping a small disc of card to a length of fine, stiff wire, then holding it over the area you need to lighten. Vibrate the dodger gently during the exposure so it doesn't leave any tell-tale marks.

Precise control

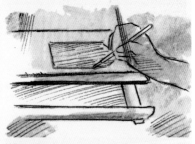

Where intricate areas require some dodging or burning-in, make a card mask by holding a sheet of black card about 6cm (2¼in) above the masking frame and then tracing the outline of the area onto it.

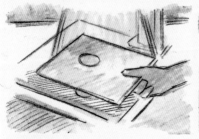

For smaller areas, cut a hole in a piece of black card and 'paint' them with light. Moving the card closer to the print reduces the size of the pool of light produced, and vice versa.

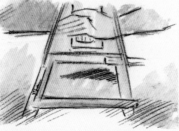

To dodge larger areas use your hand or a piece of card cut to roughly the right shape and hold it in the light path. Again, move it gently from side to side to produce a neat effect.

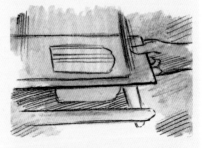

Next, carefully cut out the mask with a sharp craft knife, then hold it in the light path while you expose the final print, so that the required area is either lightened or darkened.

Black marks These marks indicate scratches on the negative, which allow too much light through to the printing paper. Severe scratches can't be corrected, but you can bleach out the marks on the print.

Area too light or too dark The exposure you use may be correct for most of the shot, but with high-contrast negatives you may still have areas that are too light or dark. Either problem can be remedied by dodging and burning-in.

Part of picture obscured This indicates something was blocking out light from part of the print. It could have been the red swing-in filter on your enlarger, or your hand straying into the light path.

Untidy edge This happens if you don't crop out the edge of the negative using your masking frame. The rebate of the negative appears on the print as an uneven, blurred line. To get rid of it, adjust the masking frame to make a slightly smaller print size.

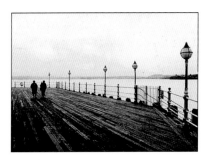

Princess Pier, Torquay, England
This pair of pictures shows the most common use for burning-in – to record detail in a washed-out sky by giving it more exposure than the rest of the print.
Camera Olympus OM4-Ti Lens 28mm
Film Fuji Neopan 1600

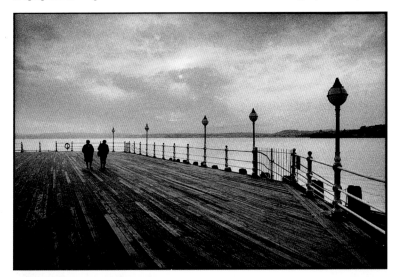

Lindisfarne, Northumberland, England
Once your darkroom experience grows you can experiment with creative techniques such as toning (see page 139), lith printing, print diffusion and so on. Here I exposed the negative through a soft-focus filter then partially bleached and sepia toned the print.
Camera Nikon F90x Lens 50mm
Film Ilford HP5 Plus

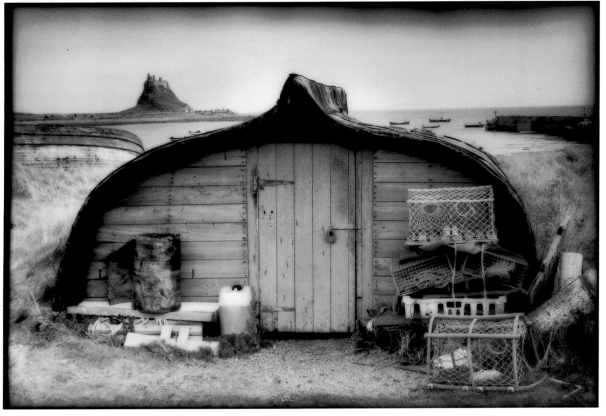

Scanning

You don't need to buy a digital camera to become involved in digital imaging – instead, slides or negatives can be scanned into a computer ready for enhancement, manipulation and outputting as colour or black-and-white prints. By working in this way you are in effect taking the best from both types of technology, because although the quality you can achieve with a digital camera is high, you still need to spend a lot more money on that camera than you would its film equivalent to obtain the same quality.

Q How does a scanner work?

When you place a print, piece of artwork, negative or slide in a scanner, it makes a digital copy of the image in the same way that a photocopier makes a paper copy of anything placed under its hood.

This is done using a honeycomb pattern of CCDs like those found in a digital camera. Each cell in the CCD grid responds to light and creates a single pixel, so the more sensors the scanner has, the more detail it can digitize. This means higher image quality and bigger print sizes.

Compared to digital cameras, scanners are far more sensitive, so they provide a cheaper route into digital imaging.

Q Which is best – a flatbed scanner or a dedicated film scanner?

That depends. Generally, dedicated film scanners give superior results to flatbeds because they are specifically designed to handle film originals and can often extract more information from that film than a flatbed scanner could. The benefit of a flatbed scanner over a film scanner is that as well as scanning film you can scan prints and artwork. You can also scan any film format – 35mm, medium-format, panoramic, 5x4in and so on.

Film scanners designed for 35mm film only aren't too expensive and they're also relatively compact, so if you only shoot that format, a film scanner is your best option.

However, if you shoot larger formats (I shoot everything from 35mm to 6x17cm), a flatbed scanner will cost you far less than a film scanner but still offer high image quality – certainly high enough to produce big enlargements or have images published in books and magazines.

The key when buying a flatbed scanner is to look at models that come with special holders for film and a transparency hood so you can scan film without further expense. Some models also have a separate drawer for film holders.

Q What features should I look for when buying a scanner?

Having decided between a flatbed or film scanner, here are the main characteristics you need to consider.

 Resolution

This is a numerical expression of image quality and refers to the number of pixels a scanner can create from an inch of picture. The higher this number is, the better. A good-quality 35mm film scanner will have a resolution of 4000dpi or more, but it needs to be higher than for a flatbed because it's designed to scan originals that only measure 24x36mm, so more sensors are required to pull out sufficient information. A flatbed scanner, on the other hand, may have an optical resolution of 3200dpi. Don't be fooled into thinking that this means it's inferior though.

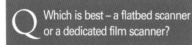

Film scanners like the Nikon Coolpix 4000 (above) are ideal if you only shoot a single film format – in this case 35mm – whereas flatbed scanner like the Epson Perfection 3200 (right) allow you to scan all film formats, as well as prints and artwork.

Bit depth

To create photo-realistic pictures you need a palette of 16.7 million different colours, more commonly referred to as 24-bit. When shopping for a scanner you should only really look at models that offer 24-bit resolution or higher.

Optical and interpolated
The resolution of a scanner is often quoted in two ways – as optical and interpolated. Ignore the latter. Only the optical resolution gives a true indication of the image quality possible by telling you how many sensor cells the scanner is equipped with.

Interpolated resolution tells you how high the resolution can go if new pixels are added to the recorded ones, but interpolated images are never as sharp because computer-generated pixels are added to mimic ones nearby.

Dynamic range
This figure refers to a scanner's ability to detect highlight and shadow detail in colour slides. Film scanners usually have a higher dynamic range than flatbeds, which means they produce scans with better highlight and shadow detail. A figure of 3.0 or above is sufficient in a high-quality scanner.

Software
When you buy a scanner it usually comes with both a standalone software package and a Photoshop plug-in. Which you use is entirely up to you. Standalone software tends to be faster and uses less memory, but plug-ins such as Silverfast work within Photoshop so once an image has been

scanned, the software closes automatically, leaving you in Photoshop to manipulate the image (see page 80). This saves time and makes the process of scanning then manipulating more straightforward.

Computer interfaces
Once an image has been scanned, the digital data has to be transferred to your computer from the scanner via connecting cables. At present, FireWire is the fastest system available, followed by USB (Universal Serial Bus) (though new, faster systems are sure to appear in the future) and current systems are relatively fast unless your scanning generates huge files (100MB or more).

Q Do you have any tips on scanning slides and negatives?

Although you could unpack a brand new scanner, plug it in, connect it to your computer and be scanning images in a matter of minutes, producing high-quality scans that you can turn into photo-quality inkjet prints takes practice and experience. Here are a few tips to get you started:

1 Make sure the original piece of film or print is free of dust and hairs, otherwise you will have to spend time cleaning it up. If you are using a flatbed scanner, the glass plate should also be kept spotlessly clean.

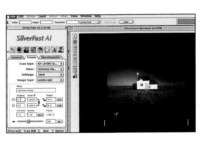

2 Make a preview scan first so you can assess the image and allow the scanner software to judge the exposure. You can also make changes to brightness, contrast and colour balance before producing the final high-res scan.

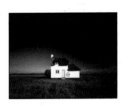

3 Crop the image tightly so there's no white space around it – not only will this make the file size bigger than necessary, but the white space will fool your scanner software into thinking that the actual image is lighter than it really is.

---

4 Make sure there are no preset functions in operation that could affect the quality of the scan. It's important to keep contrast down. You can always increase it later, but if contrast is too high when you make the scan the results may be disappointing.

5 When it comes to deciding on the size of the scanned image, it's better to go for a higher resolution than you need as you can always downsize later. If your intention is to make a print, the resolution should be at least 200dpi and for reproduction in books,

magazines and other printed media it should be 300dpi. In both cases, select an output size that's bigger than you need. So, for example, if you want to make a 16x12in print, set output size at 16x20in. This means the file size will be bigger 50MB or more isn't uncommon – but that needn't be a problem. An alternative way to scan is by setting scanner resolution to its maximum and scanning the original at 100 per cent.

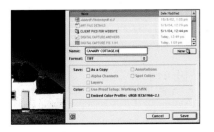

6 Save the scanned image as a TIFF file to maximize image quality. JPEG is a lossy format which means you lose quality every time you re-save.

7 Don't expect miracles. If you don't start out with a high-quality, sharp original, you can't expect the scan to be. Also, film originals give better scans than prints, so it's preferable to scan a 35mm negative than a print made from it – especially the 6x4in enprints produced by commercial processing labs.

Image manipulation

Digital technology has opened up a whole new world of creativity for photographers. For the first time, complicated techniques that took years of practice to master can now be achieved quickly, easily and with great precision. Images can be enhanced until they're perfect and manipulated to create effects that would be impossible using traditional photographic processes.

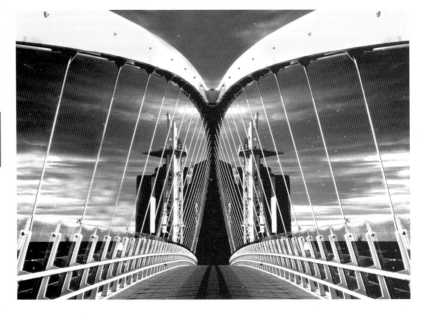

*Salford Quays, Manchester, England
Here I copied half of the original photo, flipped it, and joined the two halves together in Photoshop to create a mirror image. I then adjusted levels, brightness and contrast until I was happy with the result.*
Camera Nikon F90x Lens 28mm
Filter Orange Film Ilford FP4 Plus

Q What equipment do I need to get started in digital imaging?

The heart of any digital imaging system is the computer. The make or model you buy doesn't really matter, providing that it has an up-to-date processor and plenty of memory and hard disk space.

- At least 256MB of RAM (Rapid Access Memory) is essential, though the cost of memory is low these days so many photographers have as much RAM installed as their computer will take – usually 1GB or more.
- You will also need plenty of hard disk space to store software and images – 60GB or more is common.
- A CD-ROM drive that allows you to both read and record CDs is largely standard issue on computers today, though it's worth spending a little more and including a DVD read/write facility as DVDs offer much more storage space than CDs and are becoming a more economical and practical way to store digital images.
- A good quality monitor is essential and ideally it should have a screen size of at least 15 inches so you have enough space to work on an image and access imaging tools without endless scrolling.
- If you use a digital camera then you can download images straight to your computer, but if you shoot film you will need a scanner so you can digitize the originals (see Scanning, page 78).
- Finally, the fruits of all your labour at the computer will usually be a print, so to produce your own you need a decent printer (see Digital printing, page 84).

Q Which imaging software would you recommend?

There are many different software options on the market today and as your experience grows you will be able to take advantage of them. However, if you are looking for the ultimate package, and don't want to have to buy more than one piece of software, Adobe Photoshop is the only image-editing tool you will ever need. Photoshop is the industry standard among both professionals and enthusiast photographers and is such a versatile tool that anything you can do in a darkroom, you can do in Photoshop and much more besides. There are dozens of instructional books published on Photoshop to help you learn more.

The full Photoshop package is quite expensive and includes many features that as an amateur you may never use. But fortunately, there is a less costly alternative – Photoshop Elements – which provides just the key elements of the program – all the tools you need to begin enhancing your and perfecting photos digitally.

Q There are lots of different tools in Photoshop – can you tell me what they do?

It's not just Photoshop that has lots of tools – all imaging software packages do. And though they may differ slightly, in most cases they work in the same way. Here's a rundown of the most common.

Marquee Allows you to select rectangular or elliptical areas of the image and work on them in isolation.

Move Use this to move individual Layers or selected areas around and position them precisely.

Lasso Allows you to select odd-shaped areas by effectively drawing around it.

Magic wand Selects pixels that have a similar colour.

Crop tool Use this to crop an image to a new shape and improve the composition.

Slice tool Allows you to divide the image into rectangular sections – you can ignore this for now.

Healing tool Removes dust, scratches, blemishes, and wrinkles from your photographs and preserves the original shading, tonality, and texture in the retouched area.

Paintbrush/Pencil Allows you to draw or colour areas of an image. The brush has a softer edge.

Rubber Stamp Lets you copy/clone parts of an image to remove unwanted elements including dust/hairs/scratches or to add additional elements cloned from those already in the photo (such as extending a sky or similar).

History and Art History brush Use it to undo certain areas and create painterly effects.

Eraser/background eraser/magic eraser Use it to rub out unwanted areas of an image – either small and specific points or large areas.

Gradient Produces a smooth transition from one colour to another.

Blur/sharpen/smudge Use this tool to blur or sharpen specific areas, such as blurring the edge of an image.

Dodge/burn/sponge Allows you to selectively lighten/darken areas of an image with precision.

Path and pen selection Free drawing pen tools for advanced users.

Type tool Allows you to add type directly onto an image.

Line and shape tool Draw single pixel lines or wider and add shapes or arrowheads.

Notes/annotation tool Add text or sound notes to a file.

Eyedropper/colour sampler/ measure Lets you sample and replicate any colour from an image and measure distance/angles.

Hand Lets you navigate around an image quickly.

Zoom Enlarges the image so you can retouch with precision.

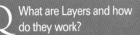

Q What are Layers and how do they work?

Layers are one of the most versatile and useful aspects of Photoshop, though initially they seem very complicated so photographers tend to avoid them.

Put simply, Layers works like transparent sheets of film laid over a photograph. You can put things in each layer, such as elements from different photographs, and combine them, as well as adding text or filter effects to images, then blend the images to achieve exactly what you want. Layers can also be removed quickly and easily if they don't work and the original image remains unaffected. This gives you enormous creative control, so it's worth spending time getting to grips with them.

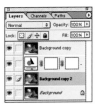

Layers are one of the most versatile tools at your disposal so it's worth learning how to use them.

Q How can I store digital images to free up hard disk space on my computer?

The most cost-effective is to copy them onto recordable CDs (CD-R) which are inexpensive and hold 650MB of memory. Recordable DVD (DVD-R) is also becoming more affordable and computers are now being made with DVD-writers installed. Each disk will hold 3.9GB so they're ideal if you want to archive collections or store lots of big image files.

Q Is it possible to convert a colour image into black and white?

Having scanned your colour photograph, or downloaded it from your camera, make a copy. Next, select Image›Adjustments› Desaturate and all colour will be removed. This makes a basic black-and-white image.

Of course, this is only the start – you can then lighten and darken selected areas (dodge and burn) as you would a conventional black-and-white print, adjust contrast and so on until you are happy with the end result.

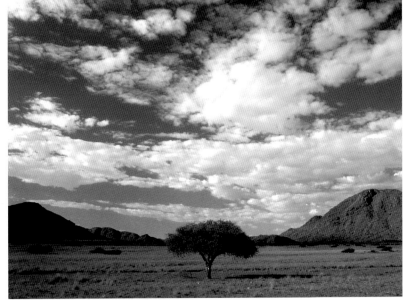

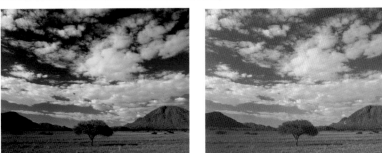

Solitaire, Namibia
The colour shot (left) was desaturated, leaving a rather flat mono version (right). This was then transformed using Levels in Photoshop to create a powerful black-and-white print (top).
Camera Pentax 67 Lens 45mm Filter Polarizer Film Fujichrome Velvia 50

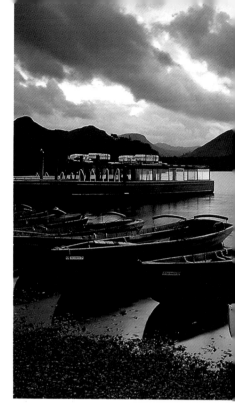

Q Can you talk me through some of the basic Photoshop controls once I have scanned a photo?

Photoshop is such complex software that whole books have been written on it, so don't expect to understand it overnight – you must spend time trying different things out, making mistakes and learning from them. To get you started, here are the first eight steps you will need to take:

STEP 1 Open and copy the image
Drag and drop the image icon onto the Photoshop icon on your computer's desktop and it will open the software and import the image. If the image has just been scanned you will need to name it – select File›Save As, and save it as a Photoshop (PSD) file. It's important to make a copy of the original, just in case you mess up.

STEP 2 Level the picture
Sometimes you may find that a picture looks off-square, such as a landscape with a sloping horizon. To rectify this, select Image› Rotate Canvas› Arbitrary then type in the amount of rotation required, such as 1°, then click on CW (clockwise) or CCW (counter clockwise). If this is too much or too little, try again.

STEP 3 Crop the image
Once you have rotated the image as required to level it off, you can crop the edges to remove any unwanted canvas. Cropping can also be used to improve the composition or to create a portrait format image from one originally shot in landscape format. To do this select the crop tool, crop the image as required then click return.

STEP 4 Remove dust and blemishes
To do this, enlarge the image on your computer monitor so the blemishes are clearly visible – I have exaggerated the effect here so you can see it clearly. Next, select the Rubber stamp tool or Healing tool in Photoshop. Both allow you to cover up blemishes by selecting pixels from another part of the image – such as the area next to the blemish - and dropping them over the blemish itself. You can vary the size/shape of the stamp/number of pixels and how hard or soft the effect is.

STEP 5 Adjust brightness and contrast
Although modern scanning software allows you to adjust things like exposure before the final scan is made, you may still decide

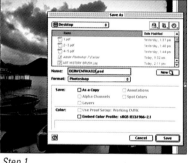

Step 1

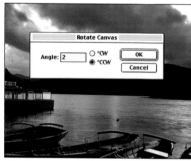

Step 2

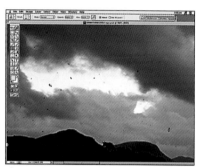

Step 4

Aldburgh, Suffolk, England
The original photograph shows obvious converging verticals as I had to lean back to include the top of the building.
Camera Nikon F90x Lens 28mm
Filter Polarizer Film Fujichrome Velvia 50

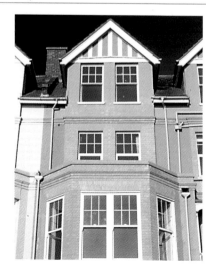
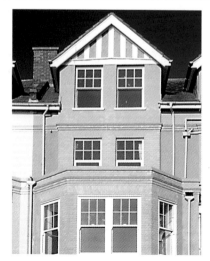

The final, corrected image looks much more effective, though it only took two minutes to complete the transformation.

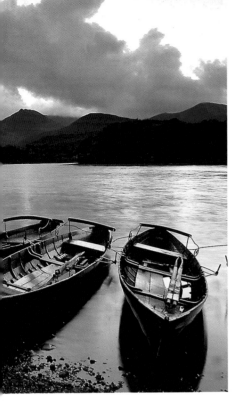

magic, but what is deemed 'correct' may not be what you want, so instead you can select Image›Adjustments›Levels and make the changes yourself. Image›Adjustments› Brightness/Contrast can also be used to lighten or darken images and adjust contrast.

STEP 6 Colour correction

Photoshop has a number of controls and tools that allow you to adjust the colour content of an image. If you select Image›Adjustments you will see various options including Curves, Colour Balance, Hue/Saturation, Replace Colour, Selective Colour; all these features can be used to help you produce perfect results.

Sometimes you may need to correct a colour cast created by artificial lighting such as tungsten; warm-up photographs taken in shade outdoors; or enhance a picture by boosting colour saturation.

STEP 7 Improve sharpness

Images from scanners or digital cameras usually require some degree of sharpening, while images that suffer from slight unsharpness can be corrected – within reason. This should always be the last step.

The Unsharp Mask filter in Photoshop – Filter›Sharpen›Unsharp Mask – is the most effective sharpening tool and has three variables – Amount, Radius and Threshold.

Amount should usually be set to 150–200 per cent, though it will go as high as 500 per cent. Radius controls the size of the halo surrounding each pixel that has been sharpened. Start with a setting from 1.0–2.5. Threshold controls which pixels are affected. The lower the setting the more pixels are sharpened.

Experiment with all three controls until you're happy with the effect. The higher the Amount is set to, the lower the Radius and Threshold should be. Don't be tempted to over sharpen as the image will look strange, and keep an eye on shadows and skies which show the effects more clearly.

STEP 8 Having completed all these steps, you should have a clean, well exposed and colour balanced image. However, this is just the beginning of what you can do – the rest is limited only by your imagination!

that the image is too light or too dark, or that contrast needs adjusting. A quick solution is to select Image› Adjustments› Auto Levels and let Photoshop perform its

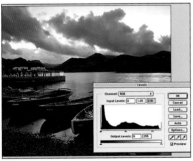

Step 5

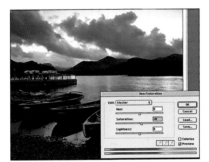

Step 6

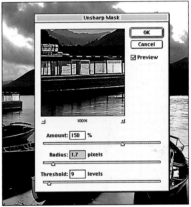

Step 7

Q I've heard you can correct converging verticals in Photoshop. Is that true?

Yes, you no longer need to buy an expensive perspective control lens because Photoshop can be used to do the same job for free!

To do this follow these steps:
• Open up your picture then choose Select›All to select it – this places a dashed line around your image.
• Select View›Show›Grid to display a grid of lines over the image which will aid the correction of the leaning verticals. See Step 1.

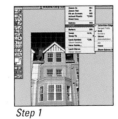

Step 1

• Select Edit›Transform›Distort then click on the top left corner of the picture and drag the cursor out gently to the left – as you drag it the wall on that side will begin to straighten. Use the grid as a guide and stop when the vertical lines loom okay.
• Repeat this action for the right side and tweak both sides until the verticals are vertical. See Step 2.

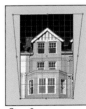

Step 2

• Press the return key on your keyboard to process the transformation then select View›Show›Grid and uncheck the grid so it disappears from your picture.
• If the image looks rather squat now, select Image›Image Size, uncheck the Constrain Proportions box and increase the height of the image by 5–10 per cent. This should make it appear more normal.

Digital printing

Although many photographers still use a conventional darkroom to make colour and black-and-white prints from film originals, a growing number are now abandoning traditional wet processes in favour of the speed and convenience of the digital 'lightroom'. Given the level of technology now accessible to enthusiast photographers, this comes as no surprise. However, to produce high-quality prints digitally, you still need knowledge, experience and skill.

Q What factors should I consider when choosing a printer?

The most important decision you need to make is how big you would like the maximum print size to be. For most photographers, A3 or A3+ seems to offer the best compromise between the cost of the printer itself and maximum print size – A3+ is 48.3x32.9cm (19x13in). A4 printers, 21x29.7cm (8½ x 12in), are ideal if you're working on a budget, but you will almost certainly want to make bigger prints than that in the future so it's worth saving a little longer for an A3 or A3+. Printers capable of producing prints at A2 or bigger, 42x59.4cm (17x24in) are available, but they're expensive to buy and run, and you will rarely want to make prints as large as this.

Other factors to consider are that the printer offers photo-quality printing, it accepts six or seven colour inks, and that it can be fitted with individual ink bottles or cartridges ideally, to save on waste.

Q What's the difference between an inkjet printer and a dye sublimation printer?

As the name suggests, inkjet printers work by placing millions of tiny dots of ink onto a sheet of printing paper (or other printable medium). The more dots per inch (dpi) the printer has, the better the image quality.

Modern inkjet printers tend to use up to six colours – yellow, magenta, light magenta, cyan, light cyan and black. Some also use a light black ink as well for greater tonal control.

Dye sublimation printers work by merging separate colour layers of yellow, cyan and magenta, plus a protection layer to avoid print damage.

The vast majority of photographers use inkjet printers as they're less expensive and can be used to make prints on a wide range of materials – paper, card, transparencies and more.

The Epson Stylus photo 1290 is still one of the most popular inkjet printers among photographers. It's affordably priced but capable of superb quality prints up to A3+ 48.3x32.9cm (19x13in) in size.

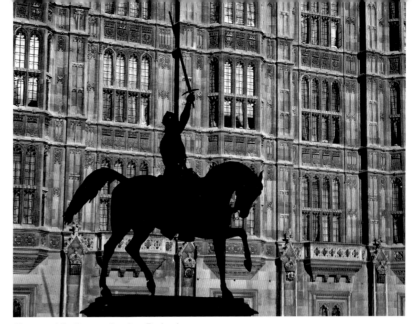

Q Can I make black-and-white prints using normal colour ink cartridges?

Yes, you can, although photographers who are producing a lot of black-and-white prints often tend to have a second dedicated printer purely for black-and-white work and this is loaded with a black-and-white ink set. Quad Black inks by Lyson are the most common type used for black-and-white printing. These sets consist of black, dark grey, mid grey and light grey inks to give full tonal control, and they also avoid colour casts so you can produce true black-and-white prints.

Small Gamut ink sets are also used for black and white. They give you the option to create interesting toning effects such as sepia or selenium.

Houses of Parliament, London, England
Although it is possible to produce black-and-white prints using normal colour ink sets, better results are possible from specialist inks such as Lyson Quad Blacks.
Camera Nikon F90x Lens 80–200mm Film Ilford FP4 Plus

Q Do I have to use ink cartridges and paper from the same manufacturer as my printer?

Generally speaking, yes. If you stick to the same brand for printer, media and ink, you will achieve the highest possible image quality. However, successful digital printing isn't always about optimum quality – it's also about creativity – so never be afraid to experiment with papers from other manufacturers, or different makes of ink. The key is not to use cheap inks – they can cause problems with clogging or the printer head and aren't always as stable as the maker's own inks.

Q What's the difference between dpi and ppi?

Dpi stands for dots per inch while ppi stands for pixels per inch. Digital cameras and scanners create images digitally using pixels – tiny squares of colour information. The more pixels per inch the image has, the finer the resolution of that image will be.

Inkjet printers create photo-realistic prints by placing tiny dots of coloured ink on the printing paper. The more dots per inch a print is produced with, the greater image quality will be generally. So, ppi is used in relation to digital cameras and scanners, and dpi is used in relation to printers.

Q Do inkjet prints fade over time?

Sadly, yes, but then any type of photographic print will fade eventually, so inkjet printing is no less stable than conventional silver-based printing in either colour or black and white. When inkjet printing first became accessible, the inks used were very unstable and early dye-based inks could fade within a matter of weeks. Nowadays the situation is much better and the latest inks claim stability for 30 years or more. If archival quality is important to you, stick with pigment-based inks rather than dye-based.

Q What's the benefit of using a continuous ink system instead of single ink cartridges?

Cost saving is the main benefit of using a continuous ink system. Single ink cartridges are relatively inexpensive to buy, although they are far less economical in the long run because when one colour runs out you have to discard the whole cartridge and replace it with a new one. Continuous ink systems are much more expensive up-front as you have to buy each ink as a separate item. However, in the long term you will definately save money as you only replace each individual ink as it runs out. This also helps to avoid wastage.

Buying each ink colour as a separate cartridge saves both ink and money long term by minimizing wastage.

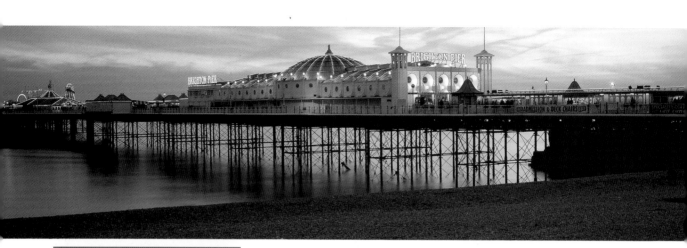

 Q **What's the best resolution to print at?**

The standard printing resolution chosen by photographers is 300dpi, though this tends to be because dpi and ppi are commonly confused. The number of pixels in your image (ppi) does not need to be the same as the print resolution in dpi, as each pixel in your image may be reproduced using up to six of the printer's coloured dots.

Making inkjet prints at a resolution of 240–360dpi will produce good results for all but the very largest prints. What you shouldn't do is automatically print with your printer set to its highest resolution as it will take a lot longer to generate the print and the increase in quality won't necessarily be noticeable on the final print.

 Q **Which type of printing paper should I use?**

That depends on the type of result you want, as choice of paper will have a huge influence on the look and feel of the print.

Initially your best bet is to stick with glossy photo paper as this type will produce the crispest results with the brightest colours and richest shadows, just like glossy photo paper such as Ilfochrome. However, once you have mastered the basics of digital printing, don't be afraid to experiment – there are literally hundreds of different printing papers available now including textured art papers to give your prints a handmade feel.

If you work in black and white, art papers can be especially effective and it's now possible to create black-and-white prints digitally that are just as convincing as those made in a traditional darkroom.

This comparison shows how print resolution affects image quality. The main picture is a frame reproduction of the original photograph.

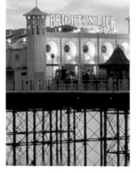 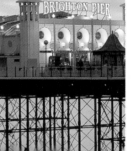 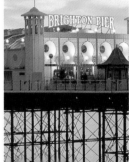

At 100dpi resolution is too low to give photo-quality results. You can see that the image is soft.

At 200dpi resolution is much better but not quite photo-quality. This will be obvious at close viewing distances.

Increasing resolution to 300dpi does the trick – there'd be no great benefit printing at a higher dpi than this.

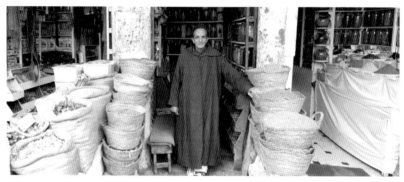

Shopkeeper, Marrakech, Morocco
Digital printing needn't restrict your creativity – there are many different inkjet papers available now that allow you to produce stunning fine-art prints.

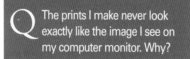 **Q** **The prints I make never look exactly like the image I see on my computer monitor. Why?**

This is almost certainly because your computer's monitor isn't calibrated correctly to show accurate colours, so the image it presents you with isn't totally realistic. The room lighting you use, or sunlight striking the monitor can also cause problems with colour accuracy.

Monitors need to be calibrated regularly. There are special pieces of equipment available to do this, though Photoshop comes supplied with Adobe Gamma Correction, which is simple to use.

Calibrating your printer may also be necessary so it produces acceptable results with different brands of printing paper.

Q Can you talk me, step-by-step, through making an inkjet print?

Printing from digital files is actually very straightforward if you have a good-quality scan or captured image to work from. Assuming you have, here's what to do next.

Step 1 Open the image file in Photoshop by double-clicking on the icon or dragging and dropping the file onto the Photoshop icon on your computer's desktop.

Step 2 Check the size of the image by selecting Image>Image size. This will tell you what the maximum print size can be depending on the resolution you set. Ideally, the resolution needs to be at least 200ppi, though most photographers use 300ppi. In this example with resolution at 300ppi, the maximum print size is just under 9x6in (22x15cm).

Q I have a digital camera but no computer. How can I make my own prints?

There are numerous printers now available that bypass the need for a computer. All you do is connect your digital camera direct to the printer and you can make prints from images stored on its memory card. Some models also have a memory card slot so that you can take the card from the camera, insert it into the printer and print away.

A growing number of desktop inkjet printers can be used without a computer, while compact dye sublimation printers are also available that you can carry everywhere and use to make prints on location.

Direct printers allow you to print photographs from your digital camera without the need for a computer.

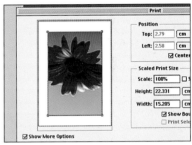
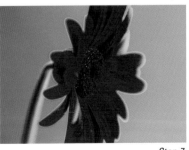
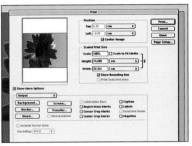
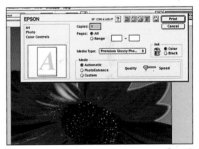
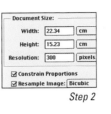
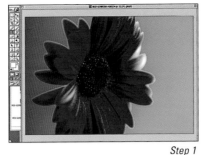

Step 1

Step 2

Step 3 Select File>Page set-up from the menu bar at the top of the monitor and select either landscape or portrait format for the orientation of the print, plus the size of the printing paper you are using, such as A4. You can also select setting at this stage such as whether you want a margin or not, and if you want the image to be centred on the paper.

Step 3

Step 4 Select File>Print with Preview. This dialog box tells you various things, such as if the image size is too big for the page if you print it at 100 per cent, what the maximum output size is, if the image orientation matches that of the printing paper and so on.

Step 4

Step 5 In the previous screen grab you could see that the image size was smaller than the paper at 100 per cent, but the image itself needed to be turned in its side to match the orientation of the paper. This was done by selecting Image>Rotate Canvas>90°CW. You can now see from the preview that the image fits onto the page and leaves a good-sized border.

Step 5

Step 6 The next stage is to click on Print in the dialog box, or use a suitable keyboard shortcut, to bring up the print with preview dialog box. This will open a further dialog box where you can select the paper type being used – in this case Premium Glossy Photo Paper – or the closest match, check the quality setting, that the printer is set to colour printing, and finally, having checked that you have some paper in the printer, hit the print button.

Step 6

Step 7 If all goes well you should end up with a high-quality, photo-realistic print from your digital file. If not, consider possible problems with monitor and printer calibration. As your experience grows you can also create your own profiles to perfect the results. Don't expect overnight success though.

Step 7

One final tip – if you're planning to make a big print such as A3 or A3+, it's a good idea to produce a smaller proof print first to check that everything is right before you make the final print. This can save ink and printing paper.

Digital printing 87

Problem solving

Making mistakes is an important part of the photographic learning process – if we got everything right on our first attempt, much of the challenge and excitement would be lost. Knowing what caused those mistakes and how they can be rectified is equally important though, otherwise you will continue to make them and eventually this could compromise your progress as a photographer.

Most photographic problems are easy to identify, and their cause can usually be related to one of three things: user error, equipment error, or processing error. Once you've established which it is, solving the problem and making sure it doesn't happen again is relatively straightforward.

Q A lot of my pictures are ruined by camera shake. What's the easiest way to overcome this?

Camera shake is caused by accidental movement of the camera during the moment of exposure, and produces images with slight or obvious blur across the whole frame. This is usually a result of using a shutter speed that's too slow for handholding with a certain lens, or because the position you have adopted is unsteady.

Camera shake can also occur when the camera is mounted on a tripod, either because the reflex mirror creates vibrations when you trip the shutter, or you create vibrations when you press the shutter release with your finger.

The following steps should help prevent it.

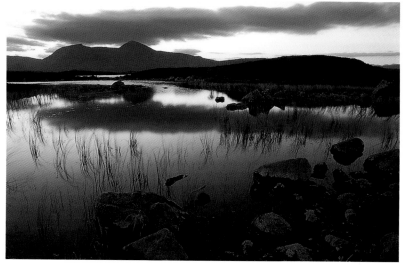

Rannoch Moor, Scotland
If you want to take sharp pictures in low light, keeping your camera stable is vital. The best way to do that is using a sturdy tripod.
Camera Nikon F90x Lens 28mm Film Fujichrome Velvia 50

When handholding:

1 Use a shutter speed that at least matches the focal length of the lens – 1/250sec with a 200mm lens, 1/60sec with a 50mm lens, 1/500sec with a 300–500mm lens, and so on.
2 If you're using a long telephoto lens or are forced to set slower shutter speeds, rest the lens against a wall or post, or crouch down to provide a more stable support for the camera.
3 Always adopt a stable position, and hold the camera properly – refer back to Cameras (page 12) for details.
4 Use a tripod whenever possible.

When using a tripod:

1 If your camera has a mirror lock, use it to reduce vibrations but let the camera settle down for a few seconds after locking up the mirror before you go ahead and take the picture.

2 Always trip the shutter with a cable release so you don't have to touch the camera. If you don't have one, set the self-timer on your camera so there's a delay between pressing the shutter release and the picture being taken. This allows the camera to settle down before an exposure is made.
3 Make sure your tripod is set up properly, and only use the centre column when necessary as it's the least stable part of the tripod.
4 In strong winds, weight the tripod down with your gadget bag to increase stability, or hang a bag of sand or stones under the tripod.
5 When using long, heavy lenses, mount the lens, rather than the camera, on the tripod so it's balanced.

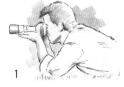
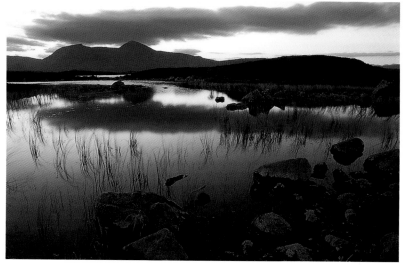
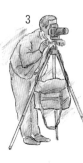
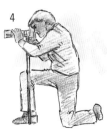

Here are just a few of the methods you can use to keep your camera steady and ensure sharp pictures.

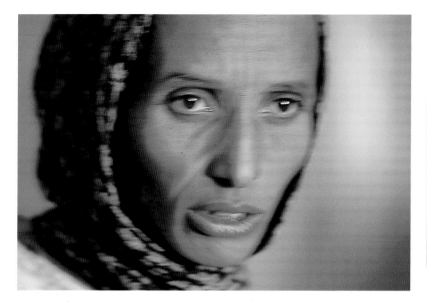

No matter how good a picture is, if it suffers from camera shake or inaccurate focusing, there's only one place for it – the bin!

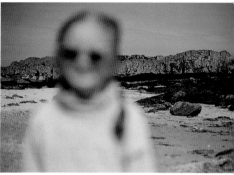

If your main subject is off-centre, some autofocus cameras with a focusing sensor in the centre of the viewfinder will focus on the background, so you end up with a picture like this.

Q I wear glasses, but have trouble focusing when I'm wearing them. What do you suggest?

Many SLRs and compacts have a dioptre correction lens built into the viewfinder eyepiece which you can adjust to suit your eyesight so you needn't wear spectacles when taking pictures. Alternatively, most cameras can be fitted with correction lenses that are available from photo dealers in different +/- dioptre strengths.

If both options are out, try fitting a rubber eyecup to your camera's viewfinder so you can press your spectacle lens against it and cut out stray light.

Q Why is it that I still get out-of-focus pictures, even though my camera has autofocusing?

Virtually all autofocus cameras have a small focusing sensor marked in the centre of the viewfinder – or several sensors around the viewfinder that can be activated for off-centre subjects.

To make sure your main subject comes out sharply focused you must place this sensor over it while focusing. This is particularly important with compact cameras, as you can't see what the lens has focused on. With most cameras you can lock the focus by half-depressing the

shutter release and holding it down. This allows you to focus on your subject then recompose the shot as you wish before taking the final picture.

Inaccurate focusing can also result when you try to focus on an area of low contrast or texture, such as a white wall, or because you're too close to your subject. If the former problem occurs, focus on something else that's a similar distance from the camera, lock the focus, then recompose. With the latter, check the minimum focusing distance of the lens and don't move any closer than that.

Q I took some pictures recently and the corners were very dark. What do you think caused this?

The problem you refer to is known as cut-off or vignetting, and it's caused by an attachment that's fitted to the front of your lens, obscuring its angle of view. This could be a lens hood that's too narrow, a filter holder that's too small, or because you've fitted too many screw-in filters to the lens at once. Wide-angle lenses are especially prone to cut-off due to their extensive angle of view.

Once you've identified the cause, solving it is easy – make sure the lens hood you use is designed for that particular focal length, switch to a bigger filter holder, or avoid using more than one or two screw-in filters on your lens at once.

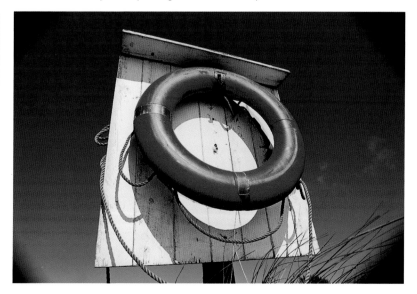

The main cause of vignetting is using a filter holder on your lens that's too small, or too many filters together. This is the effect you end up with.

*Does this look familiar?
If so, the problem is with you, not the
processing lab, as the film was accidentally
loaded into the camera twice.*

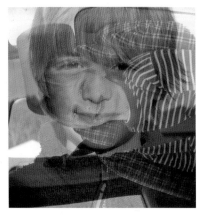

*Sound of Sleat, Highland, Scotland
If you don't want colour filter effects
to be corrected when shooting colour
negative film, remember to tell the
processor they were used.*
Camera Nikon F90x Lens 80–200mm
Filter Blue 80A Film Fujichrome Velvia 50

Q I used some coloured filters
with colour negative film, but
the prints looked normal. Why?

The automatic printing systems used in
most processing labs are designed to give
correct colour balance, so they often treat
the effects of coloured filters as a mistake
and compensate for them by adding the
opposite colour. To prevent this happening,
inform the lab that you've used coloured
filters on certain shots, so the technicians
will know that any casts are intentional.

Q Half the pictures from a roll I shot
were ruined by light patches.
Was this a processing fault?

It sounds like some of the shots were
fogged due to exposure to light before the
film was processed. Check the negatives as
well to see if they suffer from the same
problem. If so, it's probable that you
accidentally opened the camera back
halfway through the film so part of it was
fogged. If the fogging is only on the prints,
the printing paper must have been exposed
to light by mistake, so inform the lab and
ask them to reprint.

Other causes of fogging could be a light
leak in your camera or the film cassette, or
due to loading a new roll of film in bright
sunlight – always do this in the shade.

Q I got a set of prints back from
the lab, and every shot is
ouble exposed. Is this my fault?

This often happens to beginners, and they
nearly always try to blame the poor
processing lab. Unfortunately, double
exposure of this type is caused by
accidentally running the same roll of film
through the camera twice, so only you are
to blame, I'm afraid.

To make sure it doesn't happen again,
always rewind a used film completely back
into the cassette, so you can't forget it has
already been used and try to reload it, and
have used film processed immediately after
you've shot it.

If you remove a partly used roll of film
with the intention of reloading at a later
date, mark the number of shots already
used on the leader with an indelible pen.
When you reload, wind onto the
appropriate frame by firing off the shots
already taken with the lens cap on so they
aren't double exposed.

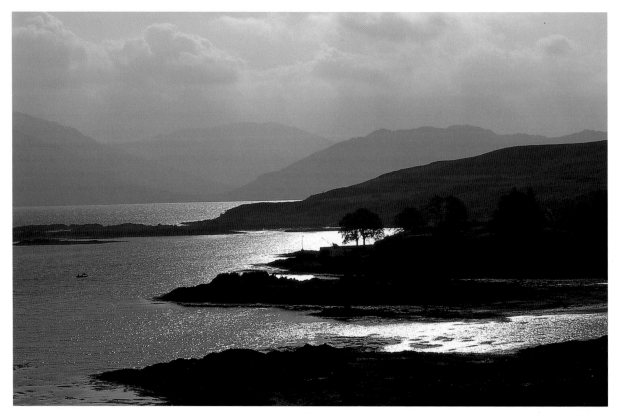

part three
subjects

Portraits

If a picture is worth a thousand words, it's probably a portrait. Pictures of people account for more film shot per capita than just about every other subject put together, and are perhaps the biggest single reason why people pick up a camera at all. Most of the people-pictures we take, however, could never be described as true portraits. Usually they're hastily grabbed snapshots and often the sentimental value of those pictures far outweighs the need for technical perfection.

Portraiture serves the same purpose, but its aim is to capture the character of a person on film. A successful portrait should tell us something about the subject. This may seem like an impossible task, but each and every one of us gives off powerful signals that tell the rest of the world how we're feeling. The job of the photographer is to watch those signals and capture them.

Q Which lenses are best for portraiture?

The ideal lens for general use – particularly head and shoulders portraits – is a short telephoto with a focal length of 85–105mm. This is chosen mainly because its slight foreshortening of perspective flatters the human face. The depth of field provided by a short telephoto is also shallow at wide apertures, so you can throw distracting backgrounds out of focus to concentrate attention on your subject.

Most serious portrait photographers use an 85mm, 100mm or 105mm prime lens with a wide aperture of f/1.8 or f/2.8. However, the same focal length setting on a tele zoom is equally suitable, even though the maximum aperture is usually smaller – f/4 or f/5.6. Longer focal lengths can be used effectively, but the increased camera-to-subject distance makes them impractical for general use.

A 50mm standard lens is also handy providing you don't try to fill the frame with just your subject's face, while a 28mm or 35mm wide-angle is invaluable for taking environmental portraits that reveal your subject in their surroundings.

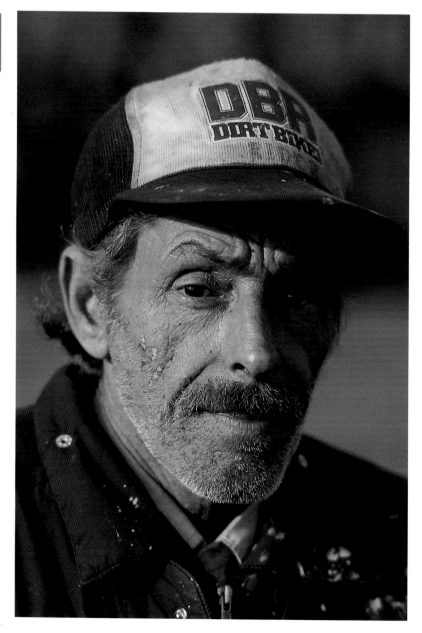

Dirt biker
This character portrait was taken from close range using an 85mm lens – a favourite among portrait photographers as it flatters facial features. Setting a wide aperture – f/2.8 – reduced depth of field so the background was thrown well out of focus, concentrating attention on the main subject.
Camera Olympus OM4-Ti Lens 85mm
Film Fujichrome RDP100

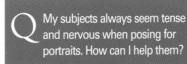

Q Are there any preliminary steps I can take before commencing a portrait session to ensure the shoot runs smoothly?

The golden rule of portraiture is Be Prepared. Before your subject arrives, make sure you're organized and ready in all respects. Decide where the pictures will be taken – indoors or out? – think about props, clothing and poses, make sure your cameras are loaded with film and that you have all your equipment at hand, and set up the background and lighting ready for the first shot.

If you get all these tasks out of the way you'll be able to start work the minute your subject appears, and to give them your undivided attention so that successful pictures result. If not, they will have to hang around waiting, and this will exacerbate the nerves they're probably already experiencing.

Being unprepared also means you start the shoot in a panic, rather than being in total control, and this invariably leads to silly mistakes being made, like getting the exposure wrong, or forgetting to set the correct film speed on your camera.

Q My subjects always seem tense and nervous when posing for portraits. How can I help them?

Few people feel confident in front of a camera, so if the shoot is to be a success you must put a lot of effort into making your subject feel at ease.

The easiest way to do this is simply by chatting to them. Talk about their hobbies, the news, politics, ancient history, anything

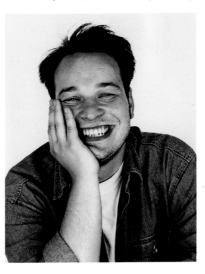

to break the ice and help them forget about the camera. It's also a good idea to involve them in the shoot by explaining what kind of effect you're trying to produce, why you're moving the lights around, how you want them to pose and so on. You could even let them look through the viewfinder while you take their position, so they've got an idea of what you're seeing.

Feedback is equally important. When things are going well, say so to bolster their confidence, and when you're not completely happy with something, be polite and make suggestions rather than showing your frustration. Communication should be a constant factor throughout the shoot, so you gradually build up a rapport with your subject and eventually they stop worrying about the camera.

Final touches like playing background music, making sure the location is warm, and taking regular breaks, will also help to oil the wheels of success.

Damon
Once you establish a rapport with your subject they will feel at ease in front of the camera, allowing you to capture relaxed, natural expressions.
Camera Pentax 67 Lens 165mm
Film Fujichrome RDP100 cross-processed

USING WINDOWLIGHT

The daylight flooding in through a window of your home is perfect for portraiture, and with a little care can be used to create a range of effects.

North-facing windows are ideal when you want soft, low-contrast lighting as any light entering them is reflected – for the best results shoot in bright but slightly overcast conditions. South-facing windows admit direct sunlight at certain times of day, so you can obtain totally different results – the warm light of late afternoon is ideal as it casts attractive shadows.

The traditional approach is to pose your subject with the window on one side, so half their face is lit and the other half is thrown into shadow. In dull weather this creates a very moody effect, but in stronger light contrast will be high so you should ideally position a white reflector opposite the window so it bounces light back into the shadows. The light can also be softened by taping a sheet of tracing paper to the window.

For more even lighting, shoot with your back to the window so that the light floods across your subject's features.

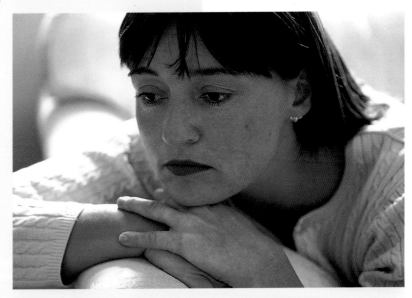

Alternatively, use the window as a background and bounce light into your subject's face with a reflector. By exposing carefully, the window will then burn out to create an atmospheric high-key effect behind your subject.

Alison
The soft light of a dull day was used for this portrait, with the subject positioned 2m (6½ft) opposite a large window.
Camera Nikon F90x Lens 85mm
Film Fujichrome Sensia 100

Q How can I encourage my subject to produce interesting facial expressions?

Simply asking your subject to smile rarely works because a true smile can't be produced to order; it has to be natural. Similarly, while asking your subject to say certain words like 'Russia' or 'whiskey' may animate their face slightly, it's not ideal – unless you choose a funny word that makes them laugh out loud.

The best way to elicit interesting expressions is by talking to your subject and shooting as they respond. If you want a serious expression, strike up a serious conversation, or if you want a more light-hearted response, tell a joke. You could even try asking your subject to tell a joke while you capture their uniquely personal expressions and mannerisms.

If you've succeeded in putting your subject at ease during the earlier stages

of the shoot you can also ask them to give a certain look – mean, moody, serious. Merely trying this is often enough to generate more spontaneous, natural expressions because they'll find the whole thing amusing. Patience and timing are the keys to success.

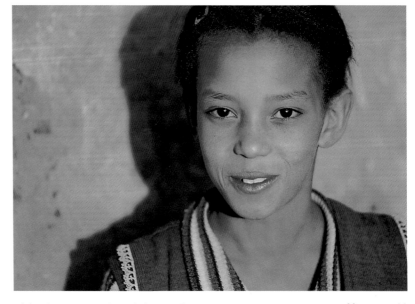

Moroccan girl
Early morning and late afternoon are ideal times of day for outdoor portraiture – the warm light adds a flattering glow to our skin, and in this case the sun itself has created attractive catchlights in the girl's eye.
Camera Nikon F90x Lens 80–200mm zoom
Film Fujichrome Sensia II 100

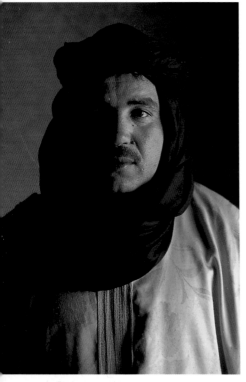

Berber man
Don't always expect your subject to smile and appear jolly – their mood on the day may be sombre rather than happy, for a start, and often, portraits that capture a thoughtful, serious side to your subject are more successful than those that show them smiling from ear to ear.
Camera Nikon F90x Lens 50mm
Film Fujichrome Sensia II 100

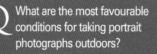

Q What are the most favourable conditions for taking portrait photographs outdoors?

Successful outdoor portraits can be taken in virtually any conditions, though some demand a little more care than others. Harsh sunlight is your worst enemy. It casts deep, black shadows across your subject's face, makes their eye sockets look dark and lifeless, and is very harsh on delicate skin tones. To prevent this, turn your subject away from the sun and bounce light onto their face with a reflector, or use a burst of fill-in flash to lower contrast. Alternatively, move into the shade where the light is much softer and shadows weaker.

Earlier or later in the day when the sun is low in the sky, the light has a beautiful warmth that makes skin tones glow. The light can still be harsh though, so your best bet is to keep the sun on one side of your subject if facing it causes them to squint.

Finally, the diffuse, shadowless light of an overcast day can produce very flattering results, though it's a good idea to put an 81A or 81B warm-up filter on your lens to balance the slight blue cast in the light, otherwise skin tones may look a little pale.

Q Does the background play an important role in portraiture?

Only if you make a bad choice. Ideally the background should be plain and simple, so it doesn't attract too much attention and your subject stands out against it, but if it competes for attention with your subject, the impact of the portrait will be reduced.

Indoors, a plain wall or sheet of card can be used as a background. White, cream and black are popular colours because they're very neutral, but brighter hues can work well when used carefully. Mottled or spattered backgrounds made from painted canvas also look attractive. Avoid fancy patterned wallpaper at all costs. Outdoors, foliage, stonework and other natural features work a treat, especially if they're in shadow.

If the background you use has an obvious pattern or texture, set your lens to a wide aperture such as f/4 or f/5.6, so it's thrown well out of focus. You can check how it will record before shooting by pressing the stopdown preview button on your camera or lens. If it's still too obvious, simply set an even wider aperture, or move your subject further away from the background.

POSING YOUR SUBJECT

Few people feel confident standing in front of a camera, so you must give your subject plenty of advice when it comes to posing. If you fail to do this they will end up feeling very tense, and it will make your job of capturing their personality all the more difficult. Posing is vital because it helps dictate the aesthetic success of a picture.

The good news is that there are only so many different poses to work with and they've all been done countless times before, so a quick flick through a few copies of photographic or fashion magazines will provide lots of useful ideas for you to be getting on with. You can also dictate the pose to a certain extent by providing a chair for your subject to sit on, or by taking the pictures in a specific location.

The main priority is that your subject feels totally comfortable – if they're not, then they will never be relaxed in front of the camera.

Here are a few suggestions.

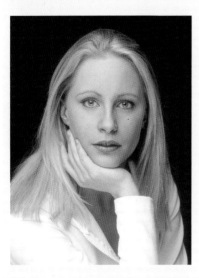

Hands can look clumsy floating around the frame. One way around this is to ask your subject to place one hand on their chin or the side of their face. A flat hand is more flattering for women while a fist looks more masculine on portraits of men.

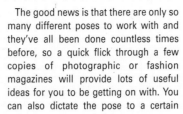
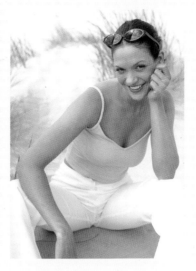

Asking your subject to sit down will make them feel more comfortable, but make sure their pose doesn't become wooden and boring – here the relaxed sitting position suits the subject's expression and clothes.

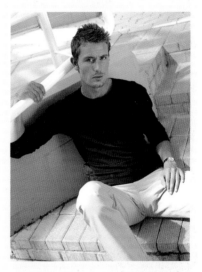

Giving your subject something to lean on will help them relax and also dictate the way they pose. Walls, tables, chairs, railings, fences – anything can be used providing it suits the style of the portrait and of your subject.

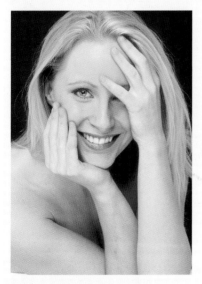

If your subject is confident in front of the camera, try using their hands in a more creative way – here they frame the model's face and draw your eye towards her relaxed expression.

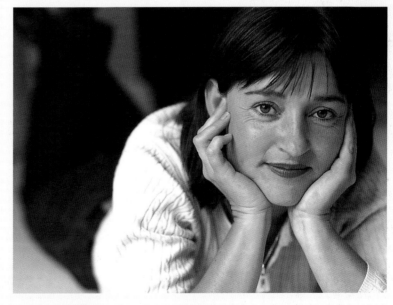

Reclining poses can work well if your subject is feeling relaxed – though you will need to work from a low level as well to avoid the pictures looking awkward.

Q How can I overcome cosmetic problems such as baldness or a double chin?

In an ideal world everyone would be perfectly proportioned and infinitely attractive. Unfortunately, it isn't an ideal world, so there will undoubtedly come a time when you have to photograph a less than perfect specimen!

Here are a few hints on how to overcome common problems.

Bald patch Shoot from a slightly lower viewpoint – only a few inches – so the top of your subject's head doesn't appear in the shot. Also ask them to keep their head upright – it's tempting to look down if the camera seems low.

Long noses These can be played down by using a slightly longer lens than normal, such as a 135mm or 200mm, so the extra compression of perspective makes the nose look considerably shorter. Also shoot head-on rather than from the side so that the length of your subject's nose isn't revealed.

Double chin A slightly higher shooting angle usually does the trick here, because you'll be looking down on your subject and their neck will be partially obscured by their chin.

Skin blemishes Spots and rashes are emphasized by side-lighting because it reveals all the texture in the skin, so avoid it at all costs. Instead, use even frontal lighting – a softbox either side of the camera and a reflector below your subject's chin is ideal, or if you're taking pictures outdoors in bright sunlight, keep the sun either behind your subject or behind the camera.

Q What's an environmental portrait?

A portrait that depicts your subject in their surroundings, whether it's at work, at home or enjoying a hobby or sport. The advantage of an environmental portrait compared to a traditional headshot is that it tells the viewer a lot about the subject. The extra elements included in the shot, such as where they live or work, or their personal possessions, also make for a more interesting composition and provide you with many different options.

Q What type of film is best to use for portraiture?

Accurate rendition of skin tones is important in portraiture, so you need a film that will give satisfying results. You should also consider fine grain and pinpoint sharpness.

Your best bet is to experiment with a range of different films and see which you prefer. The vivid colours of Fujichrome Velvia 50 and 100F look superb with most subjects, but skin tones tend to come out far too warm so this film is usually avoided. Fujichrome Provia 100F or Astia, on the other hand, give more attractive results and are favoured by many portrait photographers. Kodak Ektachrome E100 S and E100 SW slide films are also renowned for lovely

STUDIO LIGHTING TECHNIQUES

If you have access to studio lighting equipment, an endless range of moods and effects can be created and you can exercise total control over the direction and strength of light falling on your subject.

In the beginning your best bet is to start off with one light and see how changing its position around your subject alters the effect obtained. You'd be surprised just how flexible one flash unit or tungsten spot can be, especially if you fit a brolly or softbox to it to soften the light, and use a couple of reflectors to bounce the light around.

Once you've had a little experience, further lights can then be added to give you more control. The thing to remember is that no matter how many lights are used only one will provide the main illumination, so this is the light on which the exposure for the whole shot should be based. The rest are used to balance the shadows or create specific effects.

The set of pictures below shows how you can vary the mood of a portrait quite dramatically just by using different lighting set-ups.

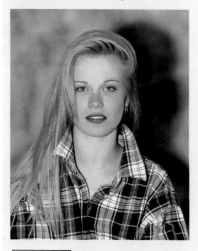

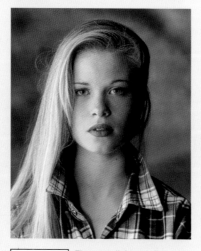

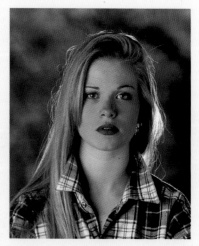

 Here just one bare light was positioned at 45 degrees to the left of the subject. Note the harshness of the light and strong shadows, which don't really make for a flattering result.

 The same light was fitted with a softbox to spread the light. Shadows are now much weaker and the light is very flattering – you can produce successful results with this set-up alone.

 Here a single light was placed directly behind the model's head to create the halo effect around her hair, while a large reflector placed near the camera bounced light from the flash back onto her face.

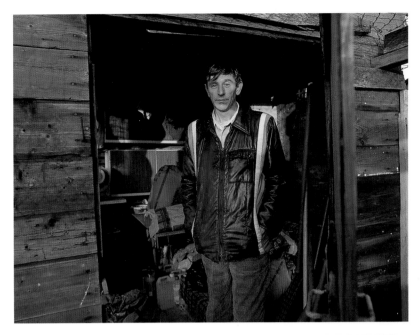

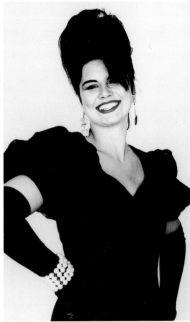

Gardener
Taking a step back and showing your subject in their own surroundings can create a more revealing portrait than if you simply photographed their head and shoulders.
Camera Pentax 67 Lens 105mm
Film Fujichrome RDP100

colour rendition. If you prefer print film to slide, Agfa Portrait 160, Kodak Portra 160 NC and 400 NC are preferred for portraits.

Fast, grainy films such as Fujichrome RSP1600 or Fujicolor Superior 1600 can also produce atmospheric and moody portraits – especially if you shoot in soft, warm light.

Finally, don't forget black and white – it's perfect for powerful portraits because the lack of colour focuses attention on your subject and produces much simpler results. General-purpose films such as Ilford FP4 Plus and HP5 Plus are ideal.

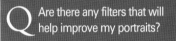

Q Are there any filters that will help improve my portraits?

The 81-series warm-up filters are handy for enhancing the light and making your subject's skin look healthy. Use them in dull weather to counteract blueness in the light.

Soft-focus filters are also useful for increasing the mood of a portrait by adding an overall soft glow or a soft spot that keeps your subject's face sharp but softens the picture edges.

Sally
This portrait was taken on colour slide film then cross-processed in C-41 chemistry. This has increased contrast and colour saturation (see page 136).
Camera Pentax 67 Lens 165mm
Film Fujichrome RDP100

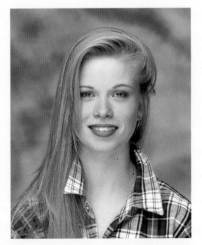

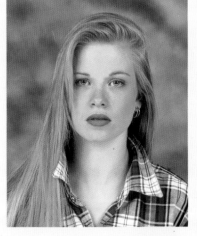

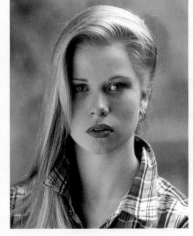

For this shot the photographer used a single flash unit and softbox positioned above the model and pointing down, plus a large silver reflector under her chin to bounce light into the shadows.

This time, two flash units fitted with softboxes were placed above and either side of the camera, while a reflector was placed under the model to soften the shadows. Note the different catchlights.

One light and a softbox was placed above, behind and to one side of the model so it illuminated her hair, while a reflector placed opposite the flash and in front of the model bounced light into her face.

Kids

Kids can be a photographer's best friend and worst enemy all rolled in to one. Their innocence, boundless enthusiasm and lack of inhibitions make them a joyous subject to photograph. But at the same time, they also have the ability to drive a photographer crazy within minutes. Ask them to stand and they'll sit. Ask them to smile and they'll stare blankly at the camera. Spend ages setting up a shot, and they get up and go! We've all faced this battle many times before, but that's what makes photographing kids so challenging and rewarding. If you accept it rather than trying to fight it you'll produce some of the best pictures of your life.

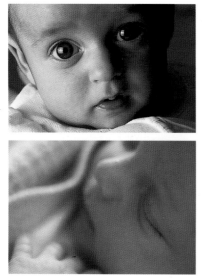

Kitty
Babies are relatively easy to photograph because they're less active than older children – though their attention span is short and they tend to sleep a lot! These three photographs give you an idea of what's possible – the top portrait was taken using a single studio light with the baby sat on her mother's lap, while the two close-ups were shot in natural daylight.
Camera Nikon F90x Lens 105mm macro
Film Fuji Sensia II 100 and Sensia 400

Q Got any suggestions about how I might photograph a baby?

Compared to toddlers and older kids, babies are a really easy to photograph. They can't protest or do a disappearing act as soon as a camera is produced, so you can spend as long as you like taking perfect pictures. Unfortunately, all they tend to do is sleep or eat, so trying to capture a facial expression other than a yawn is tricky.

If you're the father, why not take a camera along and capture the birth? The light levels are rather low in hospitals, so load fast film to avoid camera shake – ISO 400 may be fast enough, but ISO 1000 is a safer bet. Flash is an option, but its harshness tends to ruin the atmosphere.

Once the baby is home you have all the time in the world to take lots of pictures. A good approach is to place the baby on a blanket or bed or ask an adult to cradle it and sit by a window. Use reflectors to fill in the shadows and create very soft, even illumination of your subject.

With a macro lens or the close-up facility on a zoom you can move in close to take frame-filling pictures of the baby's face, its tiny hands, or delicate toes. For really moody portraits, load the camera with fast, grainy film, and fit a soft-focus filter to the lens. If you're using slower film, mount the camera on a tripod and wait until the baby is still before shooting.

A camera should also be kept handy to capture all those momentous events like the first smile, the first bath, and some months later, the first faltering steps. And don't forget to take pictures of the latest addition to the family with its proud grandparents or older brothers and sisters.

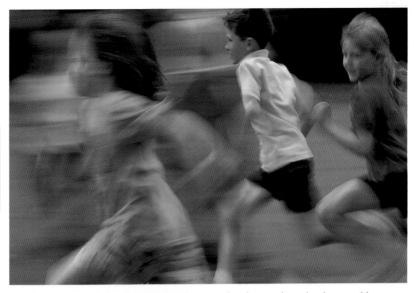

Running race
Events such as your child's school sports day can be a great source of unusual pictures. In this case I panned the camera while using a slow (1/8sec) shutter speed to create an impressionistic shot of the 50-metre dash.
Camera Nikon F90x Lens 80–200mm zoom
Film Fujichrome Velvia 50

Q My kids always get fidgety and lose interest after a few minutes of being photographed. How can I hold their attention?

Trying to keep a young child in one place for very long is always tricky, especially if they haven't got anything to do. Boredom quickly sets in, and before you know it they're up and away.

The easiest way to solve this problem is by giving them something to do. Not only will it keep them happy, but they'll also forget about the camera and you'll be able to take more natural pictures.

A favourite cuddly toy or an ice cream should do the trick with toddlers, while a pet rabbit, kitten or puppy dog will keep infants occupied for ages and generate some lovely expressions. An alternative approach is to offer your subject a small reward for their cooperation, like a bar of chocolate or a trip to a burger bar. Kids will do anything if they've got a good reason.

Older kids like to be taken more seriously, so ask them to show off their favourite possession, like a new bike, or talk to them about their hobbies. Asking a child to dress up like mum or dad for a picture also guarantees success – especially if you give them full access to the clothes, the make-up and the shoes!

Q Should I photograph my kids in a formal portrait situation, or just take pictures as and when the opportunity arises?

The formal approach can work well, providing you get everything set up beforehand so your subject isn't kept waiting. Test the lighting on an adult model, make sure the camera is ready and loaded, then once your subject arrives begin immediately and keep the shoot brief – ten minutes seems like a lifetime to a kid.

Generally, however, your best bet is to keep a camera handy at all times and just grab pictures when an opportunity arises – kids washing the car, kicking a football around the back garden, paddling in the sea or playing with their grandparents are all common events worth documenting.

In other words, make photographing your kids a natural and regular part of daily life rather than a special activity. Not only will this produce lots of great pictures, but your subjects will also grow accustomed to you wielding a camera and it will become perfectly normal for them.

Noah
A garden hose on a hot summer's day is guaranteed to give your kids hours of fun – and provide you with the perfect opportunity to take lots of great pictures. Just don't get too close!
Camera Nikon F5 Lens 80–200mm zoom
Film Fujichrome Sensia II 100

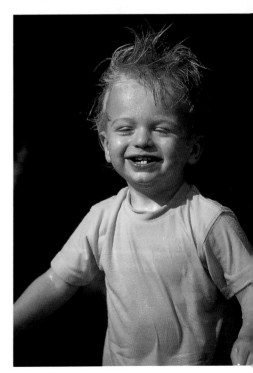

TIPS FOR SUCCESS

Whole books have been written on how to photograph kids, but there are a handful of golden rules that should be obeyed if you want to take successful pictures and make sure your subject is willing to cooperate the next time.

1 Never, ever lose your temper when things aren't going according to plan. If your subject isn't interested, call the shoot off and try again another day rather than forcing the issue. It's impossible to take good pictures if you're frustrated, and any bad vibes will be instantly picked up by your subject.

2 Always get down to your subject's eye-level. If you tower above them like a giant the results will look odd because the child is forced to look up. It can also make them feel uneasy and intimidated.
3 Kids aren't stupid, so don't treat them as such. When giving instructions be firm but polite, just like you would with an adult, and take an active interest in what they have to say or any ideas they have to offer.
4 Don't put your camera down too soon. It's inevitable that your kids will start performing the minute you stop shooting, so stay put and don't be afraid to use a lot of film.

Noah
Children are easier to photograph
outdoors in natural daylight than inside
in the confines of a studio environment –
simply because the former approach is less
formal and intimidating. I keep a camera
handy at all times – these days a digital
compact – so I can grab pictures
at every opportunity.
Camera Nikon F90x Lens 80–200mm zoom
Film Fujichrome Velvia 50

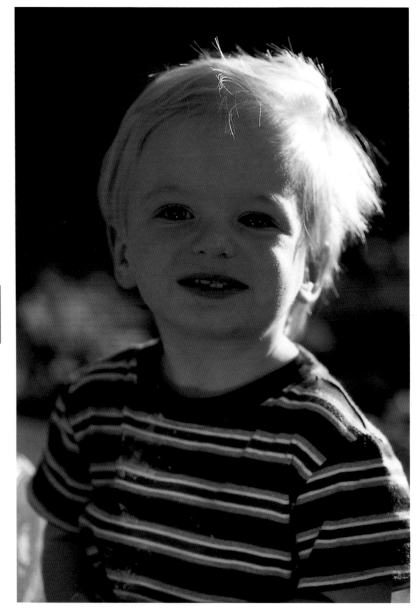

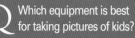

Q **Which equipment is best
for taking pictures of kids?**

Given the spontaneous nature of children
you need a camera that can be used quickly
and instinctively.

Modern compacts are ideal for keeping
handy at all times so you never miss the
chance to take a picture, because their
automation allows you to just point and
shoot in an instant. For general use,
however, the extra control offered by an
SLR will be a great benefit. Autofocusing
can be useful, but is by no means essential
if you practise your manual focusing skills.

As for lenses, a short telephoto or zoom
setting of 85–105mm is perfect for frame-
filling head and shoulder portraits, while
longer focal lengths can be useful for
candid or action shots of children taken at
a greater distance. Wide-angle lenses are
useful too. You can take stunning pictures
by using a 24mm or 28mm lens from close
range to create unusual distortions, or
simply to include your subject's
surroundings in the frame.

Other items to consider are a flashgun, so
you can take pictures indoors with slow
film, reflectors to bounce the light around
when taking pictures outdoors or by
windowlight, and a tripod to prevent
camera shake when using slow shutter
speeds. For general use both indoors and
out, use a slowish film of ISO50 or 100,
which will give pin-sharp, virtually grain-
free results. Faster film of ISO400 and
above is a useful standby if you want to
take handheld pictures in low light, or to
produce more moody effects.

Q **Do I need to change my
approach when photographing
kids of different age groups?**

All kids must be given the same amount of
attention and patience, but the ways in
which you photograph them will differ
simply because their needs and demands
differ with age. Toddlers, for example, are
very mischievous and inquisitive. Being
able to walk gives them endless freedom to
explore, and they love fiddling around with
anything that isn't nailed down – pressing
the buttons on the TV, hi-fi and video,
emptying the cupboards, knocking things
flying, or covering the room with toys.

By the age of a year or so they're also
aware of the camera and able to respond to
it and your prompts, so you can capture
wonderful animated moments as they have
fun, or sit watching you with a confused
look on their face. Everyday routines
provide great opportunities for pictures, like
bath time, dressing, potty training, eating
and drinking. And don't just concentrate on
the happy times – temper tantrums and
tears are as much a part of growing up as
anything else.

As kids get older they become interested
in other things and their personality
becomes more established. They can also
follow your instructions, enabling you to
explain exactly what you want them to do,

and they begin to develop hobbies and interests that can become an integral part of your picture-taking.

Capture your children kicking their first football, riding their first bikes, baking cakes, painting pictures or making dolls' dresses. Days out, birthday parties, games with friends, holidays and school plays and concerts also provide endless opportunities to capture those formative years on film, so try to make the most of them while you can, as all too soon they'll be gone.

Once they reach the teenage years, kids aren't kids any longer and tend to be less inclined to pose for the camera. They tend to become self-conscious, and hate the idea of being photographed in case their spots are captured, or their friends find out. This can easily be overcome with a little persuasion, but you need to tread carefully and treat your subjects like adults. Let them decide what to wear, and how to pose, and allow them to make decisions about the type of pictures taken. If you involve them at all stages they may begin to enjoy it, and you can produce some poignant portraits.

LIGHTING FOR KIDS

The key to success with child photography is keeping things as simple as possible at every stage so you have less to worry about – that includes the lighting.

Windowlight is an ideal source as it produces soft, flattering illumination and can be used at a moment's notice. With babies and toddlers all you have to do is place their cot or high chair close to a window, position a large reflector opposite to bounce light into the shadows, and fire away. Older children can be asked to stand or sit by a suitable window.

Bright but slightly overcast weather creates very soft light but keeps the light level high enough for you to shoot at decent shutter speeds on ISO400 film. If you need to soften the light further just hang net curtains over the window or tape a sheet of tracing paper to the glass. Warm, late-afternoon sunlight flooding through a window also works well.

Electronic flash is another option, but it must be used carefully to give attractive results. Rather than firing the flash directly at your subject, bounce the light off a wall, ceiling or large reflector, so it's softened and shadows are weakened. Alternatively, fit a bounce attachment to the flashgun itself, or take the gun off the camera and hold it to one side so you have control over the direction of the light in relation to your subject.

Outdoors, successful pictures can be taken in just about any conditions. Just one point: if you're shooting in bright sunlight, make sure your subject isn't looking towards the sun otherwise they'll squint and will quickly feel uncomfortable. Instead, keep the sun behind them, and use a reflector or a burst of fill-in flash to bounce light onto their face.

In the studio all sorts of lighting set-ups can be used to produce exactly the effect you want. Don't be too ambitious though. You can produce superb results with just one light and a couple of reflectors – the less equipment you use, the more you can concentrate on your subject. See Portraits (page 96) for specific lighting set-ups.

I decided to try something different here and used a single candle as the only source of illumination. Not only did this create attractive, atmospheric lighting, but Noah was also fascinated by the candle so I captured some great expressions.
Camera Nikon F90x Lens 50mm
Film Fujichrome Sensia 400 at ISO1600

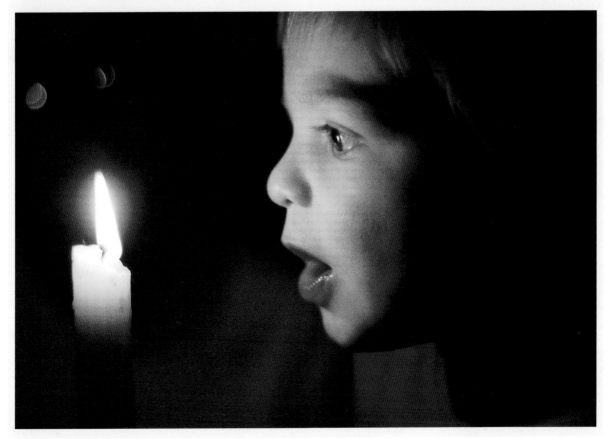

Travel

Blackpool, Bangkok, Barbados – wherever you go on your annual holidays you're going to discover an endless range of things to photograph. All those new sights, sounds and smells have an intoxicating effect on photographers, and often, more film is consumed in that traditional two-week period than the rest of the year put together.

There's a big difference between taking a few snapshots for the family album and creating a serious photographic record of your stay, though. Travel photography is a subject that requires dedication, hard work and patience, so if you want to return home with a selection of successful pictures you'll need to bear a few essential factors in mind.

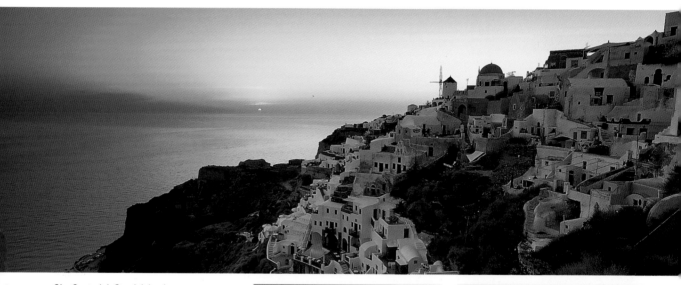

Oia, Santorini, Greek Islands
The key to travel photography is trying to capture the character of a location in a single image. This view of Oia, for example, is symbolic of not only Santorini, but the whole Greek Island idyll – pretty whitewashed towns, amazing sea views and beautiful sunsets.
Camera Hasselblad Xpan Lens 45mm
Filters 0.9ND grad and 81D warm-up
Film Fujichrome Velvia 50

Q Is it worth doing a little research on my chosen destination before I leave home?

Definitely. The more homework you do before leaving home, the better prepared you'll be to make the most of your destination's photographic potential because you'll have a clearer idea of what to expect when you arrive and this will save valuable time.

Go on the Internet or check through some guidebooks to find out about interesting places or special events worth visiting. Speak to your travel agent about local transport, so you can get around once you're there, and jot any useful information in a notebook.

Once you arrive it's also a good idea to make a bee-line for the postcard stands. The pictures may not be brilliant, but they'll give you a good idea of what there is to photograph in the area and where the best viewpoints are.

Q How much equipment should I take on holiday with me?

How long is a piece of string? Most photographers drive themselves to despair deciding which gear to take and which to leave behind, simply because once you've left home it's too late to wish you'd packed a certain lens or filter.

If your primary concern is taking snapshots, a zoom compact or an SLR fitted with a standard zoom will suffice. But if your intentions are more serious you'll need more than that. Use the following checklist as a guide.

- Two 35mm SLR bodies if you have them, so you can use different film types in each, such as colour and black and white.
- Lenses from 28 to 200mm for general use. This range can be covered by 28–70mm and 70–210mm zooms if you need to keep the weight of your kit down, or a selection of prime lenses.
- A 1.4x or 2x teleconverter will provide a

lightweight means of increasing the power of your lenses for the occasional long telephoto shot.

- A portable flashgun for taking pictures indoors or for fill-in in bright sunlight.
- A lightweight tripod for low-light and indoor photography in available light.
- Filters: a polarizer is essential to deepen blue sky and reduce reflections in water; 81A and 81B warm-ups to enhance the natural light; 0.3 and 0.6 neutral density graduates to tone down the sky; plus any of your other favourite filters such as sunset and soft-focus.
- Accessories: cable release, lens cleaning kit, plenty of spare batteries for cameras and flashguns, notebook for logging location details, lens hoods to prevent flare in bright light.
- A photographic backpack that will hold all the equipment and be comfortable to carry all day.

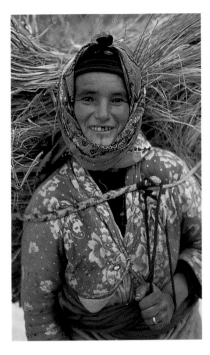

Berber Woman, Todra Gorge, Morocco
Treat the people you encounter with respect and dignity and you will return home with some great travel portraits. I encountered this woman while she watered her goats in a mountain stream. Rather than try to grab a candid picture, I asked permission to photograph her and this resulted in a much more natural portrait.
Camera Nikon F90x Lens 50mm Film Fujichrome Sensia II 100

CAPTURING FAMOUS LANDMARKS

We've all photographed famous tourist attractions on our holidays – Big Ben, the Statue of Liberty, the Eiffel Tower, the Taj Mahal. But how many of you could honestly say those pictures were original? Very few, if the truth were known.

The problem is that when we see impressive subjects like this our natural instinct is to start shooting away excitedly. Problems of access and battling through crowds also limit our options somewhat, and many famous sights even have suggested vantage points to take good pictures from. So we use them, we follow the crowds, and we end up with pictures that are identical to the millions of others that have already been taken.

It doesn't have to be that way though, and with a little effort you'll find ways of taking pictures that are totally original and show your subject in a whole new light.

For a start, you could try shooting from a different angle. Leave the crowds behind and go for a wander to see if you can snatch a glimpse of your subject from somewhere else – up that hill in the distance, or down another street.

Experimenting with different lenses can also make a big difference. While most people fire away with a standard or wide-angle, why not back off and use a telephoto instead, or vice versa? Don't be so keen to include the whole thing either – homing in on smaller details can produce pictures that are far more interesting, provided that the subject is still identifiable.

Lastly, if you're staying close by, rise at dawn so you can use the beautiful early morning light while the crowds are still in bed, or return at night when the crowds have dispersed, and take your picture then.

Leaning Tower of Pisa, Italy
There are many creative techniques you can employ to make your travel pictures more original – especially now that digital technology is so accessible. For this simple shot I copied the original slide on to Polaroid instant film then produced an image transfer on watercolour paper.
Camera Olympus OM4-Ti Lens 200mm Film Fujichrome Velvia 50

Q How should I go about taking pictures of the local people?

Carefully and politely. Imagine you were walking down the high street, minding your own business, when suddenly a foreign tourist jumped out from behind a tree and started taking your picture. How would you feel? Confused, surprised, and rather annoyed no doubt.

Well, it's exactly the same for the people we photograph every year on our holidays. So if you want total strangers to cooperate with your wishes then treat them with respect and courtesy. Instead of sneaking pictures with a long telephoto lens, approach your subject and ask their permission. Show a genuine interest in them, without being patronizing, and try to strike up a conversation – even if you have to resort to sign language.

In most countries the people are more than happy to be photographed, but some cultures and religions aren't. You may also be asked for money in developing countries. At least by making your intentions clear you'll discover this. Then it's up to you to decide whether to proceed without risking a confrontation.

Approaching your subject also gives you more control over the pictures. You can pose them in attractive light, and encourage interesting expressions. All in all this will lead to better results.

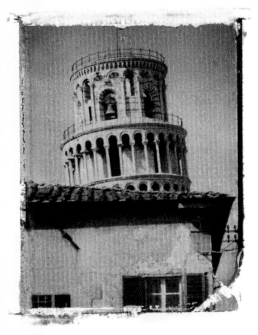

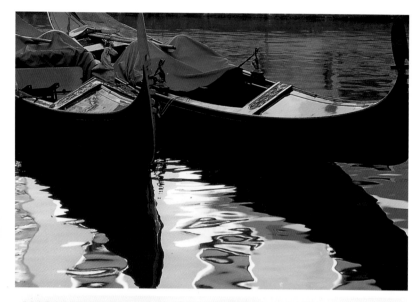

Gondolas, Venice, Italy
The most powerful travel images are often the simplest, so don't be afraid to look for symbolic subjects and telling details, as well as grand views. This graphic photograph sums up the character of Venice as well as any other.
Camera Nikon F90x Lens 80–200mm zoom
Film Fujichrome Velvia 50

Q How can I capture the atmosphere of a foreign location, so when people see the pictures they get a sense of being there?

It seems like a rather tall order, but that's what successful travel photography is all about: capturing the character of a place. The pictures used in brochures and guidebooks do that, and the photographers who take them go to great lengths to make it possible.

There's no magical formula, unfortunately. It's a simple case of being responsive to what's around you and getting under the skin of a place so you react to it with your camera in a positive way, rather than taking dispassionate snapshots. You need to explore your chosen location. Spend time absorbing the atmosphere, let the sights, sounds and smells influence you, then try to record those feelings in the best way possible – remembering that photography is a visual medium only.

On a more practical level you also need to ask yourself what it is about your location that makes it so interesting and inviting. The beaches? The sea? The architecture? The people? A combination of all these things? The answer to these questions should lead you in the right direction when it comes to taking pictures.

Finally, make an effort to take pictures in the best possible conditions. Rise early and stay out late each day, so you're there when the light is wonderful and things are happening. And pay great attention to detail when taking each picture. Take care with the composition, be patient and wait until everything falls into place, and return to the same spot time after time if necessary. Travel photography is hard work and requires much dedication, but the rewards are immense.

AVOIDING EXPOSURE ERROR

In certain parts of the world, lighting conditions and the type of subjects encountered are totally different from what you'll find in your own country, so you need to take extra care when sorting out the exposure for pictures.

The main areas of concern are subjects that reflect a lot of light, such as whitewashed buildings, sandy beaches and the sea. If you just fire away without a care, chances are your camera's meter will be fooled by the high reflectance and cause underexposure. To prevent this, take a meter reading then increase the exposure to prevent error – especially when large areas of brightness are included in the shot (see Exposure, page 46).

In countries south of the equator the light is also very intense, especially around the middle hours of the day when the sun is overhead. This creates very high contrast with a brightness range that's too high for your film to fully record. To prevent disappointment you must therefore decide which is the most important part of the scene and expose accordingly. With slide film, exposing for the highlights is recommended, but with negative film you're better off choosing an exposure that will record some detail in the shadows, as the highlights can be burned-in at the printing stage.

Santorini, Greek Islands
Bright sky and reflective buildings can easily fool your camera into underexposure. For this shot I used a handheld meter to take an incident light reading of the light falling onto the church walls.
Camera Nikon F90x Lens 20mm
Filter Polarizer Film Fujichrome Velvia 50

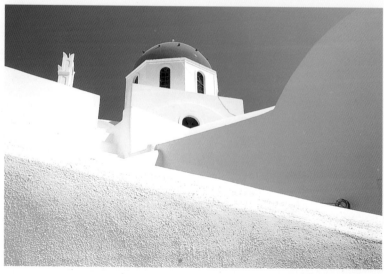

Q Do I need to worry about X-ray machines in airports damaging my film?

No, not any more. X-ray machines used to be renowned for fogging photographic film, but modern systems use low dosages that cause no problems.

The only time you should try to get a hand search is if you'll be passing through several airport terminals, each requiring an X-ray inspection, as X-ray damage is cumulative. Fast film is also more susceptible to damage than slow film, although recent tests have shown that it would take literally hundreds of passes to cause any problems.

Minimize the risk by carrying your film in hand luggage. The chance of a hand search will also be increased if each film is removed from its box and placed in clear plastic tubs for easier inspection.

 Q Should I buy my film in my home country, or once I arrive at my holiday destination?

To a certain extent that depends upon where you're going. Most major cities around the world carry stocks of all types of film, but it's a wise precaution to take what you'll need with you. If not, you may find your favourite stock is not available, and in touristy areas film does tend to cost much more than you are accustomed to paying.

As for the amount, that will be determined by how serious your intentions are. In photogenic areas it's easy to use between five and ten rolls per day. Your best bet is to work out how much you think you'll need then double it – unused film can always be brought home again and used at a later date, but there's nothing worse than running out of film.

Q I always get hassle from airline check-in staff about the size of my backpack, which is my hand luggage. What's the solution?

Airlines are becoming stricter and stricter about baggage allowances, so try and remove as much of the weight from your backpack as you can. Your backpack should be as close to the 15kg hand luggage weight limit as possible – you may get away with being a couple of kilograms over, but if it weighs nearly double your allowance, you're going to face problems.

 Q Do I need to take proof of purchase of my equipment on holiday with me? Also, is it worth insuring my gear?

If you're taking a lot of expensive gear with you it's always a good idea to carry proof of purchase, if only to prevent problems with customs when you arrive at your holiday destination and when you return home.

As for insurance, it's an absolute must. Check your home insurance policy to see if the equipment is covered in foreign countries, and if not, take out a 'new for old' policy to cover it for the duration of your trip. If you take a chance and don't take out a policy, you will only regret it if anything goes wrong.

Some items can be packed in your main luggage to be stored in the aircraft's hold – cameras and lenses carefully wrapped in bubble-wrap or clothing will be well protected – as will filters, light meters, tripods and other accessories.

Another suggestion is to put some heavy items in your jacket pockets so that it keeps your hand luggage weight down. Check-in staff will never ask you to step onto the scales to weigh yourself, so it doesn't matter how much weight you carry on your person – photographers' waistcoats are ideal for this purpose as they contain lots of useful pockets.

Q When's the best time to take pictures outdoors?

As a general rule you should avoid taking important pictures from about 10am to 4pm in summer as the light's harsh, and with the sun overhead everything looks rather flat and uninspiring. This is particularly true in hot parts of the world as the light is extremely strong – though you can produce stunning graphic shots of buildings and monuments in the middle of the day.

Any time outside this period is ideal, although the most attractive conditions occur during the first couple of hours after sunrise, and during the last hour before sunset, when the sun is low in the sky and the light has a beautiful warmth.

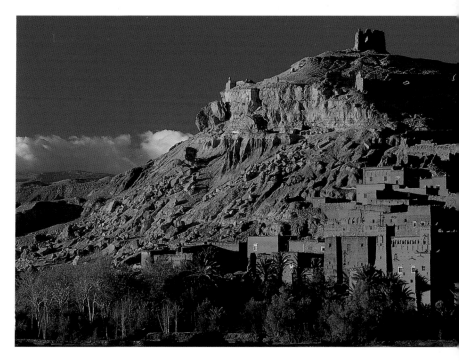

Kasbah Ait Benhaddou, Morocco
Early morning and, in this case, late afternoon are the most photogenic times of day to shoot scenic pictures. Warm sunlight and long shadows make everything look amazing – all you have to do is capture it on film.
Camera Nikon F5 Lens 80–200mm zoom
Filter Polarizer Film Fujichrome Velvia 50

Candids

Candid photography offers a great release from the confines of formal portraiture. Instead of having to worry about lighting, posing and putting your subject at ease, your aim is simply to wander around, looking for opportunities to capture ordinary people going about their daily lives. To do this successfully you need quick reflexes and a certain amount of self-confidence. Turning your camera on a complete stranger can be a very unnerving experience, mainly because of the embarrassment you feel if your subject catches you in the act. But as your experience grows this will fade, and you'll find it's possible to photograph people unawares in intimate situations.

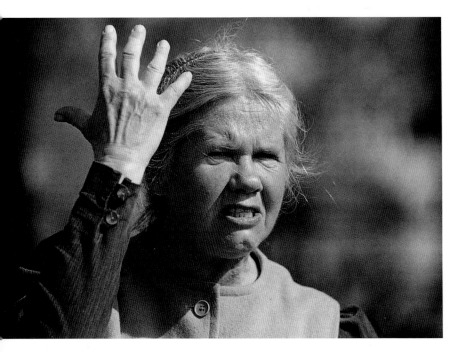

Speaker's Corner, London, England
I mainly use an 80–200mm telezoom lens for candid photography – the longer end of the focal length range is powerful enough to obtain frame-filling pictures from a reasonable distance while shallow depth of field at wide apertures throws the background well out of focus.
Camera Nikon F90x Lens 80–200mm f/2.8 zoom Film Ilford HP5 Plus

FROM THE HIP

A great way to take candids in a crowd, or places where your subjects might not be too happy about being photographed, is by shooting with the camera at your waist level.

This technique is rather hit and miss, because you can't see exactly what's going to appear on the final shot, but the low angle of the camera can produce eye-catching results and there's no risk of being spotted.

All you have to do is preset the focusing to a suitable distance estimate of how far away your subject is, then simply stand opposite your subject and press the shutter release gently. Wide-angle lenses are ideal for this type of photography, because as well as including a lot in the frame they also give great depth of field so your focusing needn't be totally accurate.

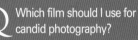
Q Which lenses are best for candid photography?

It's tempting to use the longest lens in your gadget bag so you can keep your distance. However, for general use a 70–210mm tele-zoom or 200mm telephoto is ideal because it will allow you to take frame-filling pictures from several metres away. Also, by setting a wide aperture of f/4 or f/5.6, any distracting background details will be thrown out of focus so your subject becomes the centre of attention.

Longer lenses tend to be more suitable in situations where potential subjects are a long way off. At a football match, for example, you could use a 300mm or 400mm telephoto to pick out people from the crowd and capture the emotion on their faces when a goal is scored.

Wide-angle lenses are also perfect for candid photography at close quarters. Because the angle of view is so great you can photograph people in a crowd or demonstration without pointing the camera directly at them, so they will not realize what you're doing.

Q Which film should I use for candid photography?

For general use ISO100 film is ideal. In bright conditions it will give you an exposure of 1/500sec at f/5.6, which is fast enough to prevent camera shake when handholding a telezoom or telephoto lens. The image quality is also excellent.

In duller weather, the extra speed of ISO400 film will come in handy for keeping the shutter speed up, while indoors you'll need to load up with film of ISO1000 or above to cope with the lower light levels.

Q Where should I go to find candid subjects?

Wherever people gather there will be interesting candid subjects. In your local town centre, for example, you'll see the whole gamut of human emotions on display: frustrated mothers carrying heavy bags of shopping, old folk chatting on a bench, young lovers in fond embrace, traffic wardens arguing with angry motorists... Markets, funfairs and sporting events are also worth checking out.

Don't forget about your own family and friends. If you take a camera along to parties, or on walks and holidays you'll have lots of opportunities to shoot candids, and because the people know you, they won't pay too much attention if the camera is spotted.

Q How can I remain unobtrusive so people don't know I'm taking their picture?

By making sure they have nothing to be suspicious about. If you wander into the middle of a market square with a huge gadget bag and three SLRs swinging from your neck you'll stand out like a sore thumb. But walk around with just one camera and lens in your hand and hardly anyone will notice you.

Even better, take a compact rather than an SLR. Not only will it be smaller and harder to see, but people tend not to associate them with serious photography, so you'll be ignored.

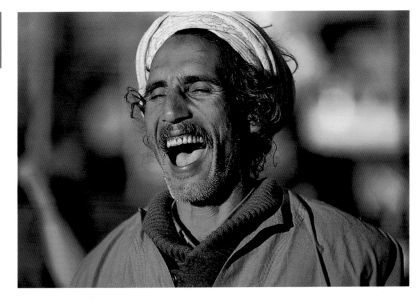

Marrakech, Morocco
Travel provides great opportunities for candid photography. I photographed this man entertaining the crowds in the Djemaa el Fna – he was too engrossed to notice me taking his picture.
Camera Nikon F90x Lens 80–200mm zoom
Film Fujichrome Sensia II 100

Q I seem to spend ages fumbling with my camera when trying to take candids, and the moment is missed. How can I avoid this?

Get to know your camera gear inside out so you can operate it instinctively.

Once you've spotted someone who might make a good candid subject, preset the focus either by guessing or focusing on something a similar distance away. The exposure should also be set, or you could switch to aperture priority, set a wide aperture, and the camera will set the required shutter speed automatically.

All you have to do then is raise the camera to your eye, quickly check the focusing is accurate and trip the shutter before anyone has a clue what's going on.

Q Am I breaking the law by photographing people without their permission?

Privacy laws are changing all the time as press photographers and paparazzi are challenged for invading the lives of celebrities and public figures. However, this is unlikely to affect an enthusiast photographer taking a few street pictures. Providing you're in a public place and not causing a nuisance you should be okay.

The only time you need to be careful is if a candid picture is published and the caption is defamatory to the subject. Calling an old man a tramp just because he looks a little untidy, for example, could have you facing a lawsuit.

Similarly, if someone takes offence at being photographed, be polite and apologetic to diffuse the situation.

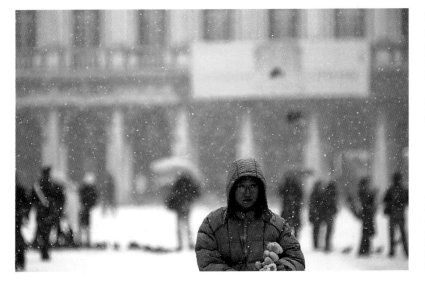

Venice, Italy
Your subject doesn't have to fill the frame to make a successful candid shot – I noticed this tourist in St Mark's Square looking rather despondent due to unexpected snow so I intentionally kept him small in the frame to show him as part of his surroundings.
Camera Nikon F90x Lens 80–200mm zoom
Film Fujichrome Provia 400

Landscapes

Successful landscape photography is all about watching, waiting and walking. You need to get to know the landscape, understand its rhythms, and let yourself be influenced by what you see. You need to wait until the light is just right before tripping your camera's shutter. But perhaps most important of all, you need to walk, and walk, and walk some more. Rarely are the best landscapes captured from the side of the road, or a footpath that is frequented by everyone else, and it is only by getting off the beaten track that you will discover those magical scenes that no one else sees.

Q What lenses would you recommend for a keen landscape photographer?

The vast majority of landscape photographers use wide-angle lenses almost exclusively because they offer several distinct advantages.

For a start, you can include a much greater area in the viewfinder than is visible with the naked eye. The wide angle of view also makes it possible to create powerful compositions, by emphasizing foreground interest to add a strong sense of distance and scale to your pictures. Also, wide-angle lenses give extensive depth of field at small apertures, so you can keep everything in the scene sharp, from the immediate foreground to the distant background.

For general use, a 24mm or 28mm wide-angle lens is ideal for photographing landscapes, although even wider optics

Bedruthan Steps, Cornwall, England
Wide-angle lenses are invaluable for landscape photography as they allow you to emphasize foreground interest to create a sense of depth and scale. This picture was taken with the equivalent of a 28mm lens – the most versatile for general use.
Camera Ebony RSW45 Lens 90mm
Filters Polarizer, 0.6ND grad and 81B warm-up
Film Fujichrome Velvia 50

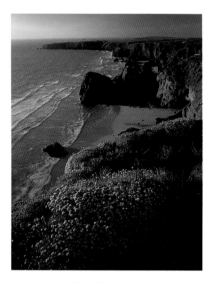

such as a 17mm or 20mm lens can produce staggering results when used carefully.

Telephoto lenses come into their own when you want to isolate a small part of a scene – an old farm at the base of enormous cliffs, or reflections in a lake, perhaps. Because telephotos compress perspective they can also be used to make the elements in a scene appear crowded together. This works well on shots of mountain ranges or distant hills and adds dramatic tension to a picture. In terms of focal length, telephotos from 85–300mm are the most useful. Anything longer tends to be too heavy to carry around.

Namib Desert, Namibia
Use a telephoto or telezoom lens to isolate smaller features in the landscape. Such features get lost in wide-angle compositions.
Camera Nikon F90x Lens 80–200mm zoom
Filters 81C warm-up and polarizer
Film Fujichrome Velvia 50

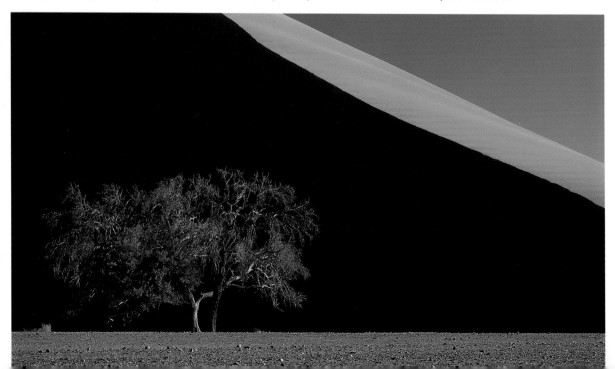

Q What is the best time of day to photograph the landscape?

An appreciation of light is an essential aspect of landscape photography. As the sun arcs across the sky each day the colour, harshness and intensity of the light changes, and each permutation transforms both the physical appearance and mood of the landscape.

Generally you will obtain the best results during early morning or late afternoon. Not only is the light lovely and warm but, with the sun low in the sky, raking shadows are cast across the landscape to reveal texture and form in even the flattest scenes.

You can also take superb pictures at dawn, when the sky is alive with colour and veils of mist hang over rivers and lakes and in valley bottoms, or at dusk, when golden shafts of sunlight make even the dullest scenes look beautiful.

In bright, sunny weather, the worst time to shoot is around midday. With the sun almost overhead the light is far too harsh and shadows are very strong, making the landscape look flat and featureless. The only exception to this is during late autumn and winter, when the sun never climbs very high in the sky and the light is attractive from dawn to dusk – often giving you more effective hours of shooting in a day than you would get in mid-summer (and you don't have to rise so early to catch the sunrise – which is essential!).

The only way to catch the light at its best is by spending time outdoors, observing the magic spell it casts on the landscape. When you arrive at a location, ask yourself if the light could look better. Sometimes you may only have to wait for a few minutes until a cloud passes over; at others you will have to return a few hours later when the sun's position has changed, or on another day.

This may seem like a rather laborious way of going about your business, and it may take several return visits before you get The Shot, but in the end your efforts will be amply rewarded. For more details see Lighting (page 54).

Val d'Orcia, Tuscany, Italy
Misty weather reduces the landscape to a series of pale tones and overlapping forms, especially in mountainous areas. Dawn is the best time to photograph mist – for this picture I had to start shooting before the sun rose and started to burn off the mist.
Camera Pentax 67 Lens 165mm
Filter 81C warm-up Film Fujichrome Velvia 50

THE LANDSCAPER'S KIT

Portability is an important factor to consider when putting together equipment for landscape photography. You need an outfit that will cope with all your picture-taking needs, but be light enough to carry long distances over rough terrain. Many landscape photographers use medium-format equipment for improved image quality. However, 35mm gear is perfectly adequate, and a kit containing the following items would cater for pretty much all your needs:

- **Two 35mm AF SLR bodies with sophisticated metering and a choice of exposure modes.**
- **A mix of prime and zoom lenses covering focal lengths from 20mm to 200mm, plus a 1.4x teleconverter.**
- **Sturdy tripod and head – this tripod is made from lightweight carbon fibre.**
- **Electronic release to fire the camera's shutter when it's tripod-mounted.**
- **A selection of filters including polarizers, warm-ups and neutral density graduates.**
- **Filter holder and adaptor rings for all lenses.**
- **Cleaning accessories for cameras, lenses and filters.**
- **A waterproof 'stuff sack' to cover the camera in the event of sudden rain.**
- **Maps of the location being visited plus a compass – invaluable for establishing sunrise and sunset positions.**
- **Handheld spotmeter for precise metering.**
- **Grey card doubles as lens shade to prevent flare.**
- **Plenty of slow-speed film such as Fujichrome Velvia for general use, plus black and white and infrared.**
- **Heavy-duty photographic backpack to store and protect all this equipment and make carrying it long distances less of a pain in the back.**

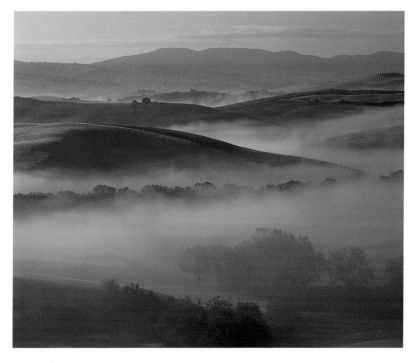

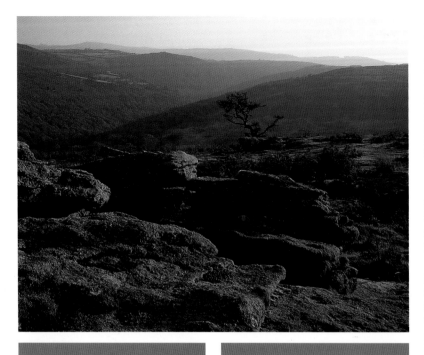

Q I live in a boring part of the country. How can I ever hope to take interesting pictures?

Ah, this is a common complaint of budding landscape photographers. Unfortunately though, it's a poor excuse for producing second-rate pictures.

Successful landscape photography is all about using light and composition to make the most of a scene, not being surrounded by beautiful scenery. Even the most stunning location looks dull and dismal if it's captured in grey, rainy weather, but a relatively boring location will look magical if it's brought to life by the camera of a skilled photographer in amazing light.

So, instead of feeling left out because there's nothing interesting to photograph where you live, rise to the challenge. The more you explore an area the more you'll get to know it, and that's when you'll start discovering the real beauty that's eluded you so far.

Q Have you got any tips for creating interesting compositions?

The main thing to consider when photographing the landscape is that you're taking a three-dimensional subject and cramming it into two, so to retain that feeling of depth and scale you need to compose your pictures carefully. The final result should also be visually pleasing, with the various elements in the scene linked together so the viewer's eye is naturally carried up through the scene from the foreground to the background.

When you discover a scene that shows promise, a good way to start is by seeking out some kind of foreground interest such as a wall, stream, hedge or rocks to provide a logical entry point into the picture and add scale. If this feature creates a natural line, so much the better as it will carry the eye through the scene as well.

A wide-angle lens will allow you to emphasize foreground features, and their 'weight' can be controlled by varying shooting distance and camera height. The closer you are and the lower the camera, the more the foreground will dominate the shot. The picture should also be composed so that there are other interesting features in the middle distance and background for the eye to move to – almost as if the scene

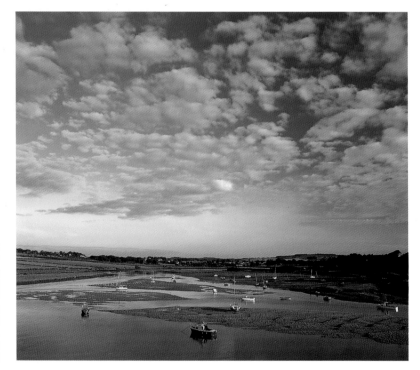

were on different planes, with one carrying the eye to the next. If one feature acts as a focal point, such as an isolated farm house or a single tree, position it off-centre (see rule of thirds in Composition, page 59).

Finally, the amount of sky you include can make a big difference to the compositional balance of a picture. If the sky is full of interesting cloud patterns you shouldn't be afraid to make a feature of it, but as a guide including only a narrow band of sky – no more than the top third of the picture area – will give you a pleasing result in the final picture.

With telephoto landscapes your priorities change somewhat. It becomes more difficult to emphasize depth because perspective is foreshortened by the lens, so you're better off going for a more graphic effect. Try to emphasize repeated patterns or shapes, and planes of colour or tone in the landscape, including perhaps just one element as a focal point so the eye has something to settle on.

Q What's the best type of film for landscape photography?

In general most landscape photographers prefer to use slow film, with a speed of ISO50 to 100. The main reason for this is it gives optimum image quality, with fine grain, rich colours and superb sharpness.

In terms of specific brands, that's really up to you. Fujichrome slide film is preferred by many landscape photographers because it produces very bright images with deeply saturated colours – particularly greens. However, others swear by Kodak Ektachrome and Elitechrome films.

Whichever you choose, you really can't go wrong, though Fujichrome Velvia 50 is still the favourite of discerning landscapers.

If you're looking to create something a little bit different, then try a roll or two of faster film, with a speed of ISO1600. The grain is unashamedly coarse and the colours are noticeably weaker, but in soft light or stormy weather the results can look truly beautiful.

Landscape pictures can also look stunning when shot in black and white, because the medium gives you the chance to make use of tone, texture and form rather than concentrating on colour. And if you want to create something totally different, nothing beats Kodak High Speed Mono Infrared film (see Film, page 31).

PHOTOGRAPHING WATER

Water is a common feature of the landscape. Rivers and streams wind through the countryside like a network of veins and arteries, bringing life to the land, while lakes and ponds punctuate the scenery like enormous full stops. Except for desert landscapes, wherever you go it's impossible not to find water in one form or another, and the photographic opportunities it presents are endless.

The reflections in calm water can be used to add interest to a picture – if you stand by the edge of a lake or pond in calm weather you'll be able to capture a perfect mirror image. When photographing reflections in this way, use a polarizing filter to remove any unwanted glare from the water's surface. Rivers or streams winding away into the distance can also be used to lead the eye through a scene, improving the composition immensely.

For shots of waterfalls and fast-flowing rivers, mount your camera on a tripod and use a slow shutter speed of 1/2sec or slower, so the water records as a graceful blur while static elements in the scene come out sharp. Stopping your lens down to a small aperture will help to ensure you can use a slow enough shutter speed, but if that fails you can reduce light levels by fitting a neutral density or polarizing filter to your lens (see Filters, page 22).

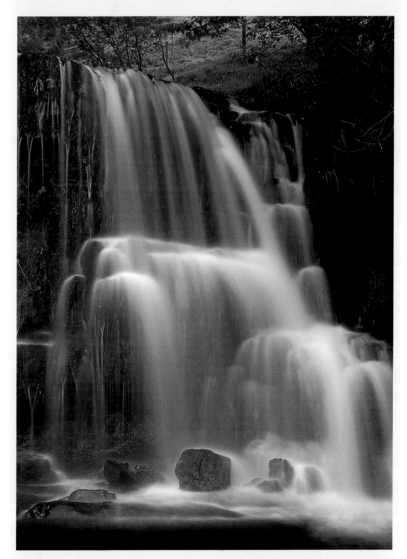

East Gill Force, Yorkshire Dales, England
Capturing moving water as a graceful blur may be something of a cliché, but the effect works beautifully – as you can see here. The exposure used was eight seconds at f/16.
Camera Pentax 67 Lens 105mm Film Fujichrome Velvia 50

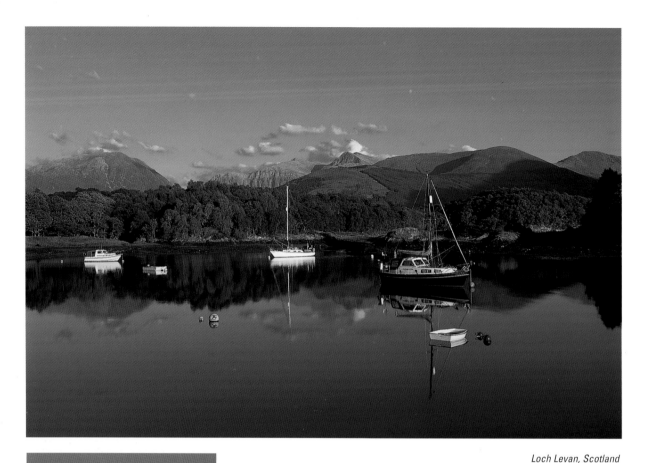

Loch Levan, Scotland
A polarizing filter is one of the most useful for landscape photography as it deepens blue sky and increases colour saturation. Here it also removed glare from the surface of the loch so the reflections were enhanced.
Camera Pentax 67 Lens 105mm Filter Polarizer Film Fujichrome Velvia 50

Q Are there any filters that can help improve my landscape pictures?

The best filters for landscape photography are generally those that enhance the good work mother nature has already done, rather than changing it and adding cheap effects. A polarizer is absolutely essential – it will remove unwanted glare from foliage, reduce surface reflections on water and generally increase colour saturation. The 81-series of warm-ups are also indispensable for balancing the slight coolness in the light on dull, cloudy days, or for enhancing warm sunlight.

But perhaps the most useful filter of all is the neutral density graduate, which allows you to reduce the difference in brightness between the sky and ground so when you expose for the landscape, the sky comes out as you remembered it with the clouds intact. Other types of graduated filter can also be used – a pink or coral grad works well at dawn and dusk to add warmth to the sky, or in dull weather – but neutral density is best for general use as it doesn't alter the natural colour of the sky.

Finally, you might want to include a soft-focus filter for the occasional shot – combine it with a warm-up filter when shooting fast, grainy film for beautiful atmospheric images – plus an orange 85-series filter or a sunset grad to really enhance dawn and dusk shots

For more about these and other filters, see Filters (page 24).

Q Is it important to use a tripod for landscape photography?

It isn't essential, but you'll find that your pictures improve if you do make the effort.

The main advantage of using a tripod is that you can set slow shutter speeds without fear of camera shake spoiling the results. In turn, this frees you to use slow film for optimum image quality, and small lens apertures to maximize depth of field.

In bright weather conditions you may find you don't need one, but early or late in the day, when light levels are much lower, it will be indispensable.

CONSULTING MAPS

The more you know about an area before visiting it, the greater your chances of taking successful pictures, so any background work that you can do will be worthwhile.

Ordnance Survey maps are particularly valuable to UK landscape photographers because they provide a great deal of information about the topography of the land. Contour lines tell you how high a particular location is in relation to surrounding scenery, while their closeness indicates how steep or gentle the gradients are. The maps also show many other useful features, such as rivers, streams, footpaths, roads, sites of ancient settlements and so on. You can even roughly calculate the best time of day to visit a particular spot once you know which direction it faces.

All this information will help you build up a mental picture of the area you intend exploring, so you have some idea of what to expect before you arrive.

Q Is landscape photography just about capturing sweeping views?

Not at all. The key to landscape photography is to capture the character of a place, and often you can do that just as effectively by concentrating on details.

A telephoto lens can be used to home in on interesting sections of a scene, for example. Or you can capture the many intricate patterns and textures that appear in the landscape, such as lichens on a dry-stone wall, the rough texture of tree bark, or autumn leaves carpeting the ground.

All you have to do is ask yourself what it is about a scene or area that you like, then answer that question with your camera in whatever way you feel is suitable.

Q Is it worth photographing the landscape in bad weather, or should I wait for the sun to come out?

Yes, bad weather is definitely worth it. The mood of the landscape changes completely in bad weather, and if you brave the elements you could be rewarded with stunning results.

The most dramatic conditions occur when sunlight breaks through during a storm and illuminates the landscape against a backdrop of black clouds. This may only last a few seconds, with the light levels

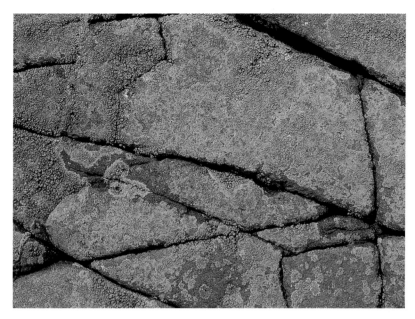

Smaller details in the landscape can be just as interesting as grand views, so don't just see things on a grand scale. Landscape photographers often concentrate on details when the weather is overcast.
Camera Pentax 67 Lens 165mm and 135mm macro Film Fujichrome Velvia 50

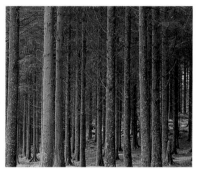

constantly changing, so you need to be ready to capture it. Use a ND graduated filter to make the sky even darker, and meter for a part of the scene that's lit by the sun. Should it start to rain while the sun is out you may also have the chance to photograph a rainbow arching across the

landscape. Position it against a dark background if you can, so its colours stand out.

Mist and fog shroud the landscape in a mysterious veil, reducing colours to soft pastel shades, and making hills and trees look like cardboard cut-outs.

The ideal time to catch mist is at dawn during autumn and winter, when it floats serenely above water and hangs in valleys like a ghostly shroud. You need to act quickly though, because once the sun comes up it quickly burns away. When photographing fog, try to include one or two bold features to act as a focal point, otherwise you'll end up with a murky sea of grey and nothing else. A church spire, hills or tall trees are ideal.

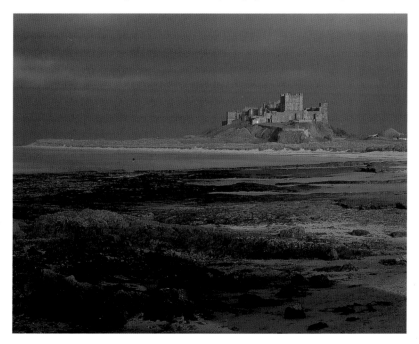

Bamburgh Castle, Northumberland, England Stormy weather produces the most dramatic conditions for landscape photography, though you risk a soaking by staying outdoors in such conditions. This shot was taken minutes before sunset, when the sun broke through the cloudy sky and illuminated the castle.
Camera Pentax 67 Lens 165mm
Filter 81C warm-up Film Fujichrome Velvia 50

Sport and action

The essence of sport and action photography lies in capturing the drama and excitement of moving subjects. To do this successfully you must be familiar with your equipment, and have knowledge of the subject, so you can anticipate what's going to happen next.

Allied to sound knowledge is the ability to react quickly. The most rewarding photo opportunities rarely give any prior warning before happening, so you must be ready at all times, able to focus quickly and accurately, and able to trip the shutter at precisely the right moment.

For someone used to static subjects such as landscapes, this can come as something of a shock. Even relatively slow subjects appear to be travelling at breakneck speed when viewed through a telephoto lens, and capturing them on film seems like an impossibility. But don't worry, with practice, the seemingly impossible suddenly becomes relatively easy, just like driving a car – and remember how frightening that was the first time you tried it!

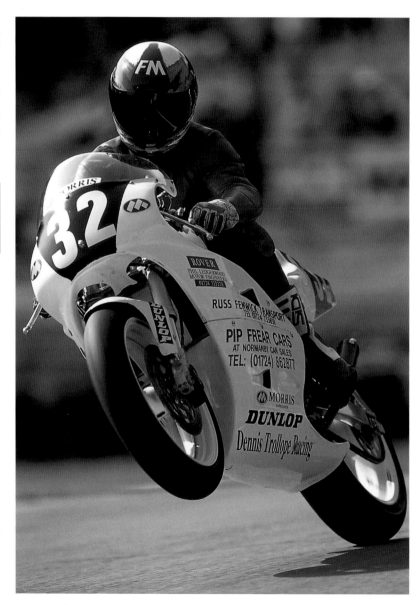

Taking stunning pictures like this requires immense skill. Timing and focusing is critical, as you only have a fraction of a second to trip your camera's shutter before the subject moves out of frame and out of focus. A shutter speed of 1/640sec was used to make sure the biker was frozen.
Camera Canon EOS 1N Lens 500mm f/4.5
Film Fujichrome Sensia 100

Q Are long telephoto lenses essential for sports photography?

Again, it depends what your subject is. For sporting events that occur some distance from the camera, a powerful tele will be essential to fill the frame. Photographers covering athletics, motorsport and field events such as football and rugby rarely use lenses shorter than 400mm, and often resort to 500mm or even 600mm optics. Cricket is even worse, requiring lenses up to 800mm for wicket shots.

But these are extremes, and you'll find that if you go along to local venues, or cover more accessible sports, the top end of a 70–210mm or 75–300mm zoom will be fine. If not, you can always increase its power with a 1.4x or 2x teleconverter.

You shouldn't ignore the versatility of shorter lenses either. Action pictures are at their best when they capture the drama and excitement of an event, and that can be done just as well by shooting from close range with a 35mm or a 28mm wide-angle lens, depending on your composition.

CHOOSING THE RIGHT SHUTTER SPEED

There are three factors to consider when choosing a shutter speed to freeze subject movement: the speed your subject's travelling at, the direction it's moving in relation to the camera, and how big it is in the frame. If your subject is travelling across your path, or filling most of the frame, you'll need to use a faster shutter speed than if it's heading straight towards the camera, is small in the frame, or moving at an angle. The table, right, gives the recommended shutter speeds to freeze a variety of subjects.

Subject	Across path Full-frame (sec)	Across path Half-frame (sec)	Head-on (sec)
Jogger	1/250	1/125	1/60
Trotting horse	1/250	1/125	1/60
Sprinter	1/500	1/250	1/125
Cyclist	1/500	1/250	1/125
Car at 40mph (64kmh)	1/500	1/250	1/125
Car at 70mph (112kmh)	1/1,000	1/500	1/250
Galloping horse	1/1,000	1/500	1/250
Diver	1/1,000	1/500	1/250
Tennis serve	1/1,000	1/500	1/250
Formula 1 car	1/2,000	1/1,000	1/500
Train	1/2,000	1/1,000	1/500

Slow shutter speeds are ideal for emphasizing movement – here 1/8sec has reduced these children to an impressionistic blur. Panning was also used to enhance the effect.
Camera Nikon F90x Lens 80–200mm zoom Film Fujichrome Velvia 50

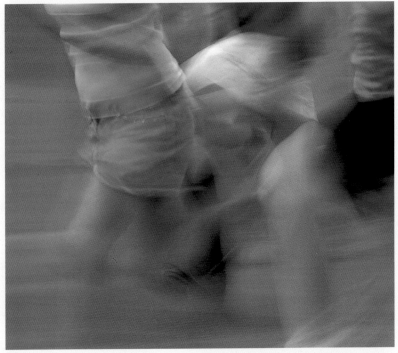

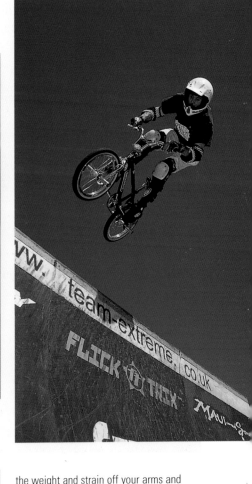

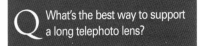

When you want to freeze a moving subject, make sure the shutter speed you use is fast enough – in this case 1/250sec was sufficient.
Camera Canon EOS 30 Lens 28–105mm Film Fujichrome Provia 100

Finally, if you're buying lenses specifically for action, choose the fastest you can afford. A 70–210mm zoom with a maximum aperture of f/2.8 is at least double the price of a 70–210mm f/4–5.6 model, for example, but the extra one or two stops will allow faster shutter speeds and slower film to be used in the same conditions. That can make all the difference between a good or great picture – especially when you're working in low light.

Q What's the best way to support a long telephoto lens?

If you refer back to Accessories (page 40) you'll see there are various forms of camera/lens support available. The favourite among sport and action photographers is undoubtedly the monopod.

Monopods are ideal for use with long, heavy telephoto lenses because they take the weight and strain off your arms and provide loads of support. This makes it far easier to focus the lens and hold it steady for extended periods of time to prevent camera shake.

Being compact and light, monopods also give you the freedom to move around so you can change position quickly and easily, and provide a nice fluid action that enables you to keep track of moving subjects without having to strain.

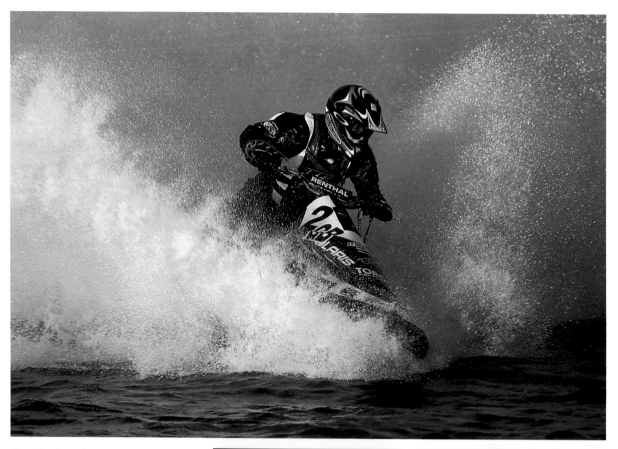

Powering through
Prefocusing your lens on a point you
expect your subject to pass is the easiest
way to ensure you get a sharply focused
picture, but you still need to time the shot
with great precision.
Camera Canon EOS 1V
Lens 500mm plus 1.4x teleconverter
Film Fujichrome Sensia 100 at ISO200

Q Do I need fast film when photographing sport and action?

That depends what you're photographing and where, but you should always use the slowest film you can get away with.

In bright weather outdoors, most sport and action photographers use ISO100 film. This may seem rather slow, but it will allow shutter speeds of 1/500 or 1/1000sec with your lens set to a wide aperture such as f/4 or f/5.6, and that's more than enough to freeze most subjects.

Faster film is only used when absolutely necessary, to ensure suitably high shutter speeds can be set. In dull weather you may find it necessary to load up with ISO200 or ISO400 film. Indoors, ISO400 tends to be the starting point, but it isn't uncommon for ISO1000 or ISO1600 film to be used.

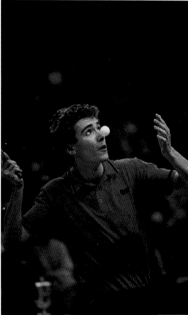

Balancing act
When shooting indoors, fast film is
required to cope with the lower light
levels. For this shot, ISO400 film was
uprated to ISO1600 and push-processed
by two stops so the photographer could
manage a fast enough shutter speed.
Camera Nikon F4 Lens 300mm
Film Fujichrome Provia 400

Q What kind of camera features will come in handy?

The ability to work quickly and instinctively is vital when trying to photograph sport and action, otherwise all the great moments will be missed while you spend time twiddling knobs and pressing buttons. Your camera should therefore be as easy to use as possible, and present all the important information in the viewfinder, such as the aperture and shutter speed set, so you don't have to keep taking the camera away from your eye.

A motor drive is also handy for saving time and allowing you to capture whole sequences of pictures in rapid succession, while shutter speeds up to at least 1/2000sec will allow you to freeze even the most fast moving of subjects.

Other than that, any type of 35mm SLR is generally suitable for sport and action photography – it's the skills of the photographer that are the most important factor. The key to successful action shots is practice, so there is only one thing to do: get out there and practise, practise and practise some more!

Q I never seem to get my subject in focus when photographing sport or action. Are there any easy solutions?

There are no easy solutions available, but there are a few techniques you can use.

If your subject follows a set course, in athletics, motor racing, track cycling and show jumping, for example, your best bet is to prefocus on a point that you know the action will pass, such as the corner of a race track, a jump, or the finish line. All you have to do then is keep your eye on that point, then just before your subject reaches it, trip the shutter. Don't wait until your subject snaps into focus, otherwise by the time you trip the shutter it will be too late and the moment will have passed.

When your subject is moving around in an irregular way, such as football or rugby players, you'll have to use a technique known as follow-focusing, which involves continually adjusting focus to keep your subject sharp until you're ready to take a picture. This is much more difficult than prefocusing, so practise on moving subjects without taking any pictures – joggers or cars driving down the road are ideal.

EMPHASIZING MOVEMENT

Don't always be tempted to set a high shutter speed and freeze your subject – often, using a slower shutter speed deliberately to introduce blur can work far better because it helps to create a feeling of motion, and it heightens the drama.

Again, the shutter speed you use depends upon how fast your subject is moving and how much blur you want. For a person jogging you could use anything from 1/30sec to 1/2sec, whereas a racing car can be blurred at 1/500sec or 1/250sec.

When emphasizing movement, most photographers use a technique known as 'panning'. This involves tripping the shutter while tracking the subject with the camera, so the background blurs but the subject remains relatively sharp.

Alternatively, use a tripod and keep it still during the exposure, so anything that's moving blurs while stationary features stay sharp. This can be used to produce eye-catching pictures of commuters rushing off a train, or crowds of shoppers.

Q Is it necessary to go to major sporting venues to take exciting action pictures?

Not at all. At most large sporting venues, in the UK at least, you need a press pass to take pictures anyway, and they're only issued to professionals with accreditation from magazines or newspapers.

A far better approach is to visit local sporting venues – most towns and cities have one – where you can get closer to your subjects without the need for a press pass, and where you don't have to jostle for position with crowds of other photographers.

Some sporting events are also better than others in terms of access. Car rallying, motocross, cyclocross, marathon running, canoeing, tennis and city-centre cycling are just a few examples of subjects that can be photographed successfully from spectator positions that are close to the action, without the need for expensive powerful telephoto lenses.

Q Will autofocusing increase my success rate?

In many situations it can, but don't take that as an indication that manual focusing is a poor second.

Autofocus SLRs offering 'servo' or Predictive mode are ideal because they continually shift focus to keep moving subjects sharp. In Predictive mode the subject's acceleration is also accounted for, and focus is adjusted at the moment of exposure to ensure a sharp result.

However, autofocusing only works well if you keep the central AF envelope over your subject. Even then, if something comes between you and your subject the lens will hunt around and you'll miss the shot. So, by all means use autofocusing, but make sure your manual focusing skills are up to scratch too.

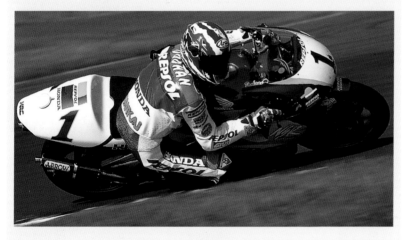

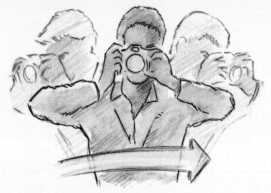

Perfect panning
The aim of panning is to keep your subject sharp but blur the background – easier said than done! In this case the subject was moving at such high speed that a shutter speed of 1/250sec was 'slow' enough to produce the desired effect.
Camera Canon EOS 1N Lens 300mm Film Fujichrome Sensia 100

Night and low light

Night time holds many mysteries and surprises for all who dare to venture into it. As the curtains of daylight are drawn across the world, everything is transformed into a glittering spectacle of colour. Floodlit buildings stand out vividly against the night sky, neon signs flicker outside pubs, clubs and bars, and a welcoming glow radiates from every window. Stepping out after dark is like entering another world. Even the most uninspiring places by day become a photographer's paradise by night, and you cannot fail to take stunning pictures.

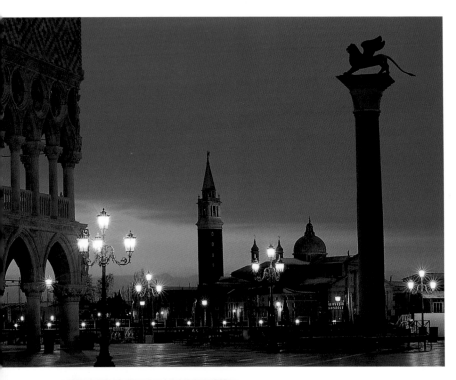

St Mark's Square, Venice
The period before sunrise (as here) and after sunset when there's still colour in the sky is the most productive period to shoot 'night' pictures as natural and artificial forms of lighting are at similar levels and the sky forms an attractive backdrop. Bracket exposures widely to be sure of getting a perfect result – I often shoot in aperture priority mode and bracket up to two stops over the metered exposure in one-third stop increments.
Camera Nikon F90x Lens 89–200mm zoom
Film Fujichrome Velvia 50

Grand Canal, Venice
This picture was taken on the same day as the one opposite, only at dusk instead of dawn. I set my telezoom lens to its longest focal length so I could fill the frame for impact. An exposure of 30sec was required, making a tripod essential.
Camera Nikon F90x Lens 80–200mm zoom
Film Fujichrome Velvia 50

Q **Is there any magical formula to getting the exposure correct when taking pictures at night?**

Many night scenes would appear to be an exposure nightmare, but multi-pattern metering systems are pretty good these days, so you'll probably find that you can achieve fairly accurate exposures by setting your camera to aperture priority exposure mode and leaving it to set the required shutter speed.

That said, no two night scenes are the same, so it's always worth bracketing exposures at least one stop over and half a stop under the exposure set by your camera – do this using the exposure compensation facility (see page 9).

The trickiest night scenes are where you have bright lights in the frame – they can fool your camera into giving too little exposure. Equally, if you have something like a floodlit tower or building that's small in the frame and set against a dark sky or an unlit landscape, the opposite is likely to occur and your camera is fooled by all the darkness into giving too much exposure so the brighter elements are overexposed. Bracketing should take care of either or both of these problems.

If you like to feel more in control, use your camera's spot metering facility to take meter readings off specific areas – blue sky at twilight is a good mid-tone so you could meter from that. Alternatively, choose a mid-tone on a building or something else in the scene that's in the same light as the main subject matter.

To give you an idea of the exposures you should expect when photographing common subjects, use the guide opposite.

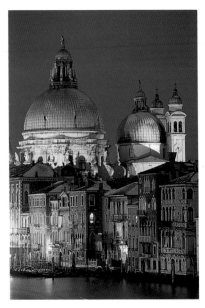

NIGHT EXPOSURE GUIDE

Subject	Aperture			
	f/5.6	f/8	f/11	f/16
Bonfire	⅛	¼	½	1
Neon signs	⅛	¼	½	1
Cityscape just after sunset	¼	½	1	2
Brightly lit city street	¼	½	1	2
Shop window	¼	½	1	2
Subject lit up by fire	1	2	4	8
Subject lit by car headlights	2	4	8	16
Floodlit building (eg church)	2	4	8	16
Subject under street light	2	4	8	16
Fairground rides (eg big wheel)	3	6	12	24
Normally lit street	4	8	16	32
Cityscape at night	4	8	16	32
Landscape by moonlight	2mins	4mins	8mins	16mins
Fireworks (aerial)	bulb (B) at f/16			
Traffic trails	bulb (B) at f/16			

Exposure in seconds for ISO100 film

For general night-time scenes such as floodlit buildings and cityscapes, where you have a mixture of artificial and manmade illumination, start shooting soon after sunset, when there's still some colour left in the sky but the manmade lighting is clearly visible.

The 'crossover' period when natural and artificial lighting is in balance doesn't last long – perhaps only 20 minutes in winter and 45 minutes in the summer – but it's the optimum window of opportunity as contrast is at a level where you won't end-up with black shadows and blown-out highlights. Colours are also at their most intense.

CAPTURING TRAFFIC TRAILS

One of the most popular night-time subjects is the colourful streaks of light created by moving traffic. To capture traffic trails you first need to find an elevated location that gives a clear view along a road, motorway, or over a roundabout – bridges and high-rise buildings are ideal. Late autumn or winter is the best time of year to shoot, as rush hour occurs at dusk. After mounting your camera on a tripod and composing the shot, all you have to do is wait for traffic to appear and trip your camera's shutter. Set your camera to bulb (B), so you can hold the shutter open using a cable release for as long as necessary.

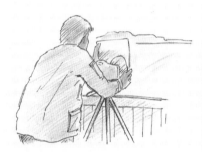

If the traffic runs out, hold a sheet of card in front of the lens while still holding the shutter open, and stop counting.

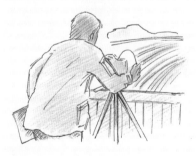

When the traffic reappears, uncover the lens so more trails can record, and resume counting down the exposure.

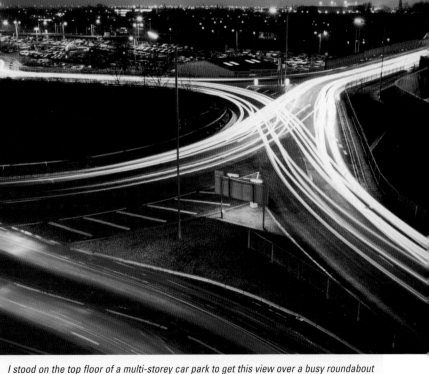

I stood on the top floor of a multi-storey car park to get this view over a busy roundabout and exposed the scene for around 60sec to ensure plenty of traffic trails recorded.
Camera Olympus OM4-Ti Lens 28mm Film Fujichrome Velvia 50

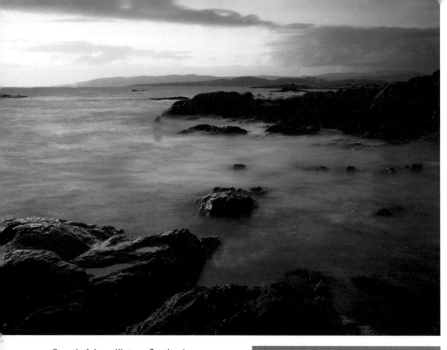

Take your pictures when you can still just about see what's going on, and set the exposure for the foreground as you would during the day – ideally using a handheld meter – and expect exposure times to run into many minutes. A neutral density graduated filter can also be used to darken down the sky if it's still quite bright.

Q **If I use fast film can I take night pictures without a tripod?**

For shots of things like people gathered around a bonfire or peering into brightly lit shop windows, fast film of ISO1000 or ISO1600 will allow you to take handheld pictures. However, for general night photography it won't because you often need a relatively small aperture to give sufficient depth of field, and that makes long exposures necessary. Image quality will also suffer due to the coarse grain and weaker colours if you use ultra-fast film, so you're better off mounting your camera on a tripod and using slow film to capture the scenes you encounter in all their glory. Most photographers use ISO50 or ISO100 film at night because it gives beautiful colours and pin-sharp results.

Sound of Jura, Kintyre, Scotland
Seascapes can look stunning at night, when a long exposure turns the sea into a beautiful mist floating on the shoreline and washing over rocks. Here I used a two-minute exposure. The vivid cool cast is partly a result of reciprocity failure brought on by the long exposure.
Camera Pentax 67 Lens 55mm
Film Fujichrome Velvia 50

Q **Can I photograph landscapes and seascapes at night?**

Yes – you can photograph anything you like. Few photographers ever try to capture the landscape at night, but the results can look amazing – especially if there's a full moon to bathe the scene in eerie light, and clouds to blur during the long exposure.

PHOTOGRAPHING FUNFAIRS

Funfairs, like firework displays, provide the photographer with endless opportunities to take exciting, colourful pictures. The techniques involved are also very similar.

For shots of fairground rides such as the big wheel and the waltzers, simply mount your camera on a tripod, set the lens to f/8 or f/11, and use an exposure of 20 or 30 seconds so the moving lights record as coloured streaks.

To photograph people having fun on the dodgem cars and other rides, combine a slow shutter speed with a burst of electronic flash, so you get both blurred and sharp images on the same picture.

The integral flashgun of your compact or SLR may cut in automatically in low light, or will have a special slow sync mode that can be set to produce this effect. Alternatively, use a portable flashgun mounted on the camera's hot shoe.

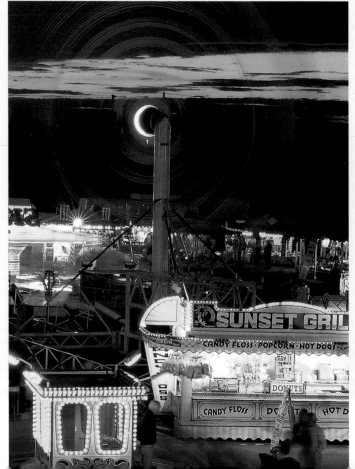

This shot was taken from a bridge overlooking the funfair. By using a telephoto lens I was able to fill the frame with colour and activity and capture the excitement of the event.
Camera Nikon F90x Lens 80–200mm zoom
Film Fujichrome Provia 100

What happens if light levels are so low that my camera meter won't give a reading?

This should rarely happen as the integral meter of modern SLRs is extremely sensitive. However, if it does happen you can overcome it by employing a little trick.

Let's say you're using ISO50 film and you want to shoot at f/16, for example, but the exposure time required is outside of the meter's range. If you set your lens to its widest aperture instead, such as f/2.8 or f/4, a much shorter exposure will be required and this may fall within the meter's range.

All you have to do then is to double the exposure every time you close the lens aperture down to the next f/stop, until you arrive back at f/16. If the meter sets 2sec at f/4, for example, the correct exposure would be 4sec at f/5.6, 8sec at f/8, 16sec at f/11 and 32sec at f/16.

An alternative method to this is to set the camera to a much higher film speed. If you can't get a reading at ISO50, for example, you probably will if you uprate the film to ISO1600. The exposure time should then be doubled every time you halve the film speed, until you arrive back at ISO50.

Marrakech, Morocco
Coloured filters can be used to make colours more intense when shooting at night – in this case I used a sunset filter to make the orange glow in the sky even more vibrant.
Camera Nikon F90x Lens 80–200mm zoom
Filter Cokin Sunset 1 Film Fujichrome Velvia 50

 Do I need special filters at night, to control the colour casts caused by artificial lighting?

That depends how realistic you want your pictures to be. If there's just a single light source in the picture, such as tungsten or sodium vapour, you can balance it using the necessary filter (see Filters, page 26). Unfortunately, general night scenes contain a mixture of several different types of light, making it impossible to deal with them all.

Your best bet is to ignore this problem, as the colour casts produced can actually improve a picture by making it more colourful than the original scene.

I've heard that something called reciprocity law failure occurs at night. What is this exactly?

The film you use in your camera is designed to give optimum results using exposures between 1sec and 1/10,000sec. If you use exposures outside that range the film loses speed, so the exposure suggested by your light meter must be increased to prevent the pictures coming out too dark. This can be a problem at night because you'll often be using exposures longer than a second.

The exact amount of increase required varies because each type of film responds differently to reciprocity failure. However, as a rule of thumb, if your camera suggests an exposure of 1sec, use 1½, if 10sec is suggested use 20, and if 1 minute is suggested use 3 minutes.

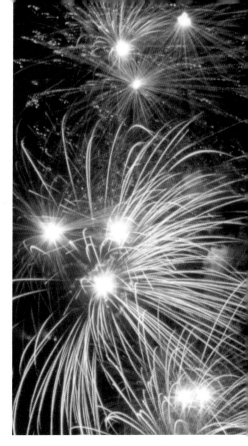

This is the result if you record several rocket bursts on a single frame of film. The key is pointing your camera at the area of sky where most fireworks explode.
Camera Olympus OM2n Lens 70–210mm zoom
Film Fujichrome RFP50

The fireworks pictures I took were a disaster. How can I have more success next time?

Forget about trying to photograph domestic fireworks, and visit a large communal display where everything is done on a bigger scale. Aerial displays also give better results than ground-based fireworks, because if you're too close smoke will obscure your view.

At the display ask a marshal where the rockets are likely to explode, then select a position that gives you a clear view.

Next, mount your camera on a tripod and compose the scene. Then set the shutter to B (bulb), trip the shutter with a cable release as the rockets launch, and hold it open as they explode. Once the first rockets die down, keep the shutter locked open, hold a piece of black card in front of the lens, then move it away when the next rockets launch. By repeating this two or three times you can capture several bursts on the same frame of film, so your pictures are packed with colourful streaks.

Night and low light 121

Nature and close-ups

Animals and birds can be photographed on several different levels, depending on your experience and interest. Family pets make a good starting point, while zoos give you the chance to photograph exotic species without travelling to the ends of the earth. Bird sanctuaries are another option worth considering, and even your own back garden.

But for the ultimate reward nothing beats stalking wildlife through the undergrowth or capturing animals and birds from the concealment of a hide. To succeed you must have the same sense of cunning as your quarry, and be willing to play a fascinating game of cat and mouse, but the satisfaction of tracking down an animal and capturing it on film just can't be beaten.

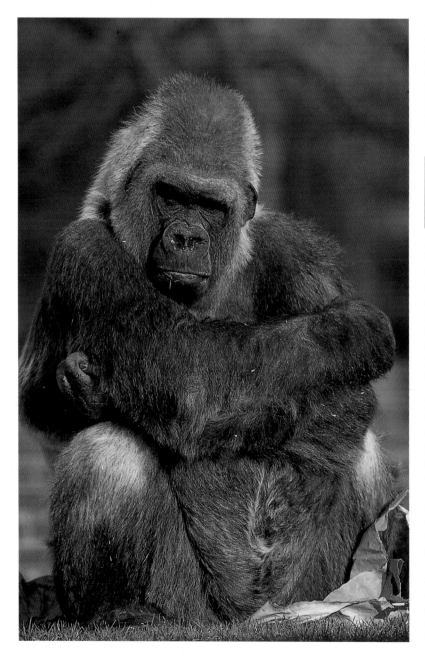

Gorilla, Paignton Zoo, Devon, England
Zoos and safari parks are ideal places to photograph animals that you might never get to see in the wild. They're also more accessible, so taking successful pictures is made easier.
Camera Canon EOS 1N
Lens 300mm plus 1.4x teleconverter
Film Fujichrome Sensia 100

 Q I'm going to the zoo and would like to photograph the animals. Have you got any advice?

Zoos and safari parks are great places to try your hand at 'wildlife' photography. Not only are they home to a vast range of species from all over the world, but the animals and birds are used to having people around, so you can get relatively close without scaring them away. They're also restricted by the confines of a cage or pen, so they can't vanish into thin air as animals in the wild have a habit of doing.

All these factors combine to make your life relatively easy. Frame-filling pictures can usually be taken with a telezoom lens, and by carefully choosing your shooting position it's often possible to exclude all signs of confinement so the pictures look as though they were shot in the wild.

The main problem is caused by wire mesh or iron bars obscuring your view. To overcome this, set your lens to its widest aperture and focus carefully on your subject. If you're using a telephoto lens of 135mm or more, the depth of field will be so shallow that the bars or mesh won't actually appear on the final shot. Doing this also renders any distracting background detail out of focus. For pictures of animals behind glass use electronic flash and press your lens up against the glass so the flash doesn't create reflections – though check first that you're allowed to use flash.

The best pictures tend to be taken at feeding time, when the animals are at their most active.

Q What kind of lenses will I need to photograph animals and birds in the wild?

Long telephoto lenses are essential for serious wildlife photography, simply because most animals and birds are very timid, making it impossible for you to get close to them.

As a minimum you may be able to get away with a 300mm for some subjects, but a 400mm, 500mm or 600mm lens is much better because it will allow you to fill the frame from further away.

If you can't afford to buy such a powerful and expensive lens, invest in a 2x teleconverter, which will double the focal length of a shorter telephoto lens – effectively turning a 300mm lens into a 600mm lens, for example.

A monopod or tripod will also come in handy for supporting the lens and preventing camera shake. Alternatively, rest it on natural supports such as a tree stump, rock or fence, and use a beanbag as a cushion so you don't damage the lens.

USING A HIDE

Working from a hide is a common practice among wildlife photographers because it allows you to get very close to animals and birds and photograph things that would otherwise be impossible.

Hides come in all shapes, sizes and forms. You can buy portable models that pack into a small carrying case and are erected like a tent. Some photographers even use small 'coffin' or 'bivouac' tents which lie close to the ground and can be set up in a small area. Or you could make you own hide using sheets of camouflaged canvas draped over poles. Whichever type you choose, it's a good idea to conceal the hide further using material found at the location, such as fallen branches, leaves, bracken and grass.

Before erecting the hide you must first find a suitable location. Nest sites, watering holes, favourite roosting grounds or feeding places are all ideal, and a few visits to the area beforehand will confirm where most of the activity takes place.

To prevent the animals or birds being frightened off, your best bet is to erect the hide some distance away, leave it for a couple of days so they get used to it, move it closer, leave it again, and so on until you reach the final position. When you go to the hide it's also a good idea to take a friend along as a decoy. He or she can leave once you're inside, and the animals will think the coast is clear.

All you have to do then is watch and wait. Have your camera mounted on a tripod so you're ready to shoot. It may take hours before you spot anything, so pack plenty of food, drink and warm clothing.

The equipment required will depend mainly on how close you are to your subject. Occasionally it's possible to erect a hide so close that a 70–210mm telezoom or 200mm telephoto lens is adequate, but generally you'll need a 400mm or 500mm.

It's also possible to take good pictures using your car as a hide. If you park in a picnic spot or clearing you may see squirrels, pheasants, rabbits, foxes etc. A telephoto lens can be rested on an open window, or supported on a monopod wedged between the door and seat. It's also a good idea to drape a coat over the window to conceal yourself from view.

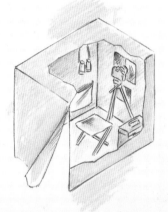

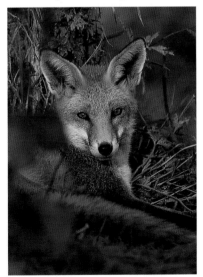

Fox in the undergrowth
Long telephoto lenses are essential for wildlife photography, allowing you to take frame-filling pictures while maintaining a respectable distance from your subject.
Camera Canon EOS1V Lens 500mm Film Fujichrome Sensia 100

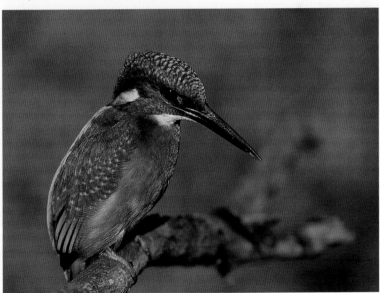

Kingfisher preparing to dive
By concealing yourself in a hide it's possible to observe and photograph animals and birds over a period of time, often from relatively close range.
Camera Canon EOS 1V Lens 100–400mm zoom at 400mm Film Fujichrome Sensia 400

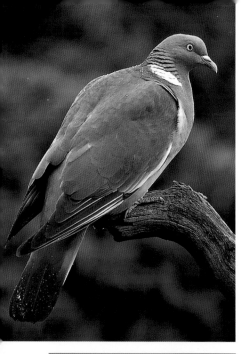

Wood pigeon
To get this excellent shot the photographer baited a branch with food to attract birds then waited inside his house with a telezoom lens.
Camera Canon EOS 1V Lens 100-400mm zoom at 400mm Film Fujichrome Sensia 100

Q Are there any laws about the photographing of animals and birds that I need to be aware of?

Certain species of animals and birds are protected by law, and it is an offence to photograph them at or near their nest or breeding site without a licence. If you would like further information about this, birdwatching and animal welfare groups are a good first port of call.

Q What's the easiest way to photograph garden birds without scaring them away?

There are various options, though the one you choose will depend upon the type of birds you want to photograph and the kind of equipment you have.

By far the easiest is to scatter food close to a window, then take your pictures through it while hiding behind the curtains. If you erect a perch from an old branch you can position it in the perfect spot to give you a clear view. All you have to do then is bait it with food for a few days so the birds become accustomed to it. The long lens of a telezoom should be powerful enough to give frame-filling pictures.

If you don't have a long enough lens for this you could mount your camera on a tripod, position it close to the perch and focus on the area where the birds land. You can then watch from indoors, and when any birds appear, trip the camera's shutter with an electronic or air release.

The main problem with this method is that it's rather hit-and-miss because you can't see through the camera's viewfinder. Also, unless your camera is fitted with a motor drive, you'll have to wind on the film manually after each shot, and this noise will frighten the birds away.

Finally, if you've got a big garden there's nothing to stop you erecting a semi-permanent hide close to the feeding site. After a while the birds will get used to it, so you can nip in and out whenever the opportunity arises.

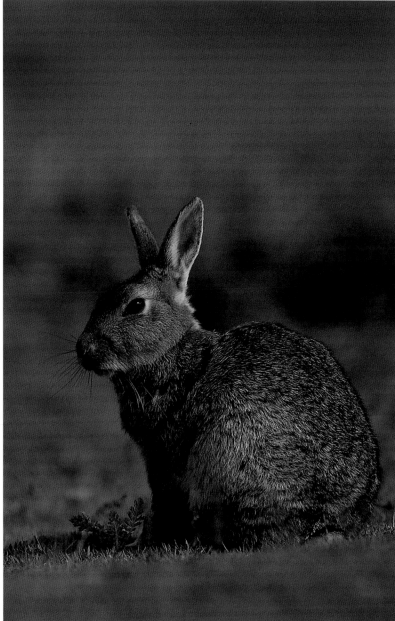

Wild rabbit
Stalking requires great dedication and patience, but the rewards make it well worth the effort – as this excellent picture shows.
Camera Canon EOS 1N Lens 300mm plus 1.4x teleconverter Film Kodachrome 200

Could you give me some advice on stalking wild animals such as deer and foxes?

Stalking is perhaps the most challenging approach to wildlife photography. Like a hunter you follow signs and clues that an animal is in the area, then get as close to it as possible without being spotted until you can take a successful picture.

This can be an incredibly exciting experience because you're working on your basic instincts; looking, listening, creeping through the undergrowth, knowing that one false move or one snapped twig could spell disaster because your subject will sense you long before you catch a glimpse of it and disappear from view in a flash.

Stalking tends to be used for larger animals, such as deer, but it is only really viable when you definitely know there's wildlife about. It can also be a very time-consuming business that demands a great deal of patience and care and often results in disappointment.

In terms of equipment, you need to travel as light as possible so you can move quietly and quickly without being seen or heard. One SLR body fitted with a long telephoto lens – 400mm, 500mm or 600mm is ideal – will take care of the hardware. A monopod or beanbag should be used to support the lens, while film and accessories can be carried in your jacket pockets.

To reduce the risk of your quarry seeing you, drab or camouflaged clothing should always be worn, along with a hat to disguise your head. You should also avoid wearing aftershave, deodorant or any kind of scent, as its smell will be picked up by your prey from a great distance, and remove any jewellery as it not only makes a noise but can reflect light that will disturb any animals in the area. Also, stay downwind of your quarry otherwise your presence will be detected very quickly.

Finally, disguise the aluminium legs on your tripod or monopod with camouflaged tape, and cover any chrome areas on your camera body with black masking tape to prevent reflections from startling any animals in the area.

Once your subject is in view, use tree stumps or foliage as a barrier so it can't see you, and sight it up in the camera's viewfinder. All you have to do then is wait for an opportune moment, and when it arises, fire away.

EQUIPMENT FOR CLOSE-UPS

There are various items of equipment that are specially designed for close-up photography. Here's a rundown of the most common.

Zoom lenses If you check your zoom you may find it has a close-up facility. Usually this gives a reproduction ratio up to 1:4 (one-quarter lifesize), so you can fill the viewfinder of your SLR with subjects around the size of a credit card.

Supplementary close-up lenses These screw to the front of your lens like filters, and reduce its minimum focusing distance. The power is measured in dioptres – usually +1, +2, +3, +4 and +10. The bigger the number, the greater the magnification. For best results, use them on prime lenses rather than zooms – 50mm is ideal.

Reversing rings These allow you to mount a lens on your camera the wrong way round so it will focus very close. Generally, by doing this you lose all electronic and mechanical linkage between the camera and lens, so the metering system and automatic aperture stopdown won't function, but there are one or two adaptors that maintain all camera functions. Image quality is high and reproduction ratios of lifesize and above are possible.

Extension tubes These are metal tubes that fit between the lens and camera body, increasing the lens-to-film distance so greater image magnification is possible. Tubes normally come in sets of three, each a different size so you can obtain various reproduction ratios. When the length of extension matches the focal length of the lens, the reproduction ratio obtained is 1:1 (lifesize). So 50mm of extension with a 50mm standard lens will give lifesize images and 100mm of extension with a 50mm lens will give 2:1 (2 x lifesize) reproduction.

Bellows These work in the same way as extension tubes, but they're adjustable so you can obtain intermediate reproduction ratios. They also allow greater extension – often up to 150mm, which gives a reproduction ratio of 3x with a 50mm standard lens. Ideally, bellows should be used on a tripod. It's also worth buying a focusing rail, which allows you to fine-tune the focusing once the tripod is in position. Some bellows units are available that maintain all camera functions including TTL metering and autofocus. You can buy bellows for medium-format as well as 35mm cameras.

Macro lens (see Lenses, page 21).

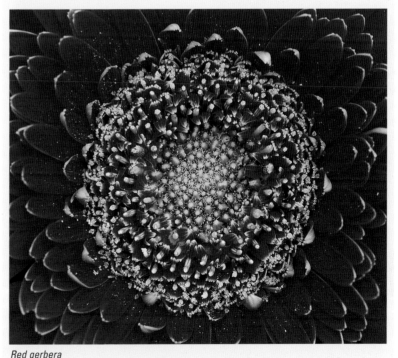

Red gerbera
This colourful close-up was taken using a 105mm macro lens, which enabled the photographer to achieve a reproduction ration of lifesize (1:1).
Camera Nikon F90x Lens Nikkor 105mm macro Film Fujichrome Sensia 100

Q What does reproduction ratio mean in close-up photography?

This term refers to the real size of your subject compared to its size on a piece of film. If you work at a reproduction ratio of 1:1, or lifesize, a subject measuring 20mm in real life will be 20mm on a 35mm slide or negative. At a ratio of 1:2, or half lifesize, it will measure 10mm on film, at 1:4 it will measure 5mm, and so on.

If you're working at ratios greater than lifesize your subject will be bigger on film than it is in real life. At a ratio of 2:1, for example, a subject measuring 10mm will measure 20mm on a 35mm piece of film.

Q What kind of subjects make good close-up pictures?

More or less anything can make a good close-up. Most nature photographers shoot close-ups because there's an infinite number of subjects waiting to be captured, including butterflies, bees, dragonflies, small mammals and insects.

You need to be very quiet and patient when photographing live subjects though, as they're easily frightened away by the slightest movement or sound. Always move slowly and carefully. Another good tip is to remember to avoid casting your shadow over the subject.

Nature is also full of beautiful patterns and textures that can be revealed if you move in close. The veins and cells in backlit leaves, ice crystals, the delicate colours of flowers and the rough surface of bark or lichen-covered stone are a few examples.

Q Sometimes my close-ups come out too dark. Do I need to increase the exposure?

That depends upon the equipment you're using. Close-up lenses and reversing rings require no exposure increases because they do not cause a light loss, so you can use the exposure your light meter suggests. However, close-up attachments such as extension tubes, bellows and macro lenses do cause a light loss that must be compensated for.

If your camera has TTL (through-the-lens) metering, as the majority of SLRs do, then any exposure increase will be taken into account automatically. If not, the exposure suggested must be increased before the picture is taken.

The table left shows the amount of exposure increase required when working at different reproduction ratios, though it is a good idea to bracket as well.

Reproduction ratio	Exposure factor	Exposure increase (in stops)
1:10	x1.2	⅓
1:5	x1.4	½
1:2.5	x2	1
1:2	x2.3	1⅓
1:1	x4	2
1.4:1	x5.8	2½
1.8:1	x7.8	3
2:1	x9	3⅓
2.4:1	x11.6	3½
3:1	x16	4

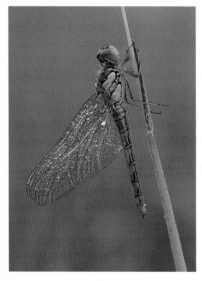

Dragonfly
Depth of field is limited at close focusing distances so you need to focus very carefully on your main subject and stop the lens down to a small aperture – in this case the photographer shot at f/16 but the background was still thrown completely out of focus.
Camera Canon EOS 1N Lens 100mm macro Film Fujichrome Sensia 100

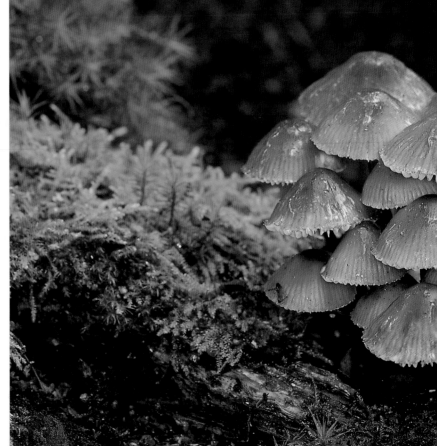

Q Whenever I take close-up pictures hardly anything comes out sharply focused. Why's that?

Because depth of field is almost non-existent at close focusing distances. You should therefore use the smallest lens aperture possible – usually f/16 or f/22 – to maximize what little depth of field there is. Careful focusing on the most important part of your subject is also vital, as you may find that only part of it is sharply recorded.

Unfortunately, using small lens apertures leads to slow shutter speeds being required, especially if you're using slow ISO50 or ISO100 film. This makes a tripod essential if you're to avoid camera shake. The shutter should also be tripped using a cable release, and if possible your camera's reflex mirror locked up as an extra precaution, to reduce vibrations. Alternatively, use electronic flash.

Fungi family
Often you find that light levels are low when shooting close-ups – especially in shady woodland. Combined with the need for a small lens aperture this makes long exposures necessary – in this case 4sec – so a sturdy tripod is essential.
Camera Canon EOS 1N Lens 100mm macro
Film Fujichrome Velvia 50

USING FLASH FOR CLOSE-UPS

The easiest way to overcome the problems of poor light and long exposures when shooting close-ups is by lighting your subject with a burst of electronic flash. Not only does this allow you to work at small apertures to maximize depth of field, but the brief burst of light will freeze any subject movement too.

If you own a dedicated flashgun you may find it will give perfectly exposed results automatically when used at close focusing distances – check the instruction book for details on how close it can be used in TTL flash mode. Special ringflash units are also available for close-up photography which fit to the front of your lens and have a circular tube surrounding it to provide even, shadowless illumination.

However, most photographers prefer to use one or two manual flashguns fitted to a special bracket and calculate the aperture required to give correct exposure.

This is done using the formula below:

$$\text{aperture} = \frac{\text{guide number (m/ISO100)}}{\text{flash-to-subject distance (m)} \times \text{(magnification + 1)}}$$

So if your flashgun has a guide number of 20, the flash-to-subject distance is 60cm, and the magnification is 0.5x (a reproduction ratio of 1:2, or half lifesize),

the aperture required is:
20/0.6 x (0.5+1) = 20/0.9 = 22.22, or when rounded up, f/22.

This aperture is correct for ISO100 film, so if you're using a different film speed it must be adjusted accordingly to prevent under- or overexposure. For ISO50 film set automatically to f/16, for ISO25 film set f/11, and for ISO200 film set f/32.

By using this formula for a range of common flash-to-subject distances, you can produce an exposure table and tape it to your flashgun.

In terms of flash position, ideally the gun should be taken off your camera's hotshoe and held closer to the lens so your subject will be evenly lit. Special brackets are available for this, and allow two guns to be used – one either side of the lens.

Finally, as you'll be using the flash from close range, low-output guns with a guide number of around 20 (m/ISO100) are powerful enough.

Tree frog
Electronic flash is an invaluable ally for the serious close-up photographer, and today's dedicated flash units make it easier than ever to achieve perfect results time after time.
Camera Canon EOS 1N Lens 100mm macro
Film Fujichrome Sensia 100

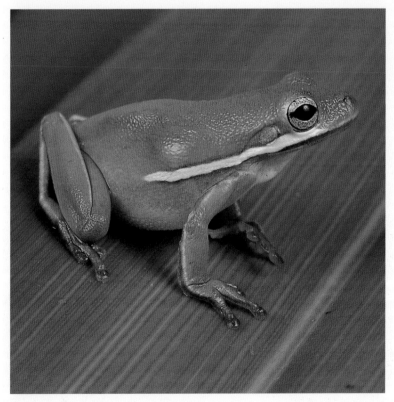

Architecture

Architecture is one of the most accessible subjects available. Everywhere you go you'll find buildings in all sizes, shapes, colours and designs presenting an endless range of photo opportunities. Even the houses on your street can be the source of excellent pictures.

The aim of the architectural photographer, like the landscape photographer, is to capture the character of the subject through careful composition and use of light. An understanding of architectural style is therefore useful, just as knowing something about a portrait subject will help you record their personality. Technical perfection is taken for granted. Buildings are static, so there's no reason why you shouldn't spend hours, even days, searching for the best viewpoint, or waiting for conditions to be right before taking a picture.

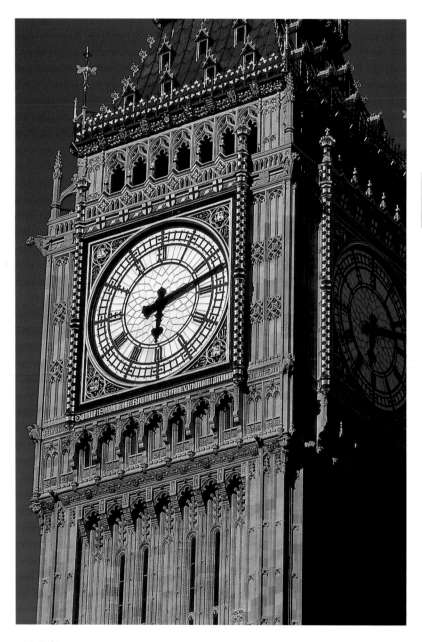

Big Ben, London, England
Early morning and late afternoon are often the best periods for architectural photography – not only is the light warm, but it strikes the building from a low angle, casting texture-revealing shadows. This shot was taken during early evening, and you can see how the light brings out the character of the mellow stonework.
Camera Nikon F5 Lens 80–200mm zoom
Filter Polarizer Film Fujichrome Velvia 50

Q When is the best time of day to photograph buildings?

The quality of light falling on your subject building influences both its physical appearance and atmosphere, so the timing of your photographic shoot must be given plenty of thought.

Professional architectural photographers regularly check the weather forecast so they know what kind of weather to expect. Maps and plans are also studied to establish where the light will be in relation to the building at different times of day – in some cases the light is perfect for only a few days each year.

Different types of buildings also suit different forms of light. Old structures tend to look their best during late afternoon, when warm sunlight makes the stonework glow. The beauty of modern architecture, on the other hand, is shown in brighter, crisper light, when blue sky can be used as a backdrop and the strong lines are fully revealed. Reflections can also be captured in glass-fronted buildings when the facade is in shade and the sun is bearing down on buildings opposite.

Dull, overcast weather tends to be unsuitable as the soft light hides texture and reduces depth, while the harsh light of midday is avoided because it causes contrast problems. That's not to say you should always stick to ideal conditions, of course. Harsh sunlight can work well if you are trying to create a bold, abstract image, while misty dawn light is perfect for adding mood to pictures of old buildings.

The appearance of a building is also changed dramatically once daylight fades. Tall buildings look stunning with the last rays of sunlight glancing across their facade, and once artificial illumination takes over at night you can produce excellent pictures of all types of buildings, from the local café to majestic cityscapes.

Q Whenever I photograph buildings they always appear to be toppling over. How can I avoid this?

The problem you're referring to, known as converging verticals, is common in architectural photography. It's caused when you try to photograph a tall building from close range, and are forced to tilt the camera up to include the whole structure in the shot. By tilting the camera, the vertical sides of the building appear to lean inwards, and in some cases this gives the appearance that the building is about to fall over on top of you.

To avoid converging verticals you must keep the back of the camera and the film plane parallel to the front of the subject building. This is best done using a shift or perspective control (PC) lens, which has an adjustable front element that can be moved up to include the top of the building without tilting the camera (see Lenses, page 21). Other options include:

- Backing off until you can include the whole building without tilting the camera. This usually gives you lots of empty foreground space, which can be filled with a colourful flower bed, path or gateway, for example.
- Shooting from a higher viewpoint so you're looking straight across at the building rather than up at it. Often, standing on a wall or stepladder will provide enough height. If not, there may be a suitable building opposite.
- Shooting from further away with a telephoto lens, so you don't have to tilt the camera so much and the effect of converging verticals is minimized.

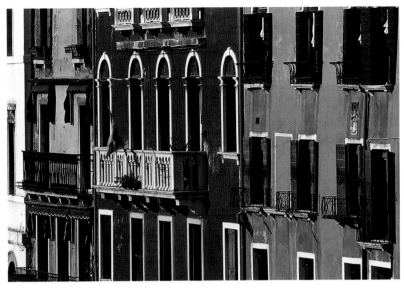

Venice, Italy
Though wide-angle lenses are often first choice for architectural photography, a telephoto or telezoom lens is also invaluable for filling the frame and compressing perspective to create dramatic compositions.
Camera Nikon F90x Lens 80–200mm zoom Filter Polarizer Film Fujichrome Velvia 50

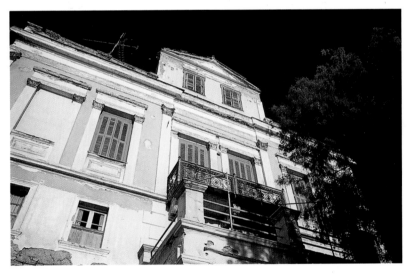

Aegina, Greek Islands
When converging verticals can't be avoided, your best bet is to exaggerate them by moving in close to the subject building and shooting it through a wide-angle lens, so the vertical sides lean dramatically.
Camera Olympus OM2n Lens 21mm Filter Polarizer Film Fujichrome RFP50

Q Which lenses are most suited to architectural photography?

Most architectural photographers prefer wide-angle lenses, simply because they allow large buildings to be captured from relatively close range. They also give you plenty of control over the composition – foreground interest or frames can be included, and slight changes of viewpoint can totally change the feel of the shot. For general use a 28mm or 35mm lens is ideal, while an ultra-wide 17mm or 20mm lens is ideal for creating dramatic perspective.

Don't ignore your telephoto or telezoom lenses though. Focal lengths from 80 to 200mm are perfect for isolating interesting architectural details, such as the gargoyles on a church, or the pattern of windows in an office block. Telephotos can also be used to take dramatic pictures of distant buildings, or to fill the frame with city skylines and compress perspective.

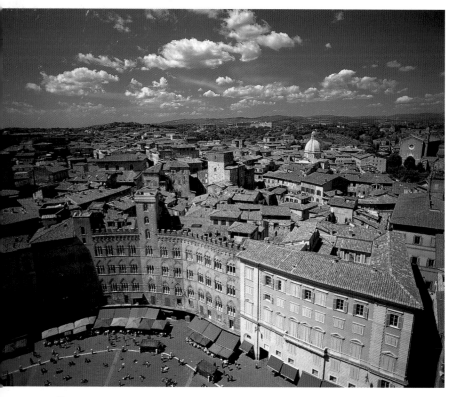

Siena, Italy
Shooting from a higher or lower viewpoint than usual can produce stunning results because it gives us an alternative perspective. In this case I shot from the small window of a tower so I was able to include both the square below and the town's terracotta rooftops.
Camera Pentax 67 Lens 45mm Filter Polarizer Film Fujichrome Velvia 50

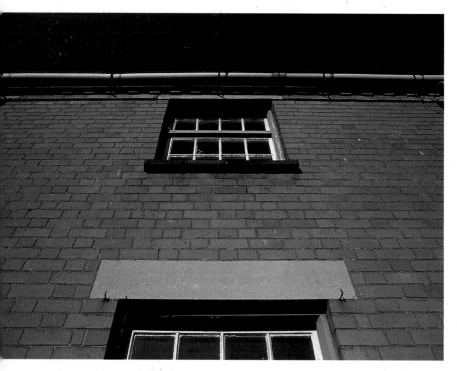

Bozeat, Northamptonshire, England
A polarizer is the most useful filter for architectural photography – here it saturated the colour of the bright red brickwork, and deepened the blue sky overhead.
Camera Olympus OM4-Ti Lens 28mm Filter Polarizer Film Fujichrome Velvia 50

Q When I photograph buildings, they're always partially obscured by shade. What do you suggest?

This is a common problem in built-up areas. Usually the shadows of buildings opposite are cast across the one you're trying to photograph for most of the day, causing problems with contrast. It's only when the sun's almost overhead that you get a clear view. The trouble is, by that time – around midday – the light's too harsh.

Your best bet is to photograph the building during early morning or late afternoon, when it's completely in shade and contrast levels are more manageable.

Q What's the best viewpoint to photograph buildings from?

The best viewpoint is the one that captures a building at its most impressive, and that can only be discovered by spending time looking from all angles.

Buildings shot square-on look attractive, but the lack of depth tends to produce rather flat results. To avoid this, and give an impression of three dimensions, move towards one corner so the side as well as the facade is revealed. Shooting from a very high or low angle can also work well, as it presents a view we're not used to seeing from eye-level.

When you're wandering around, look for other features that can be included to make the composition more attractive – such as the overhanging branches of a tree, pillars and gate posts, flower beds and ponds or lakes that may include a reflection of the subject buildings.

Q Which filters are best for architectural photography?

A polarizer is invaluable for saturating colour, deepening blue sky and removing unwanted reflection from windows. You'll also find an 81A or 81B warm-up useful for enhancing warm sunlight to make buildings glow, and neutral density graduates for reducing contrast between the sky and your subject building.

For interior shots it's worth using 80A and 80B blue filters, to balance the orange cast from tungsten lighting, and an FLD filter to balance the green cast from fluorescents.

Q **Are architectural details worth photographing?**

If you look closely at a building you'll see many different architectural details, from the steel and concrete frames of modern architecture, to the fluted columns and ornate cornices of older structures.

In a wide-angle shot these details tend to get lost against the sheer size of the whole building, but when captured in isolation they come to life and create excellent pictures in their own right. Modern architecture is full of patterns and abstracts due to the repetitious design, while older stone buildings reveal wonderful textures, colours and magnificent examples of stone masonry that have withstood centuries of exposure to the elements.

So in answer to the question, yes, architectural details are worth photographing, and make a perfect 'theme' to help improve your eye for a picture.

Marrakech, Morocco
Architectural details are just as interesting photographically as entire buildings.
Camera Nikon F90x Lens 80–200mm zoom
Film Fujichrome Velvia 50

Q **I'd like to take some pictures of the town I live in. Where's the best place to shoot from?**

Town and cityscapes always look their best when they are captured from a high viewpoint, so you can include large areas and lots of detail in the frame – shooting from ground level is limiting because often you can't see beyond the first row of buildings and this doesn't make for particularly interesting photographs.

If you look around there's bound to be a high viewpoint somewhere. I suggest you try the top floor of the multi-storey car park, a nearby hillside, the tower of your local church, or a bridge. Failing that, you could try asking permission to shoot from the window of a local office block.

As long as you get a high enough viewpoint and use the rules of composition you should be able to take striking photos that capture the spirit of the place you live.

INTERIORS

Photographing interiors is far trickier than photographing exteriors. More often than not you have limited space, low light levels, and artificial illumination that presents problems with colour casts.

The first problem can be overcome by using a wide-angle lens. Usually a 24mm or 28mm lens should do the trick, but in small buildings a 20mm or even 17mm will be better. Make sure you compose the shot carefully to avoid converging verticals – stand on a chair or stepladder if necessary.

Low light levels dictate that a tripod is almost always essential if you want to use slow film for optimum image quality. Unfortunately, few stately homes and castles allow the use of tripods, so you'll have to find some other form of support – some people carry a pocket tripod and rest it on a step or banister. Flash isn't a viable solution as your gun won't be powerful enough to cover the whole interior. Flashguns tend to be banned anyway in such places, as they distract other visitors.

In old buildings the lighting is also uneven. Small windows and artificial sources are only effective over limited areas, so you end up with bright highlights and deep shadows, and the contrast is too high for your film to record fully. The only way to overcome this is by taking a meter reading from the extremes of brightness, then using the average of the two as a compromise. Alternatively, light the dark areas with flash if possible. Where a building is lit by daylight only it's a good idea to shoot on an overcast day, when contrast is lower.

Modern buildings don't suffer from this problem as the interior lighting is better. Artificial sources tend to be used, so you must filter the light to prevent colour casts on daylight film (see Filters, page 26).

When there's a mixture of light sources, such as tungsten and fluorescent, shoot on colour negative film so the colour balance can be controlled at the printing stage.

Tangier, Morocco
The interior of this hotel was well lit thanks to large windows allowing lots of daylight to flood in. Care was still taken to avoid dark corners, though, and I bracketed exposures to ensure I came away with a successful picture.
Camera Nikon F90x Lens 20mm
Film Fujichrome Velvia 50

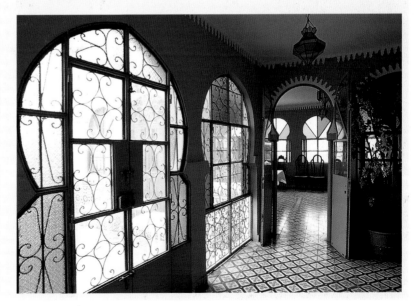

Still lifes

It may not offer the excitement of action, the cunning of candids or the scale of landscapes, but still-life photography is a challenging and highly rewarding subject that really tests your creativity, imagination and technical skills to the limit.

What makes still life different from other disciplines is that you can't just point a camera and fire away. Before a picture can be taken you must first find suitable objects, create a pleasing composition and carefully light them to bring out their aesthetic appeal. Firing your camera's shutter is the last step in a process that can take anything from a few minutes to several days.

To many photographers this seems like a waste of valuable time, but the satisfaction to be gained from producing a successful still life is immense, simply because you have total control over every stage of the process, from start to finish.

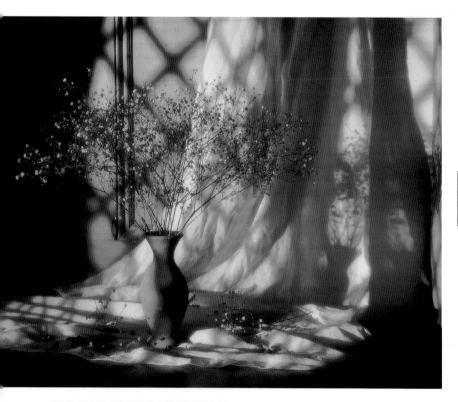

Gypsophelia and Muslin
This atmospheric still life was inspired by the golden light and shadow pattern being cast on an old door in my former home. I knew it would make a great backdrop for a still life, so I pushed a table against the door, draped a sheet of muslin, then placed the vase of dried flowers on the table. To complete the effect, the picture was taken through a soft-focus filter to add mood.
Camera Pentax 67 Lens 105mm
Filter Soft-focus Film Fujichrome Velvia 50

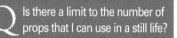

Q Is there a limit to the number of props that I can use in a still life?

No, but you must be able to justify the presence of each item, otherwise they shouldn't be included. It's easy to overcomplicate a composition by adding more and more props, but this usually creates a confusing clutter rather than a pleasing picture.

The solution is to keep things simple and take it slowly. Start off with an empty table and one or two key props, then add more and vary their position in relation to one another until you come up with a pleasing, balanced composition – sometimes you may only need one or two items.

Don't worry if the composition looks a little gappy – the space between the props is as important as the props themselves in terms of the overall visual balance of the shot, so avoid trying to fill every vacant space with something else. Often one or two objects in plenty of space can produce superb results.

Finally, try to make your compositions look natural and lifelike, rather than being too ordered and tidy. There's nothing wrong with continuing the still life outside the

Q I'd love to try photographing still lifes, but can't think of any good ideas. Any suggestions?

For many photographers, finding suitable props for still-life photography is a major stumbling block, but a quick search around your home will reveal a broad range of interesting subjects.

Something as ordinary as a bowl of fruit or a pile of fresh vegetables can be turned into interesting pictures with a little thought. Then there are ornaments, cutlery,

clocks and watches, old bottles, rusty tools, gardening implements and so on. Collections are also ideal, whether they're stamps, seashells, coins, postcards, war medals, candlesticks, or model planes. Alternatively you could devise a theme, such as Christmas, the swinging sixties, your favourite colour or a specific shape, then look around for suitable objects.

The key is to look at simple objects in terms of their colours, textures and shapes, rather than what they really are. By doing this you'll find it's possible to turn almost anything into a successful still life.

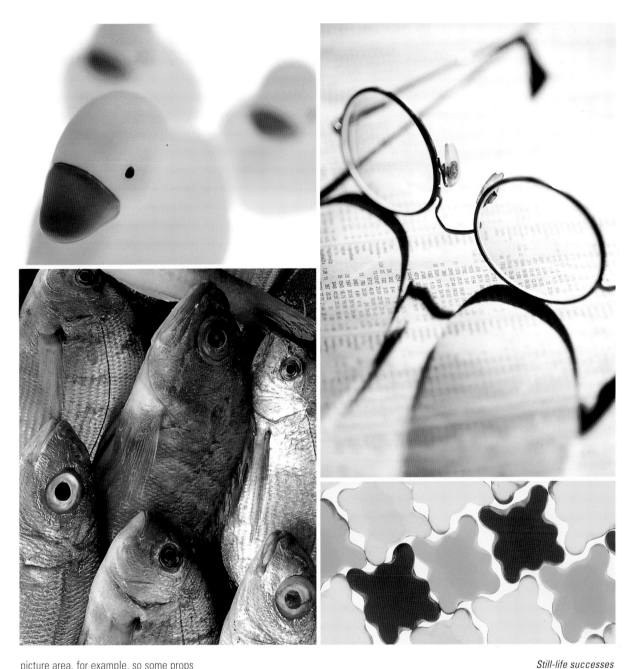

Still-life successes
Successful still-life pictures can be created using anything – you just need imagination.
The fish were shot on a market stall in Morocco; the ducks and sweets were placed on a
lightbox; while the spectacles were lit with a projector so long shadows were cast.
Camera Nikon F90x Lens 50mm and 105mm macro Film Fujichrome Velvia 50

picture area, for example, so some props are cut off at the frame edges. This tends to produce better results than a still life that fits perfectly into the camera's viewfinder, because it adds intrigue.

Q What special equipment do I need to photograph still lifes?

A great advantage of still lifes is that you can create professional results with the minimum of equipment – a simple, manual 35mm SLR and standard zoom is all you need to get started, plus a macro lens or close-up attachment for small objects.

The only other major items required are a tripod to keep your camera steady and in position, plus a cable release to prevent camera shake when using long exposures. Reflectors are invaluable for bouncing the light around to fill in shadows or create highlights on certain props. Make them in different sizes from sheets of white card and polystyrene, silver foil stuck to card, or small mirrors that can be precisely angled

to bounce light around or direct on to specific areas to create highlights.

In terms of film, most photographers stick to slow materials of ISO50–100 for still lifes as they offer optimum image quality and resolution of fine detail. But don't be afraid to try out faster film of ISO1000 or above – the coarse grain and softer colours can produce beautiful images when used on suitable subjects.

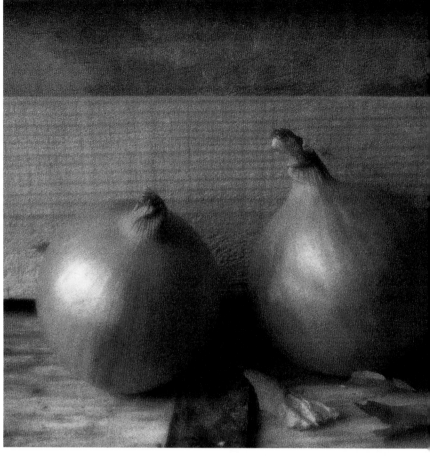

Trio of onions
You can make a background for still lifes from literally anything. In this case I wanted something neutral that would add to the rustic feel of the picture, so I used the side of an old wooden crate.
Camera Olympus OM4-Ti Lens 50mm
Film Agfachrome 1000RS

Q What kind of things make good backgrounds for still lifes?

That depends on your subject more than anything else. If you want to keep things as simple as possible a sheet of black card or velvet will provide an uncluttered backdrop that emphasizes the shape of sleek, shiny objects. White backgrounds are also ideal when you want a very clean, crisp feel.

For a more rustic, textured feel try using an old tarpaulin or canvas sheet, or make your own textured background by painting canvas or a cotton sheet with emulsion.

For still-life shots of small objects all kinds of materials can be used. Black perspex is ideal if you want to produce clean reflections, while oiled slate works well with shiny things because its texture emphasizes the smoothness of the props.

A pile of bricks, an old door covered in peeling paint, the back of a leather jacket or rusting corrugated metal sheet are other materials worth considering.

Queen of hearts
A slide projector can be a versatile source of light for still lifes as the projector can be positioned anywhere in relation to your props. I often place slides in the projector as well, to add colour and patterns to the light.
Camera Nikon F90x Lens 105mm macro Film Fujichrome Sensia II 100

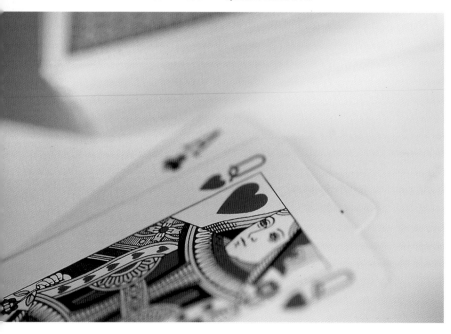

Q I'm unsure about the best lighting to use for still lifes. Could you advise me?

The type of lighting used for a still life not only determines the overall mood of the shot, but also how well the shapes of the objects are revealed, how strong the colours look, and if texture is visible.

As a starting point, the daylight flooding in through the windows of your home is ideal. All you have to do is position a table next to a large window, then erect a background sweep from card or canvas and arrange your still life on it.

Shoot during late afternoon and warm, low-angle side-lighting will cast long shadows that reveal texture and form in the props. The soft light of an overcast day is also ideal if you want a more delicate effect, and can be controlled using reflectors to bounce the light around.

An alternative source of light is your portable flashgun. If you connect the gun to your camera with a sync lead it can be

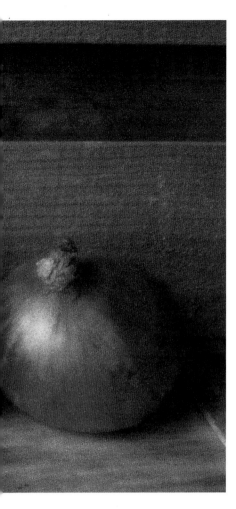

FOUND STILL LIFES

If you don't fancy the idea of taking a selection of objects and turning them into an interesting composition, another approach is to photograph things as you find them in situ.

Found still lifes can consist of virtually anything: pebbles and seashells on the beach, autumn leaves and fir cones beneath a tree, a pair of old boots on the garage floor, crushed tin cans by the side of the road, an old car overgrown by weeds, fishing tackle laid out on the riverbank, piles of plant pots behind the greenhouse... If you keep your eyes peeled while you're wandering around you'll come across all kinds of things.

Usually found still lifes are photographed using natural daylight. However, it's worth carrying a reflector in your gadget bag to bounce light into the shadows and produce more attractive results. Fill-in flash can also be used for the same purpose. When composing the picture, don't worry about whether or not the subject is actually identifiable, and don't be afraid to move objects around in the composition if it will produce a better picture.

Old plant pots
I found these plant pots, exactly as you see them here, in the greenhouse of an abandoned market garden. Even better, they were positioned close to a window where lots of diffuse light was flooding in from the overcast sky outside. This provided perfect illumination, and all I had to do was take the picture.
Camera Mamiya C220 TLR Lens 80mm
Film Fujichrome RDP100

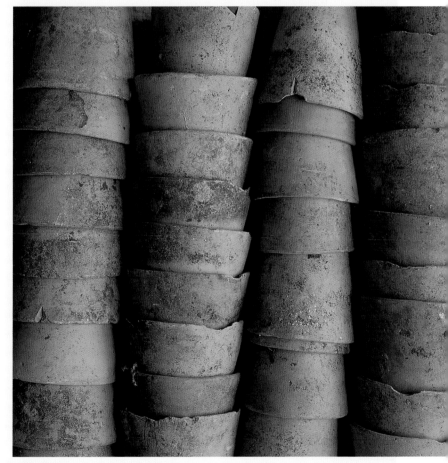

used in any position around the props. You need to soften and spread the light to produce attractive results though. This can be done either by firing it through a diffusion screen made from tracing paper, or bouncing it off a reflector.

Frontal light is ideal for revealing the colour of an object, but because shadows fall behind it the results can easily look flat, so it's best avoided for anything other than straight 'pack' shots. When you want to reveal texture and modelling, move the light to the side more, so that shadows become an integral part of the shot – with the light coming from 90 degrees, a dramatic half-light, half-shade effect will be produced that looks highly effective.

Top-lighting is another popular technique used by still-life photographers. The light is diffused using a large softbox known as a 'fish fryer' or 'swimming pool', which is suspended above the set – you could make one by stapling several sheets of tracing paper to a wooden frame. To avoid shadows, stand the props on white card so the light is reflected upwards.

Finally, your flashgun can be used to paint the still life with light. All you do is fit a paper cone to your gun so a narrow beam of light is produced, then selectively light different parts by firing the gun several times. This must be done in a dark room with your camera set to B (bulb).

A torch can be used in a similar way to the flashgun, and is capable of producing some beautiful lighting effects. As the light from a torch is constant you can also see what you're doing, and you can shine it on some areas of the still life for longer than others to vary the effect.

Special effects

Photography, like painting, is a medium that's open to infinite experimentation. Most of the time you'll use traditional techniques to produce successful images, but when the creative bug bites there are also many alternative methods waiting to be explored. You can create unusual images in-camera, in the darkroom, in your computer or using existing pictures. You can add subtle effects to enhance a picture, combine images to produce unusual multiple exposures, or completely defy reality and bring your wildest fantasies to life.

Whichever route you take, special-effects photography is a fascinating subject that will provide hours of fun and inspiration. Here are just a few of the techniques worth trying.

Q What happens if you process a of film in the wrong chemicals?

Normally the consequences of this act can be disastrous, but in recent years it has become common practice among portrait and fashion photographers as a means of creating unusual effects.

The two most common approaches are to process colour slide film as colour negative film in C-41 chemicals, so you actually obtain colour negatives from which prints can be made, or to process colour negative film as slide film in E-6 chemicals so you obtain colour slides.

Cross-processing slide film gives the most striking results – contrast and colour saturation are increased and some colours are totally transformed, depending on the film. Fujichrome Velvia, Provia and Sensia, and Agfachrome RSX II 100 are popular, but you can cross-process any slide film.

When print film is cross-processed the effect is completely different. Contrast is reduced so images look rather flat and the images usually have a dominant colour cast such as green or blue, depending on the film. This can look effective, but only on bold subjects.

If you want to cross-process slide film, rate it at the manufacturer's recommended

ISO as any exposure error can be corrected at the printing stage. However, cross-processing colour negative film tends to cause a loss of speed, so you usually need to underrate it to compensate. As a starting point, try rating ISO100 slide film at ISO25, and bracket the exposures to make sure some of the shots are perfect. Push-processing the film by one or two stops can also make a difference to the final results.

Most important of all is that you give the processing lab clear instructions so they know how to process the film. To avoid confusion, stick a label on the film cassette saying 'C-41 process', or 'E-6 process', and explain what you've done.

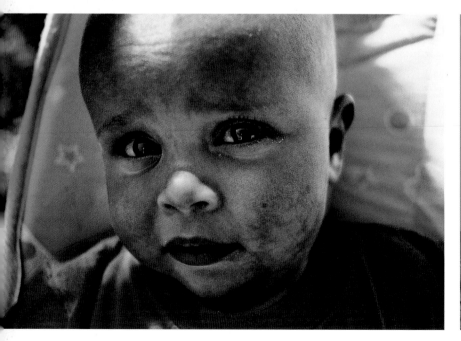

Ruis
Here's a good example of the results you can expect if you cross-process colour slide film then have prints made from the negatives.
Camera Nikon F90x Lens 28mm Film Agfachrome RSX II 100

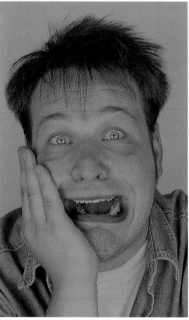

Damon
Cross-processing colour negative film also gives interesting results.
Camera Nikon F90x Lens 105mm macro Film Fuji Reala

Q I've heard of a technique where you can reveal stress patterns in plastic. How is it done?

This simple technique, known as cross-polarization works on the basis that if you place a plastic object between two polarizing filters or polarizing materials, any stress patterns in it will be revealed as vibrant colours. You can't see them with the naked eye, but when you peer through your camera's viewfinder they hit you straight between the eyes, and you can capture them on film to create colourful abstract shots.

Any clear plastic objects can be used for cross-polarization. The set squares, rulers and protractors in a kids' school geometry set are ideal. So are clear filter boxes, plastic party cups, clear medicine spoons, strips of sticky tape, pieces of stretched and torn polythene bag and so on.

If you have two polarizing filters and a slide projector you can give the technique a try. All you need to do is set up your slide projector so the lens is pointing upwards and fit a polarizing filter to it. Next, set up a sheet of glass 30cm (12in) or so above the projector and place a plastic object on the glass. All you have to do then is set up your camera over the object with a second polarizer attached to the camera lens.

Now for the clever bit. With the room in darkness and the projector turned on, peer through your viewfinder and slowly rotate the polarizer on the lens. As you do this you will see vibrant colours appear in the plastic object wherever it has been subjected to stress. This effect is a bit like a kaleidoscope – the colours and patterns change as you rotate the polarizer. When you're happy with the effect, stop rotating the polarizer and take the picture.

A much better approach is to use a lightbox and a sheet of polarizing gel. This is basically a flexible gel, like polyester studio lighting gel, but it does the same job as a normal polarizing filter. Photo dealers tend to stock it, in sheets around A4 size, 21x29.7cm (8½x12in), which is ideal.

All you do is place this gel on your lightbox, hold the corners in place with sticky tape, then position your plastic objects on top of it. The polarizer gel becomes the background to the picture, and any areas not covered by plastic objects come out pure black, which makes the pictures even more striking.

To get the effect you do exactly the same as outlined above – turn off the room lights, turn the lightbox on, then rotate the polarizer on your lens until you're happy with the effect.

A 35mm SLR is the ideal camera for cross-polarization as it gives you direct viewing through the lens so you can judge the effect with precision, and you can use the integral metering system to ensure correct exposure.

Cross-polarization
These two striking shots show the results of cross polarization to highlight stress patterns in plastic that are invisible to the human eye.
Camera Nikon F90x Lens 105mm macro
Film Fujichrome Velvia 50

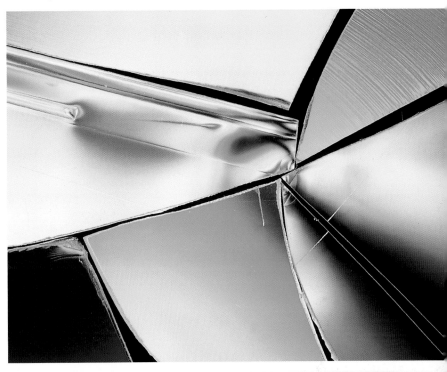

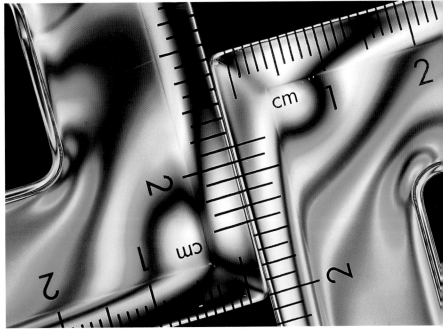

Red gerbera
This set of pictures illustrates how you can
add grain effects to existing colour slides –
both of the techniques discussed produce
good results and are very easy to use.
Camera Nikon F90x Lens 105mm macro
Film Fujichrome Sensia II 100

TOP *Original picture, no grain*
MIDDLE *Grain added digitally*
BOTTOM *Grain added by projection*

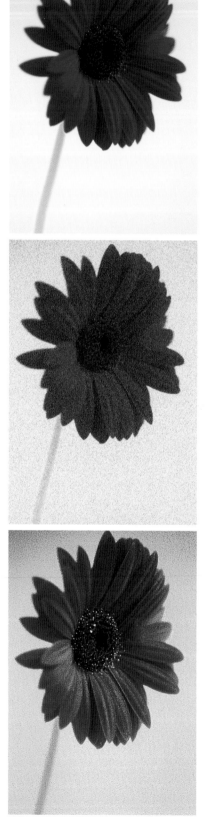

Q | **I want to add a grainy effect to some of my colour slides. Is there an easy way to do this?**

The easiest way to do anything these days is digitally, and if you have access to a computer you can add a wide range of grain effects in a matter of seconds and experiment until you have what you want.

Having scanned your photograph, open it in Adobe Photoshop then simply select Filter>Texture>Grain and play around with the sliders to vary the grain and contrast – for the picture shown here, regular grain was use. Another option is to select Filter>Noise>Add Noise and again vary the controls.

If you don't have access to a computer, a great way to add grain is by projecting your chosen slides onto a sheet of white sandpaper (Aluminium Oxide paper, available from car repair shops) then re-photographing it back onto colour slide film so the new image shows the grainy texture of the paper.

The sheets of paper are quite small, so you will need a close-focusing zoom or a close-up attachment (see page 125) to fill the frame.

The coarseness of the paper varies, so experiment with different grades. You will also need a blue 80A filter to balance the projector bulb for daylight-balanced slide film, otherwise your pictures will come out with a yellow/orange colour cast.

A third option is to have a large-format duplicate – 5x4in is ideal – made from the original 35mm slide. This will make the grain much coarser. You can then place the dupe on a lightbox and copy part of it with a macro lens to really enhance the grain.

Q | **What's the easiest way to double expose the moon on to a photograph?**

The most common method is to use a whole roll of film to photograph the moon, using your longest lens. This gives you a roll of film with the moon on each frame against a black sky. If you then re-load the film into your camera, you can re-expose each frame, photographing floodlit buildings and other night subjects, taking care not to overlap features in the second exposure and the moon.

This technique works best with traditional 35mm SLRs that have a manual film rewind and advance – modern SLRs with a motor drive tend to leave uneven gaps between each frame of film so it's quite easy to make mistakes when you come to re-expose the film.

Another option is to use your camera's multiple exposure facility – you can shoot a night scene while there's colour in the sky, then a little later when the sky is black, re-expose the same frame to the moon using a longer lens. This is a much more accurate method, but you are limited to only one shot per night.

If you want to add the moon to existing night pictures, you can do so using a lightbox in a darkened room and a camera with a multiple exposure facility.

Having set up the lightbox with a night shot on it, mask off the rest of the lightbox screen to prevent flare then copy the night shot onto slide film. Next, replace the night shot with a slide of the moon and re-expose the same frame of film to the moon.

This is easier to do if the original night shots are on medium-format because it means that you can copy the whole of the image with a macro lens on your SLR. If you copy a 35mm slide onto 35mm film, even with a 1:1 macro lens you may get the film rebate in the picture.

Finally, there's always the digital option – by far the easiest, most versatile and error-proof technique.

All you need to do is scan your night shots and a slide of the moon, select the moon image, cut out the moon from the black sky, then paste it on to a new layer. This layer can then be positioned over the night shot, the size and opacity of the moon adjusted until you're totally happy with the effect, then flatten the layers down. It's as easy as that!

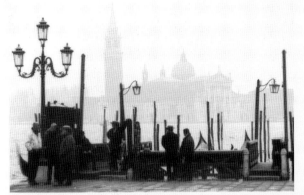
Straight print

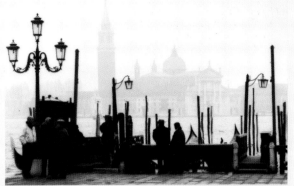
With sepia toner

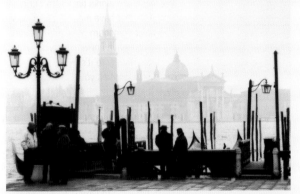
With blue toner

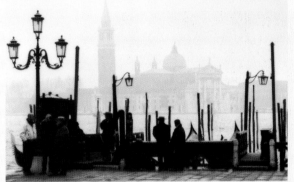
With sepia and blue

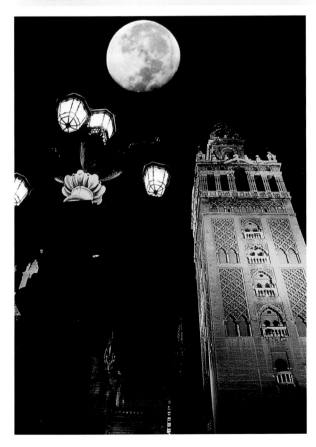

TONING PRINTS

A great way to add interest to straightforward black-and-white prints is by toning them to add an overall colour to the image.

A variety of toners are available, including sepia (warm brown), blue, green and copper, plus selenium, which creates a wide range of different colours depending upon the type of paper used.

*Venice, Italy
These four pictures show how toning can change the mood of a black-and-white print.*
Camera Nikon F90x
Lens 80–200mm zoom
Film Ilford HP5 Plus

To tone a print you need a toning kit, which can be purchased from your local photo shop, a set of developing dishes and some print tongs (see page 71). Toning can also be carried out in daylight using existing prints, and the process only takes a few minutes.

Sepia toner is a two-stage process which involves first bleaching the print to fade the image, then immersing it in a tray of toner so the image re-appears with a delicate brown colour – you can vary the effect by only partially bleaching the print, and the sepia tone can be controlled by adding more or less of the additive that comes with the kit – the more you add, the darker the colour.

All other toners involve just one bath, and you can use more than one toner on the same print – sepia followed by blue works well.

*Casares, Spain
I took the original night shot of Casares years ago, while the moon was photographed from my garden in England. I then combined the two images on a single frame of 35mm film using a lightbox and my camera's multiple exposure facility.*
Camera Pentax 67 for original shots, Nikon F5 for double exposure,
Lens 55mm and 200mm for Pentax, 105mm macro for Nikon
Film Fujichrome Velvia 50

Glossary

Q I come across a lot of terms that I don't understand. Could you explain the meaning of them?

There are hundreds of technical phrases and buzzwords used by photographers – enough to fill a whole book on their own. Here's a list of the most common.

Adobe Photoshop Image-manipulating software – the standard choice among photographers for digital imaging.

Aliasing Square pixels make curved shapes look jagged when viewed close-up. This problem can be solved using anti-aliasing software and filters.

Ambient light Available light, such as daylight, or tungsten room lighting.

Aperture Hole in the lens through which light passes en route to the film. Each aperture is given an f/number to denote its size. Large apertures have a small f/number, such as f/2.8; small apertures have a large f/number, such as f/16.

Artifacts By-products of digital processing, like noise, which degrades image quality.

ASA Old method of measuring film speed (American Standards Association).

Attachment File, such as a digital image, sent with an email.

Backlighting Shooting towards a light source, so your subject is lit from behind.

Beam splitter A mirror or prism that reflects and transmits light. They are commonly found in cameras with autofocusing or spot metering.

Bit Smallest unit of data representing on or off, 0 or 1, black or white.

Bit depth Also known as colour depth, describes the size of colour palette used to create a digital image, such as 16-bit.

Brightness range The difference in brightness, often measured in stops, between the highlights and shadows in a scene.

B setting A shutter setting that allows you to hold your camera's shutter open while the shutter release is depressed. Handy for night photography, when the exposure time required runs outside the shutter speed range on your camera.

Burning Copying images onto recordable and re-recordable CDs.

Burning-in Darkroom technique where more exposure is given to certain areas of the print, to darken them down or to reveal further detail.

Byte A small unit of computer memory (see Kilobyte, Megabyte and Gigabyte). Eight bits make a byte.

C-41 process Chemical process used to develop colour negative/print film.

Card reader A small unit like a mini disk drive that connects to your computer. Memory cards containing digital images from a digital camera are placed in the card reader's slot so that the images can be downloaded onto the computer hard disk and the card wiped clean ready for reuse.

Catadioptic lens Another name for a mirror lens.

Catchlight The reflections created by highlights or bright objects which appear in your subject's eyes and make them look more lively.

CCD (Charge-Coupled Device) Arrangement of electronic sensors that are used in autofocus cameras to aid accurate focusing, and digital cameras and scanners to resolve images – the more sensors a digital camera has in its CCD, the higher the resolution.

CDS cell Stands for Cadmium Sulphide cell, a type of light-sensitive cell found in many light meters.

CDR Recordable Compact Disc – blank compact discs used to store digital images, music and large text files. Usually have a capacity of 750MB. The least expensive way to store and archive digital images.

CDRW Compact disc that can be used more than once – CDRs can only be used once.

CD writer Hardware unit that lets you copy files onto blank recordable and re-recordable CDs – an ideal way to store digital images.

Chromogenic film Colour film that forms dyes during processing. Ilford XP2 is the only mono type available.

Cibachrome Now called Ilfochrome Classic. Ilford printing paper that allows colour prints to be made directly from colour slides.

CMYK Cyan, magenta, yellow and black (K), combinations of which produce colour images on the printed page.

Co-axial socket The socket on a camera into which you can plug a flashgun or sync cable (see your camera's manual).

Colour contrast Use of colours that clash when in close proximity to each other, such as red and blue.

Colour harmony Use of colours that look attractive together and produce a soothing result, such as green and blue.

Colour sensitivity How well film responds to light of different wavelengths – some films are more sensitive to certain wavelengths, particularly red and blue.

Colour space RGB, CMYK and LAB are all kinds of different colour space with their own characteristics.

Colour temperature Scale that is used to quantify the colour of light. Measured in units Kelvin (K).

CompactFlash One of a number of removable and reusable memory cards for digital cameras.

Compound lens A lens made up of different elements.

Compression Process that reduces the size of a digital image so that it requires less storage space, transmits faster by email and downloads faster from the Internet. This is done without physically reducing the pixel dimensions of the image.

Contrast The difference in brightness between the highlights (the brightest parts) and the shadows (the darkest parts) in a scene. When that difference is great, contrast is high; when the difference is small, contrast is low.

Contre-jour French term which means shooting into the light, or 'against the day'.

Converging verticals Problem common in architectural photography which makes buildings appear to be toppling over. It's caused when the camera back is tilted to include the top of a building.

CPU Central processing unit, another name for a microprocessor.

Crop To remove parts of an image that are not required, usually to improve the composition of the photograph.

Curves A useful tool in Photoshop for adjusting contrast, colour and brightness in a digital image.

Cut-off Darkening of the picture edges, caused when a lens hood or filter holder is too narrow for the lens, or too many screw-in filters are used together. This is also known as vignetting.

Data back Camera back that allows you to print the time and date on your pictures.

Daylight-balanced film Type of film for normal use that is designed to give correct colour rendition in light with a colour temperature of 5,500k.

Depth of field The area extending in front of and behind the point you focus on that also comes out acceptably sharp.

Depth of field preview Device that stops the lens down to the taking aperture so you can judge depth of field.

Depth of focus The distance the film plane can be moved from the lens without losing sharp focus.

Diaphragm Name given to the series of blades that form the lens aperture.

Digital zoom Optical zooms actually magnify your subject so that it looks bigger in the picture, but digital zooms merely enlarge a section of the image so image quality is reduced – rather like enlarging a small part of a negative.

DIN German method of expressing the speed of a film, still used today along with the ISO scale.

Double exposure Technique used to combine two images on the same piece of film. This can be used to creative effect but sometimes occurs as a mistake if the same film is loaded into the camera twice.

Downloading Receiving files or images from another computer, usually via the Internet or email.

DPI (dots per inch) An indication of resolution of a computer monitor, scanner or printer. The higher the resolution the better the quality. With scanners dpi refers to the number of dots per inch it can resolve, with printers it's the number of separate ink droplets per inch that are deposited.

Drum scanner Expensive scanner where images and artwork are attached to a drum that rotates at high speed while scanning.

Duotone An image constructed from two different colour channels, normally used to tone an image.

Dye sublimation A type of printer that uses a CMYK pigment-impregnated ribbon.

Dynamic range A measure of the brightness range in photographic materials and digital sensing equipment such as scanners. The higher the number, the greater the range and the better the quality.

E-4 Old colour slide film process replaced by E-6. Now only used to process Kodak Ektachrome colour infrared film.

E-6 Process used to develop just about all colour slide film except Kodachrome.

Emulsion The light-sensitive layer on film and printing paper.

Enprint Standard size of print used by processing labs, usually measuring 6x4in.

Exposure latitude Amount of over- and underexposure a film can receive and still yield acceptable results. Colour print film has a latitude of up to three stops either side of the correct exposure.

Field camera Type of large-format camera which folds down for easy carrying.

File format The way in which an image is saved and stored. See TIFF, JPEG and GIF.

Film scanner Scanner designed digitize slides and negatives and is limited to the size of film format it will accept.

Film speed Scale used to indicate the sensitivity of film to light. An ISO rating is used. The higher the ISO number, the more sensitive (fast) the film is and the less exposure it requires.

Filter factors Number indicating the amount of exposure compensation required when using certain filters.

FireWire A fast data transfer system (faster than USB) now common on computers and associated equipment.

Flare Non image-forming light that reduces image quality by lowering contrast and washing out colours.

FlashPath Adaptor that allows SmartMedia cards to be fitted into a standard floppy disk drive.

Flash sync speed Fastest shutter speed you can use with electronic flash to ensure an evenly lit picture. Varies depending upon camera type – can be anything from 1/30 to 1/250sec with most SLRs.

Flatbed scanner Scanner designed mainly to digitize flat artwork such as drawings and photographic prints, but can also be used for slides and negatives.

Focal length Distance between the near nodal point of the lens and the film plane when the lens is focused on infinity. Also used to express a lens's optical power.

Focal plane shutter Type of shutter consisting of two blades that pass in front of the film to let the light reach it. Found on all SLRs and many medium-format cameras.

Focal point Point where light rays meet after passing through the lens to give a sharp image. Also used to describe the most important element in a picture.

Fogging Accidental exposure of film or printing paper to light.

F/stop Number used to denote the size of the lens aperture.

GIF (Graphical Interchange Format) A low-grade image file format used to display images on the Internet. File sizes are small and use very little memory. GIF images are limited to 256 colours.

Gigabyte 1024 Megabytes or 1,048,576 bytes, often written as GB.

Grey card A sheet of card equivalent to the 18 per cent grey reflectance for which photographic light meters are calibrated.

Greyscale A mode used to save black-and-white images. There are 256 steps from black to white in a greyscale image.

Ground glass screen Type of focusing screen found in many cameras.

Guide number Indicates the power output of an electronic flashgun and is expressed in metres for ISO100 film.

Hard disk/drive Computer hardware that's used to store digital images, and other large files such as software and operating systems. It can either be built-in, separate or portable.

High key Type of picture where all the tones are light.

Highlights The brightest part of a subject or scene.

Histogram A graph that displays the range of tones present in a digital image as a series of vertical columns.

Hyperfocal distance Point of focus at which you can obtain optimum depth of field for the aperture set on your lens.

Incident light reading A method of measuring the light falling onto your subject rather than the light being reflected back from the subject. Incident readings are taken using a handheld light meter. See reflected metering.

Infrared filter Opaque filter that only transmits infrared light. Used with infrared film for dramatic results.

Inkjet printer Common type of printer that sprays ink droplets of varying sizes and can be used to create photo-quality prints.

Interpolation Enlarging a digital image by inserting new pixels between existing ones.

Iris Another name for the lens aperture.

ISO Abbreviation for International Standards Organization, the internationally recognized system for measuring the speed (sensitivity) of film.

JPEG Abbreviation for Joint Photographic Expert Group, a common file format that compresses images for easier storage and quicker transmission. JPEG is a 'lossy' format meaning that quality is reduced every time the image is saved.

Kelvin (K) Unit used to measure the colour temperature of light.

Key light The main light in a multi-light set-up that provides the illumination on which the exposure reading is based.

Kilobyte 1024 bytes, often written as KB.

Layered image A kind of image file that is created by placing separate image elements on top of each other in layers then blending the layers together. This is a common Photoshop technique.

Leaf shutter Type of shutter found in many medium-format and all large-format cameras. The shutter is in the lens rather than the camera body.

Levels Set of tools in Adobe Photoshop that allow you to control image brightness.

Lifesize Term used in close-up photography when the subject is the same size on film as it is in reality.

Line film High-contrast black-and-white film that eliminates almost all intermediate grey tones.

Lith film High-contrast black-and-white film that eliminates grey tones to produce stark black-and-white images.

Low key Picture that has mostly dark tones to give a dramatic, moody effect.

Magnification ratio Also known as reproduction ratio. Refers to the size of a subject on a frame of film compared to its size in real life.

Masking frame Also called an enlarging easel. Used to hold printing paper flat during exposure and allows you to create borders around the print.

Medium-format Type of camera using 120 roll film. Images sizes available are 6x4.5cm, 6x6cm, 6x7cm, 6x8cm and 6x9cm.

Megabyte 1024 Kilobytes, written as MB.

Megapixel One million pixels. Digital cameras now have several megapixels – the more it has the higher image quality is.

Microprocessor The brain of a computer. The operating speed of the processor chip is measured in Megahertz (Mhz).

Mirror lock Device found in some cameras that allows you to lock up the reflex mirror prior to taking a picture, to reduce vibrations and the risk of camera shake.

Monobloc Type of studio flash unit with its power source and controls built-in – as opposed to units that are powered by a separate generator.

Monochromatic Means 'one colour' and is often used to describe black-and-white photography or colour photography when a scene comprises different shades of the same colour.

Monopod Camera support with one leg.

Multi-coating The coating applied to most lenses and some filters to prevent flare.

Multiple exposure Technique where the same frame of film is exposed several times to create unusual effects.

Neutral density filter (ND filter) Filter that reduces the amount of light entering the lens without changing the colour of the original scene.

Neutral density graduate filter Filter that's clear on the bottom half and neutral graduate on the top half. It allows you to tone down the brightness of the sky and even out contrast when shooting landscapes so correct exposure can be achieved in both the sky and landscape. Various densities are available, from 0.3 (1 stop) to 1.2 (4 stops) to give you control.

Newton's rings Patterns caused when two transparent surfaces come into contact with each other – such as a negative in a glass negative carrier.

Noise Looks like grain in a normal photographic image and appears on digital images as brightly coloured pixels in dark areas. Most common when you're using a high ISO setting and shooting in low light.

One-shot developer A type of film developer that has to be discarded after one use only.

One-touch zoom lens Zoom design that allows you both to focus and zoom the lens using a single barrel.

Open flash Technique where the camera's shutter is locked open, usually on the B (bulb) setting, and the flash is fired at the required moment.

Optical viewfinder Direct viewing system found on some digital cameras.

Orthochromatic film Film that is insensitive to red light so it can be processed under safelight conditions. Lith film is an example.

Oxidation Process by which photographic chemicals become exhausted due to exposure to oxygen – one reason why they should be stored in full and tightly capped bottles at all times.

Panchromatic film Type of film or printing paper sensitive to all colours in the spectrum. Normal colour film, for example, is panchromatic.

Parallax error Problem encountered when using rangefinder and twin lens reflex cameras. Because the viewing and taking systems are separate what you see through the viewfinder isn't exactly the same as what the lens sees. It's most noticeable at close focusing distances, but modern compacts are corrected for it.

PC socket Socket on camera body that accepts a flash sync cable.

Peripherals Any hardware item that can be added to a computer – printers, scanners, card readers, zip drives, CD writers and so on.

Photoflood Tungsten studio light with colour temperature of 3,400K.

Photopearl Tungsten studio light with colour temperature of 3,200K.

Pinhole camera Simple camera that uses a tiny pinhole to admit light to the film inside instead of a lens.

Pixel Made up from the words Picture Element – a pixel is a tiny square of digital data, like a single tile in a mosaic.

Pixellation Unwanted effect in digital images where pixels are so large they're visible to the human eye.

Polarizing filter Type of filter that blocks out polarized light so colour saturation is increased, glare is removed and reflections are eliminated in non-metallic surfaces.

Predictive autofocusing Autofocus mode found on some SLRs that predicts how fast the subject is moving and automatically adjusts focus so when the exposure is made your subject is sharp.

Primary colours Colours that form white when combined. Red, green and blue are the three primary colours of light.

Prime lens Any lens with a fixed focal length, such as 28mm, 50mm or 300mm.

Profile The colour reproduction characteristics of an input or output device. This is used by colour management software to maintain colour accuracy in digital images when they're viewed on other computers or output as prints.

Push-processing Technique where film is rated at a higher ISO (effectively underexposed), then processed for longer to compensate.

RAM (Random Access Memory) The part of a computer that holds data while work is in progress, such as when you're working on a digital image in Photoshop. The more RAM you have, the better – 1GB is not uncommon.

Reciprocity law failure Loss of film speed caused when film is exposed for very brief or very long periods. Colour casts may also be caused (see Film, page 28).

Red eye Problem caused by light from a flashgun reflecting back off the retinas in your subject's eyes so they record as red spots. Most modern cameras now offer a red-eye reduction feature.

Reflected metering System of light reading used by a camera's integral light meter, which measures the light reflecting back off your subject rather than that falling onto it. See incident light reading.

Resolution Refers to image quality. High-resolution images are big files that contain millions of pixels and can be output as large prints. Low-resolution images make much smaller files but contain less pixels and can only stand small reproduction – such as images on websites.

RGB An image mode for colour photographs comprising red, green and blue. Each separate colour has its own channel of 256 steps.

Ringflash Flashgun with a circular tube surrounding the lens to provide even illumination of close-up subjects.

Rule of thirds Compositional formula used to place the focal point of a shot one-third into the frame for visual balance.

Scanner Item used to digitize images – slides, prints or negatives.

Scratch disk A portion of a computer's free hard disk that acts as an overflow RAM. When scratch disks are full you need to invest in more RAM.

SCSI (Small Computer Systems Interface) An older means of connecting peripherals to computers, now mainly superseded by USB and FireWire

Selenium cell Type of cell found in light meters which is sensitive to light and doesn't need a battery to work.

Selenium toner A toner that makes black-and-white prints archivally safe by converting remaining silver salts into a stable compound. Can also add a subtle colour depending upon the paper type used.

Sharpening Processing filter that makes an image look sharper by increasing contrast between pixels.

SmartMedia Type of removable and reusable memory card for digital cameras.

Snoot Conical attachment which fits to a studio light so you can direct the beam of light to where it's needed.

Softbox Attachment that fits over a studio flash unit to soften and spread the fall of the light.

Stop Term used to describe one f/stop. If you 'close down' a stop you select the next smallest aperture. If you 'open up' a stop you select the next largest aperture.

Thumbnail Low-resolution image, often used for reference purposes.

Thyristor Energy-saving circuit found in many automatic and dedicated flashguns that stores unused power to reduce recycling time.

TIFF Tagged Image File Format, the most common cross-platform image file format that doesn't reduce image quality.

Transparency Another name for a slide.

Tungsten-balanced film Film designed to give natural results under tungsten lighting.

TWAIN Cross-platform interface that allows you to acquired images from scanners and digital cameras from within your graphics application.

Universal developer Type of developer that can be used to process both black-and-white film and printing paper.

Unsharp Mask A sophisticated sharpening filter found in many digital image software applications, including Photoshop.

Upload Sending images and files to a remote computer, usually by email or to go on a website.

Uprating Rating film at a higher ISO, then push-processing it to compensate.

USB (Universal Serial Bus) A computer connectivity system that allows easy connection of peripherals to your computer.

Vanishing point The point where converging lines in a picture appear to meet in the distance, such as furrows in a ploughed field.

Variable-contrast paper Black-and-white printing paper that can produce contrast grades from 0 to 5 with the aid of filters.

Vignetting Darkening of the picture edges. See cut-off.

Waist-level finder Type of viewfinder used on many medium-format cameras that you look down on with the camera held at waist level.

White balance Control found on digital cameras that allows you to correct colour casts, such as when shooting under artificial lighting, so your pictures look natural in all conditions.

Wratten Kodak brand of gelatin filters mainly used for colour correction purposes. Favoured by professionals for their high quality, but expensive and easily damaged.

Zip Portable disk drive that accepts disks with 100MB and 250MB storage capacities.

Zone system A system devised by the late Ansel Adams that involves previsualizing how you want the final black-and-white print to look at the time of taking the picture, so you can choose the exposure carefully. The scene is divided into zones – black is zone 1 and pure white zone 9, with various densities of grey tones falling in between the two extremes.

Index

ABOUT THE AUTHOR

Lee Frost is an acclaimed photographer and best-selling author whose previous works include *The Creative Photography Handbook*, *Photos That Sell*, *The Photographers Guide to Filters* and *The A–Z of Creative Photography* (all published by David & Charles). Lee is a regular contributor to several UK photography magazines, including *Photography Monthly*, *Outdoor Photography* and *Black & White Photography*. He also leads photographic holidays and workshops.

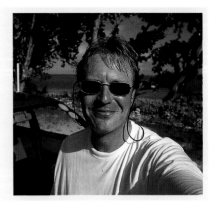